D0924926

EIGHT ESSAYS

Edmund Wilson was born on May 8, 1895, in Red Bank, New Jersey, and was educated at Princeton. He is the author of a novel, *I Thought of Daisy* (1929), two volumes of poetry, an historical study, *To the Finland Station* (1940), short stories, *Memoirs of Hecate County* (1946), and several plays. He is primarily known, however, for his works of criticism, among them *Axel's Castle* (1931), *The Triple Thinkers* (1938), *The Wound and the Bow* (1941), *Classics and Commercials* (1950), and the recent *The Shores of Light*.

Eight
Essays

BY EDMUND WILSON

DOUBLEDAY ANCHOR BOOKS

DOUBLEDAY & COMPANY, INC.

GARDEN CITY, NEW YORK, 1954

Library of Congress Catalog Card Number 54-7733

Copyright, 1938, 1941, 1951, 1952, 1953, 1954, by
Edmund Wilson
All rights reserved
Printed in the United States
First edition

The first two of these essays are reprinted from *The Wound and the Bow* and the second two from *The Triple Thinkers*, both published by the Oxford Press. The remaining four appeared in the *New Yorker* and are here for the first time collected. I have left the last three of these in their original form as reviews, believing that, in the case of editions of public and private papers, the editing, which I discuss, is an essential part of the book.

CONTENTS

EIGHT ESSAYS

DICKENS: THE TWO SCROOGES

To the Students of English 354,
University of Chicago, Summer, 1939

Of all the great English writers, Charles Dickens has received in his own country the scantiest serious attention from biographers, scholars or critics. He has become for the English middle class so much one of the articles of their creed—a favorite fish, a familiar joke, a favorite dish, a beloved Christmas ritual—that it is difficult for British pundits to recognize him as the great artist and social critic he was. Dickens had no university education, and the literary men from Oxford and Cambridge, who have lately been sifting fastidiously so much of the English heritage, have rather snubbingly let him alone. The Bloomsbury that talked about Dostoevsky ignored Dostoevsky's master, Dickens. What happens when the London of Lytton Strachey does take Dickens up is shown in Hugh Kingsmill's book, *The Sentimental Journey*, in which the man who was called by Taine "the master of all hearts" is made into one of those Victorian scarecrows with ludicrous Freudian flaws—so infantile, pretentious, and hypocritical as to deserve only a perfunctory sneer.

Since Forster's elaborate memoir, which even in the supplemented edition of Ley has never been a real biography, no authoritative book about Dickens has been published. Some of the main facts about his life have till recently been kept from the public, and now that they have finally come out they have usually been presented either by doddering Dickens-fanciers or through the medium of garrulous memoirs. Mr. Ralph Straus and Mr. T. A. Jackson have recently published studies of Dickens—the one from the psychological, the other from the Marxist, point of view—which attempt a more searching treatment; but though they contain some valuable insights, neither is really first-rate, for neither handles surely enough or carries to fundamental findings the line which it undertakes. The typical Dickens expert is an old duffer who, as Mr. Straus has said, is primarily interested in proving that Mr. Pickwick stopped at a certain inn and slept in a certain bed.

As for criticism, there has been in English one admirable critic of Dickens, George Gissing, whose prefaces and whose book on Dickens not only are the best thing on Dickens in English but stand out as one of the few really first-rate pieces of literary criticism produced by an Englishman of the end of the century. For the rest, you have mainly G. K. Chesterton, who turned out in his books on Dickens some of the best work of which he was capable and who said some excellent things, but whose writing here as elsewhere is always melting away into that peculiar pseudo-poetic booziness which verbalizes with large conceptions and ignores the most obtrusive actualities. Chesterton celebrated the jolly Dickens; and Bernard Shaw offset this picture by praising the later and gloomier Dickens and insisting on his own debt to the author of *Little Dorrit* at a time when it was taken for granted that he must derive from such foreigners as Ibsen and Nietzsche.

Chesterton asserted that time would show that Dickens was not merely one of the Victorians, but incomparably the greatest English writer of his time; and Shaw coupled his name with that of Shakespeare. It is the conviction of the present writer that both these judgments were justified. Dickens—though he cannot of course pretend to the rank where Shakespeare has few companions—was nevertheless the greatest dramatic writer that the English had had since Shakespeare, and he created the largest and most varied world. It is the purpose of this essay to show that we may find in Dickens' work today a complexity and a depth to which even Gissing and Shaw have hardly, it seems to me, done justice—an intellectual and artistic interest which makes Dickens loom very large in the whole perspective of the literature of the West.

I

The father of Charles Dickens' father was head butler in the house of John Crewe (later Lord Crewe) of Crewe Hall, Member of Parliament for Chester; and the mother of his father was a servant in the house of The Marquess of Blandford in Grosvenor Square, who was Lord Chamberlain to the Household of George III. This grandmother, after her marriage, became housekeeper at Crewe Hall, and it is assumed that it was through the patronage of her employer that her son John Dickens was given a clerkship in the Navy Pay Office.

John Dickens began at £70 a year and was in time increased to £350. But he had always had the tastes of a gentleman. He was an amiable fellow, with an elegant manner and a flowery vein of talk, who liked to entertain his friends and who could not help creating the impression of a way of life beyond his means. He was always in trouble over bills.

When Charles, who had been born (February 7, 1812) at Portsmouth and had spent most of his childhood out of London at Portsmouth, Portsea and Chatham, who had had a chance to go to the theater and to read the *Arabian Nights* and the eighteenth-century novelists, and had been taught by a tutor from Oxford, came up to London at the age of nine to join his parents, who had been obliged to return there, he was terribly shocked to find them, as a consequence of his father's debts, now living in a little back garret in one of the poorest streets of Camden Town. On February 20, 1824, when Charles was twelve, John Dickens was arrested for debt and taken to the Marshalsea Prison, announcing, as he left the house: "The sun has set upon me forever!" At home the food began to run low; and they had to pawn the household belongings till all but two rooms were bare. Charles even had to carry his books, one by one, to the pawnshop. It was presently decided that the boy should go to work at six shillings a week for a cousin who manufactured blacking; and through six months, in a rickety old house by the river, full of dirt and infested with rats, he pasted labels on blacking bottles, in the company of riverside boys who called him "the little gentleman." He wanted terribly to go on with his schooling, and couldn't grasp what had happened to him. The whole of the rest of the family moved into the Marshalsea with his father; and Charles, who had a lodging near them, went to the jail after work every evening and ate breakfast with them every morning. He was so ashamed of the situation that he would never allow his companion at the blacking warehouse, whose name was Bob Fagin, to go with him to the door of the prison, but would take leave of him and walk up the steps of a strange house and pretend to be going in. He had had a kind of nervous fits in his earlier childhood, and now these began to recur. One day at work he was seized with such an acute spasm that he had to lie down on some straw on the floor, and the boys who worked with him spent half the day applying blacking bottles of hot water to his side.

John Dickens inherited a legacy in May and got out of jail the twenty-eighth; but he let Charles keep on working in the warehouse. The little boys did their pasting next to the window in order to get the light, and people used to stop to look in at them because

they had become so quick and skilful at it. This was
an added humiliation for Charles; and one day when
John Dickens came there, he wondered how his father could bear it. At last—perhaps, Dickens thought,
as a result of what he had seen on this visit—John
quarreled with Charles's employer, and took the boy
out of the warehouse and sent him to school.

These experiences produced in Charles Dickens a
trauma from which he suffered all his life. It has been
charged by some of Dickens' critics that he indulged
himself excessively in self-pity in connection with
these hardships of his childhood; it has been pointed
out that, after all, he had only worked in the blacking
warehouse six months. But one must realize that during those months he was in a state of complete despair. For the adult in desperate straits, it is almost
always possible to imagine, if not to contrive, some
way out; for the child, from whom love and freedom
have inexplicably been taken away, no relief or release can be projected. Dickens' seizures in his black-
ing-bottle days were obviously neurotic symptoms;
and the psychologists have lately been telling us that
lasting depressions and terrors may be caused by such
cuttings-short of the natural development of childhood. For an imaginative and active boy of twelve,
six months of despair are quite enough. "No words
can express," Dickens wrote of his first introduction
to the warehouse, in a document he gave to Forster,
"the secret agony of my soul as I sunk into this companionship; compared these every day associates with
those of my happier childhood; and felt my early
hopes of growing up to be a learned and distinguished
man crushed in my breast. The deep remembrance of
the sense I had of being utterly neglected and hopeless; of the shame I felt in my position; of the misery
it was to my young heart to believe that, day by day,
what I had learned, and thought, and delighted in,
and raised my fancy and my emulation up by, was
passing away from me, never to be brought back any
more; cannot be written. My whole nature was so

penetrated with the grief and humiliation of such considerations, that even now, famous and caressed and happy, I often forget in my dreams that I have a dear wife and children; even that I am a man; and wander desolately back to that time of my life."

He never understood how his father could have abandoned him to such a situation. "I know my father," he once told Forster, "to be as kind-hearted and generous a man as ever lived in the world. Everything that I can remember of his conduct to his wife, or children, or friends, in sickness or affliction is beyond all praise. By me, as a sick child, he has watched night and day, unweariedly and patiently, many nights and days. He never undertook any business, charge or trust that he did not zealously, conscientiously, punctually, honorably discharge. His industry has always been untiring. He was proud of me, in his way, and had a great admiration of [my] comic singing. But, in the case of his temper, and the straitness of his means, he appeared to have lost utterly at this time the idea of educating me at all, and to have utterly put from him the notion that I had any claim upon him, in that regard, whatever." And Charles never forgave his mother for having wanted to keep him working in the warehouse even after his father had decided to take him out. "I never afterwards forgot," he wrote of her attitude at this time. "I never shall forget, I never can forget."

Of those months he had never been able to bring himself to speak till, just before conceiving *David Copperfield*, he wrote the fragment of autobiography he sent to Forster; and, even after he had incorporated this material in an altered form in the novel, even his wife and children were never to learn about the realities of his childhood till they read about it after his death in Forster's *Life*. But the work of Dickens' whole career was an attempt to digest these early shocks and hardships, to explain them to himself, to justify himself in relation to them, to give an intelligible and tolerable picture of a world in which such things could occur.

Behind the misfortune which had humiliated Charles was the misfortune which had humiliated his father. John Dickens was a good and affectionate man, who had done the best he was able within the limits of his personality and who had not deserved to be broken. But behind these undeserved misfortunes were sources of humiliation perhaps more disturbing still. The father of Charles Dickens' mother, also a £350-a-year clerk in the Navy Pay Office, with the title of Conductor of Money, had systematically, by returning false balances, embezzled funds to the amount of £5689 3s. 3d. over a period of seven years; and when the fraud was discovered, had fled. And the background of domestic service was for an Englishman of the nineteenth century probably felt as more disgraceful than embezzlement. Certainly the facts about Dickens' ancestry were kept hidden by Dickens himself and have, so far as I know, only been fully revealed in the memoir by Miss Gladys Storey, based on interviews with Mrs. Perugini, Dickens' last surviving daughter, which was published in England in the summer of 1939.

But all these circumstances are worth knowing and bearing in mind, because they help us to understand what Dickens was trying to say. He was less given to false moral attitudes or to fear of respectable opinion than most of the great Victorians; but just as through the offices of his friends and admirers his personal life has been screened from the public even up to our own day, in a way that would have been thought unjustified in the case of a Keats or a Byron of the earlier nineteenth century, so the meaning of Dickens' work has been obscured by that element of the conventional which Dickens himself never quite outgrew. It is necessary to see him as a man in order to appreciate him as an artist—to exorcise the spell which has bewitched him into a stuffy piece of household furniture and to give him his proper rank as the poet of that portièred and upholstered world who saw clearest through the coverings and the curtains.

II

If one approaches his first novel, *Pickwick Papers*, with these facts of Dickens' biography in mind, one is struck by certain features of the book which one may not have noticed before.

Here the subject has been set for Dickens. He was supposed to provide some sort of text for a series of comic sporting plates by Seymour—something in the vein of Surtees' *Jorrocks*. As soon, however, as Dickens' scheme gives him a chance to get away from the sporting plates and to indulge his own preoccupations, the work takes a different turn.

There are in *Pickwick Papers*, especially in the early part, a whole set of interpolated short stories which make a contrast with the narrative proper. These stories are mostly pretty bad and deserve from the literary point of view no more attention than they usually get; but, even allowing here also for an element of the conventional and popular, of the still-thriving school of Gothic horror, we are surprised to find rising to the surface already the themes which were to dominate his later work.

The first of these interludes in *Pickwick* deals with the death of a pantomime clown, reduced through drink to the direst misery, who, in the delirium of his fever, imagines that he is about to be murdered by the wife whom he has been beating. In the second story, a worthless husband also beats his wife and sets an example of bad conduct to his son; the boy commits a robbery, gets caught and convicted—in prison remains obdurate to his mother's attempts to soften his sullen heart; she dies, he repents, it is too late; he is transported, returns after seventeen years and finds no one to love or greet him; he stumbles at last upon his father, now a sodden old man in the workhouse; a scene of hatred and violence ensues: the father, filled with terror, strikes the son across the face with a stick, the son seizes the father by the throat, and the old man bursts a blood-vessel and falls dead. The third story is a document by a madman, which, like the delirium of the dying clown, gives Dickens an opportunity to exploit that vein of hysterical fancy which was to find fuller scope in *Barnaby Rudge* and which was there to figure for him the life of the imagination itself. The narrator has lived in the knowledge that he is to be the victim of hereditary insanity. At last he feels that he is going mad, but at the same moment he inherits money: men fawn upon him and praise him now, but he secretly rejoices in the sense that he is not one of them, that he is fooling them. He marries a girl, who loves another but who has been sold to him by her father and brothers; seeing his wife languish away and coming to understand the situation, fearing also lest she may hand on the family curse, he tries to kill her in her sleep with a razor; she wakes up but dies of the shock. When one of her brothers comes to reproach him, the madman throws him down and chokes him; runs amuck and is finally caught.

But it is in *The Old Man's Tale About the Queer Client* (Chapter XXI) that Dickens' obsessions appear most plainly. Here at the threshold of Dickens' work we are confronted with the Marshalsea Prison. A prisoner for debt, a "healthy, strong-made man, who could have borne almost any fatigue of active exertion," wastes away in his confinement and sees his wife and child die of grief and want. He swears to revenge their deaths on the man who has put him there. We have another long passage of delirium, at the end of which the prisoner comes to, to learn that he has inherited his father's money. At a seaside resort where he has been living, he sees a man drowning one evening: the father of the drowning man stands by and begs the ex-prisoner to save his son. But when the wronged man recognizes his father-in-law, the scoundrel who sent him to prison and who

allowed his own daughter and grandson to die, he
retaliates by letting the boy drown; then, not content
with this, he buys up, at "treble and quadruple their
nominal value," a number of loans which have been
made to the old man. These loans have been arranged
on the understanding that they are renewable up to
a certain date; but the wronged man, taking advantage of the fact that the agreement has never been
put on paper, proceeds to call them in at a time when
his father-in-law has "sustained many losses." The old
man is dispossessed of all his property and finally runs
away in order to escape prison; but his persecutor
tracks him down to a "wretched lodging"—note well:
"in Camden Town"—and there finally reveals himself and announces his implacable intention of send-
ing his persecutor to jail. The old man falls dead from
shock, and the revenger disappears.

In the meantime, the same theme has been getting
under way in the main current of the comic novel.
Mr. Pickwick has been framed by Dodson and Fogg,
and very soon—another wronged man—he will land
in the debtors' prison, where a good many of the
other characters will join him and where the whole
book will deepen with a new dimension of seriousness. The hilarity of the scene in court, in which Mr.
Pickwick is convicted of trifling with Mrs. Bardell's
affections—a scene openly borrowed from *Jorrocks*
but wonderfully transformed by Dickens, and as brilliant as the story of the fiendish revenge on the
fiendish father-in-law is bathetic—may disguise from
the reader the significance which this episode had for
Dickens. Here Dickens is one of the greatest of
humorists: it is a laughter which is never vulgar but
which discloses the vulgarity of the revered—a laughter of human ecstasy that rises like the phœnix from
the cinders to which the dismal denizens of the
tribunals have attempted to reduce decent human
beings. It represents, like the laughter of Aristophanes,
a real escape from institutions.

I shall make no attempt to discuss at length the

humor of the early Dickens. This is the aspect of his work that is best known, the only aspect that some people know. In praise of Dickens' humor, there is hardly anything new to say. The only point I want to make is that the humor of Dickens does differ from such humor as that of Aristophanes in being unable forever to inhabit an empyrean of blithe intellectual play, of charming fancies and biting good sense. Dickens' laughter is an exhilaration which already shows a trace of the hysterical. It leaps free of the prison of life; but gloom and soreness must always drag it back. Before he has finished *Pickwick* and even while he is getting him out of jail and preparing to unite the lovers, the prison will close in again on Dickens. While he is still on the last instalments of *Pickwick*, he will begin writing *Oliver Twist* —the story of a disinherited boy, consigned to a workhouse which is virtually a jail and getting away only to fall into the hands of a gang of burglars, pickpockets and prostitutes.

And now we must identify the attitudes with which Dickens' origins and his early experiences had caused him to meet mankind. The ideal of *Pickwick Papers* is a kindly retired business man, piloted through a tough and treacherous world by a shrewd servant of watchful fidelity, who perfectly knows his place: Mr. Pickwick and Sam Weller. But this picture, though real enough to its creator, soon gives way to the figure of a parentless and helpless child—a figure of which the pathos will itself be eclipsed by the horror of the last night in the condemned cell of a betrayer of others to the gallows, and by the headlong descent into hell of a brute who clubs his girl to death and who, treed like a cat by the pursuing mob, hangs himself in trying to escape.

III

Edmund Yates described Dickens' expression as "blunt" and "pleasant," but "rather defiant."

For the man of spirit whose childhood has been crushed by the cruelty of organized society, one of two attitudes is natural: that of the criminal or that of the rebel. Charles Dickens, in imagination, was to play the rôles of both, and to continue up to his death to put into them all that was most passionate in his feeling.

His interest in prisons and prisoners is evident from the very beginning. In his first book, *Sketches by Boz*, he tells how he used to gaze at Newgate with "mingled feelings of awe and respect"; and he sketches an imaginary picture of a condemned man's last night alive, which he is soon to elaborate in *Oliver Twist*. Almost the only passage in *American Notes* which shows any real readiness on Dickens' part to enter into the minds and feelings of the people among whom he is traveling is the fantasy in which he imagines the effects of a sentence of solitary confinement in a Philadelphia jail. He visited prisons wherever he went, and he later found this cruel system imitated in the jail at Lausanne. Dickens was very much gratified when the system was finally abandoned as the result of the prisoners' going mad just as he had predicted they would. He also wrote a great deal about executions. One of the vividest things in *Pictures from Italy* is a description of a guillotining; and one of the most impressive episodes in *Barnaby Rudge* is the narration—developed on a formidable scale—of the hanging of the leaders of the riots. In 1846, Dickens wrote letters to the press in protest against capital punishment for murderers, on the ground among other grounds that this created sympathy for the culprits; in 1849, after attending some executions in London with Forster, he started by writing to *The Times* an agitation which had the effect of getting public hangings abolished. Even in 1867, in the course of his second visit to America, "I have been tempted out," Dickens wrote Forster, "at three in the morning to visit one of the large police station-houses, and was so fascinated by the study of a horrible photograph-book of thieves' portraits that I couldn't put it down."

His interest in the fate of prisoners thus went a good deal farther than simple memories of the debtors' prison or notes of a court reporter. He identified himself readily with the thief, and even more readily with the murderer. The man of powerful will who finds himself opposed to society must, if he cannot upset it or if his impulse to do so is blocked, feel a compulsion to commit what society regards as one of the capital crimes against itself. With the antisocial heroes of Dostoevsky, this crime is usually murder or rape; with Dickens, it is usually murder. His obsession with murderers is attested by his topical pieces for *Household Words*; by his remarkable letter to Forster on the performance of the French actor Lemaître in a play in which he impersonated a murderer; by his expedition, on his second visit to America, to the Cambridge Medical School for the purpose of going over the ground where Professor Webster had committed a murder in his laboratory and had continued to meet his courses with parts of the body under the lid of his lecture-table. In Dickens' novels, this theme recurs with a probing of the psychology of the murderer which becomes ever more convincing and intimate. Leaving the murderers of the later Dickens till we come to his later books, we may, however, point out here that the crime and flight of Jonas Chuzzlewit already show a striking development beyond the cruder crime and flight of Sikes. The fantasies and fears of Jonas are really, as Taine remarked, the picture of a mind on the edge of insanity. What is valid and impressive in this episode is the insight into the consciousness of a man who has put himself outside human fellowship—the moment, for example, after the murder when Jonas is "not only fearful *for* himself but *of* himself" and half-expects, when he returns to his bedroom, to find himself asleep in the bed.

At times the two themes—the criminal and the

rebel—are combined in a peculiar way. *Barnaby Rudge*—which from the point of view of Dickens' comedy and character-drawing is the least satisfactory of his early books—is, up to *Martin Chuzzlewit*, the most interesting from the point of view of his deeper artistic intentions. It is the only one of these earlier novels which is not more or less picaresque and, correspondingly, more or less of an improvisation (though there is a certain amount of organization discernible in that other somber book, *Oliver Twist*); it was the only novel up to that time which Dickens had been planning and reflecting on for a long time before he wrote it: it is first mentioned in 1837, but was not written till 1841. Its immediate predecessor, *The Old Curiosity Shop*, had been simply an impromptu yarn, spun out—when Dickens discovered that the original scheme of *Master Humphrey's Clock* was not going over with his readers—from what was to have been merely a short story; but *Barnaby Rudge* was a deliberate attempt to find expression for the emotions and ideas that possessed him.

The ostensible subject of the novel is the anti-Catholic insurrection known as the "Gordon riots" which took place in London in 1780. But what is obviously in Dickens' mind is the Chartist agitation for universal suffrage and working-class representation in Parliament which, as a result of the industrial depression of those years, came to a crisis in 1840. In Manchester the cotton mills were idle, and the streets were full of threatening jobless men. In the summer of 1840 there was a strike of the whole North of England, which the authorities found it possible to put down only by firing into the working-class crowds; this was followed the next year by a brick-makers' strike, which ended in bloody riots. Now the immediate occasion for the Gordon riots had been a protest against a bill which was to remove from the English Catholics such penalties and disabilities as the sentence of life imprisonment for priests who should educate children as Catholics and the disquali-

fications of Catholics from inheriting property; but
the real causes behind the demonstration have always
remained rather obscure. It seems to indicate an indignation more violent than it is possible to account
for by mere anti-Catholic feeling that churches and
houses should have been burnt wholesale, all the
prisons of London broken open, and even the Bank
of England attacked, and that the authorities should
for several days have done so little to restrain the
rioters; and it has been supposed that public im-
patience at the prolongation of the American War,
with a general desire to get rid of George III, if not
of the monarchy itself, must have contributed to the
fury behind the uprising.

This obscurity, at any rate, allowed Dickens to
handle the whole episode in an equivocal way. On
the surface he reprobates Lord George Gordon and
the rioters for their fanatical or brutal intolerance; but
implicitly he is exploiting to the limit certain legiti-
mate grievances of the people: the neglect of the
lower classes by a cynical eighteenth-century aristocracy, and especially the penal laws which made innumerable minor offenses punishable by death. The
really important theme of the book—as Dickens
shows in his preface, when he is discussing one of the
actual occurrences on which the story is based—is the
hanging under the Shop-lifting Act of a woman who
has been dropped by her aristocratic lover and who
has forged notes to provide for her child. This theme
lies concealed, but it makes itself felt from beginning
to end of the book. And as *Pickwick*, from the moment it gets really under way, heads by instinct and,
as it were, unconsciously straight for the Fleet prison,
so *Barnaby Rudge* is deliberately directed toward
Newgate, where, as in *Pickwick* again, a group of
characters will be brought together; and the principal climax of the story will be the orgiastic burning
of the prison. This incident not only has nothing to
do with the climax of the plot, it goes in spirit quite
against the attitude which Dickens has begun by

announcing. The satisfaction he obviously feels in demolishing the sinister old prison, which, rebuilt, had oppressed him in childhood, completely obliterates the effect of his right-minded references in his preface to "those shameful tumults," which "reflect indelible disgrace upon the time in which they occurred, and all who had act or part in them." In the end, the rioters are shot down and their supposed instigators hanged; but here Dickens' *parti pris* emerges plainly: "Those who suffered as rioters were, for the most part, the weakest, meanest and most miserable among them." The son of the woman hanged for stealing, who has been one of the most violent of the mob and whose fashionable father will do nothing to save him, goes to the scaffold with courage and dignity, cursing his father and "that black tree, of which I am the ripened fruit."

Dickens has here, under the stimulus of the Chartist agitation, tried to give his own emotions an outlet through an historical novel of insurrection; but the historical episode, the contemporary moral, and the author's emotional pattern do not always coincide very well. Indeed, perhaps the best thing in the book is the creation that most runs away with the general scheme that Dickens has attempted. Dennis the hangman, although too macabre to be one of Dickens' most popular characters, is really one of his best comic inventions, and has more interesting symbolic implications than Barnaby Rudge himself. Dennis is a professional executioner, who has taken an active part in the revolt, apparently from simple motives of sadism. Knowing the unpopularity of the hangman, he makes an effort to keep his identity a secret; but he has found this rather difficult to do, because he sincerely loves his profession and cannot restrain himself from talking about it. When the mob invades Newgate, which Dennis knows so well, he directs the liberation of the prisoners; but in the end he slips away to the condemned cells, locks them against the mob and stands guard over the clamoring inmates, cracking them harshly over the knuckles when they reach their hands out over the doors. The condemned are his vested interest, which he cannot allow the rebels to touch. But the momentum of the mob forces the issue, breaks through and turns the criminals loose. When we next encounter Dennis, he is a stool pigeon, turning his former companions in to the police. But he is unable to buy immunity in this way; and he is finally hanged himself. Thus this hangman has a complex value: he is primarily a sadist who likes to kill. Yet he figures as a violator as well as a protector of prisons. In his rôle of insurgent, he attacks authority; in his rôle of hangman, makes it odious. Either way he represents on Dickens' part a blow at those institutions which the writer is pretending to endorse. There is not, except in a minor way, any other symbol of authority in the book.

The formula of *Barnaby Rudge* is more or less reproduced in the other two novels of Dickens that deal with revolutionary subjects—which, though they belong to later periods of Dickens' work, it is appropriate to consider here. In *Hard Times* (1854), he manages in much the same way to deal sympathetically with the working-class protest against intolerable industrial conditions at the same time that he lets himself out from supporting the trade-union movement. In order to be able to do this, he is obliged to resort to a special and rather implausible device. Stephen Blackpool, the honest old textile worker, who is made to argue the cause of the workers before the vulgar manufacturer Bounderby, refuses to join the union because he has promised the woman he loves that he will do nothing to get himself into trouble. He thus finds himself in the singular position of being both a victim of the blacklist and a scab. The trade-union leadership is represented only—although with a comic fidelity, recognizable even today, to a certain type of labor organizer—by an unscrupulous spell-binder whose single aim is to get hold of the workers' pennies. Old Stephen, wandering away to look for a job somewhere else, falls into a disused coal-pit which has already cost the lives of many miners, and thus becomes a martyr simultaneously to the employers and to the trade-union movement. In *A Tale of Two Cities* (1859), the moral of history is not juggled as it is in *Barnaby Rudge*, but the conflict is made to seem of less immediate reality by locating it out of England. The French people, in Dickens' picture, have been given ample provocation for breaking loose in the French Revolution; but once in revolt, they are fiends and vandals. The vengeful Madame Defarge is a creature whom—as Dickens implies—one would not find in England, and she is worsted by an Englishwoman. The immediate motive behind *A Tale of Two Cities* is no doubt, as has been suggested and as is intimated at the beginning of the last chapter, the English fear of the Second Empire after Napoleon III's Italian campaign of 1859: Dickens' impulse to write the book closely followed the attempt by Orsini to assassinate Napoleon III in the January of '58. But there is in this book as in the other two—though less angrily expressed—a threat. If the British upper classes, Dickens seems to say, will not deal with the problem of providing for the health and education of the people, they will fall victims to the brutal mob. This mob Dickens both sympathizes with and fears.

Through the whole of his early period, Dickens appears to have regarded himself as a respectable middle-class man. If Sam Weller, for all his outspokenness, never oversteps his rôle of valet, Kit in *The Old Curiosity Shop* is a model of deference toward his betters who becomes even a little disgusting.

When Dickens first visited America, in 1842, he seems to have had hopes of finding here something in the nature of that classless society which the foreign "fellow travelers" of yesterday went to seek in the Soviet Union; but, for reasons both bad and good, Dickens was driven back by what he did find into the attitude of an English gentleman, who resented the American lack of ceremony, was annoyed by the American publicity, and was pretty well put to rout by the discomfort, the poverty and the tobacco-juice which he had braved on his trip to the West. Maladjusted to the hierarchy at home, he did not fit in in the United States even so well as he did in England: some of the Americans patronized him, and others were much too familiar. The mixed attitude—here seen at its most favorable to us—which was produced when his British ideas intervened to rein in the sympathy which he tended to feel for American innovations, is well indicated by the passage in *American Notes* in which he discusses the factory-girls of Lowell. These girls have pianos in their boarding-houses and subscribe to circulating libraries, and they publish a periodical. "How very preposterous!" the writer imagines an English reader exclaiming. "These things are above their station." But what is their station? asks Dickens. "It is their station to work," he answers. "And they *do* work. . . . For myself, I know no station in which, the occupation of today cheerfully done and the occupation of tomorrow cheerfully looked to, any one of these pursuits is not most humanizing and laudable. I know no station which is rendered more endurable to the person in it, or more safe to the person out of it, by having ignorance for its associate. I know no station which has a right to monopolize the means of mutual instruction, improvement and rational entertainment; or which has even continued to be a station very long after seeking to do so." But he remarks that "it is pleasant to find that many of [the] Tales [in the library] are of the Mills, and of those who work in them; that they inculcate habits of self-denial and contentment, and teach good doctrines of enlarged benevolence." The main theme of *Nicholas Nickleby* is the efforts of Nicholas and his sister to vindicate their position as gentlefolk.

But there is also another reason why these political

novels of Dickens are unclear and unsatisfactory.
Fundamentally, he was not interested in politics. As a
reporter, he had seen a good deal of Parliament, and
he had formed a contemptuous opinion of it which
was never to change to the end of his life. The Eat-
answill elections in *Pickwick* remain the type of political activity for Dickens; the seating of Mr. Veneering in Parliament in the last of his finished novels
is hardly different. The point of view is stated satir-
ically in Chapter XII of *Bleak House*, in which a
governing-class group at a country house are made
to discuss the fate of the country in terms of the political activities of Lord Coodle, Sir Thomas Doodle,
the Duke of Foodle, the Right Honorable William
Buffy, M.P., with his associates and opponents Cuffy,
Duffy, Fuffy, etc., while their constituents are taken
for granted as "a certain large number of supernumer-
aries, who are to be occasionally addressed, and relied
upon for shouts and choruses, as on the theatrical
stage." A little later (September 30, 1855), he expresses himself explicitly in the course of a letter to
Forster: "I really am serious in thinking—and I have
given as painful consideration to the subject as a man
with children to live and suffer after him can hon-
estly give to it—that representative government is become altogether a failure with us, that the English
gentilities and subserviences render the people unfit
for it, and that the whole thing has broken down since
that great seventeenth-century time, and has no hope
in it."

In his novels from beginning to end, Dickens is
making the same point always: that to the English
governing classes the people they govern are not real.
It is one of the great purposes of Dickens to show
you these human actualities who figure for Parliament
as strategical counters and for Political Economy as
statistics; who can as a rule appear only even in histories in a generalized or idealized form. What does
a workhouse under the Poor Laws look like? What
does it feel like, taste like, smell like? How does the

holder of a post in the government look? How does he talk? what does he talk about? how will he treat you? What is the aspect of the British middle class at each of the various stages of its progress? What are the good ones like and what are the bad ones like? How do they affect you, not merely to meet at dinner, but to travel with, to work under, to live with? All these things Dickens can tell us. It has been one of the principal functions of the modern novel and drama to establish this kind of record; but few writers have been able to do it with any range at all extensive. None has surpassed Dickens.

No doubt this concrete way of looking at society may have serious limitations. Dickens was sometimes actually stupid about politics. His lack of interest in political tactics led him, it has sometimes been claimed, to mistake the actual significance of the legislation he was so prompt to criticize. Mr. T. A. Jackson has pointed out a characteristic example of Dickens' inattention to politics in his report of his first trip to America. Visiting Washington in 1842, he registers an impression of Congress very similar to his impressions of Parliament ("I may be of a cold and insensible temperament, amounting in iciness, in such matters"); and he indulges in one of his gushings of sentiment over "an aged, gray-haired man, a lasting honor to the land that gave him birth, who has done good service to his country, as his forefathers did, and who will be remembered scores upon scores of years after the worms bred in its corruption are so many grains of dust—it was but a week since this old man had stood for days upon his trial before this very body, charged with having dared to assert the infamy of that traffic which has for its accursed merchandise men and women, and their unborn children." Now this aged gray-haired man, Mr. Jackson reminds us, was none other than John Quincy Adams, who, far from being on his trial, was actually on the verge of winning in his long fight against a House resolution which had excluded petitions against slavery, and who was deliberately provoking his adversaries for purposes of propaganda. Dickens did not know that the antislavery cause, far from being hopeless, was achieving its first step toward victory. (So on his second visit to America—when, however, he was ill and exhausted—his interest in the impeachment of Andrew Johnson seems to have been limited to "a misgiving lest the great excitement . . . will damage our receipts" from his readings.) Yet his picture of the United States in 1842, at a period of brave boastings and often squalid or meager realities, has a unique and permanent value. Macaulay complained that Dickens did not understand the Manchester school of utilitarian economics which he criticized in *Hard Times*. But Dickens' criticism does not pretend to be theoretical: all he is undertaking to do is to tell us how practising believers in Manchester utilitarianism behave and how their families are likely to fare with them. His picture is strikingly collaborated by the autobiography of John Stuart Mill, who was brought up at the fountainhead of the school, in the shadow of Bentham himself. In Mill, choked with learning from his childhood, overtrained on the logical side of the mind, and collapsing into illogical despair when the lack began to make itself felt of the elements his education had neglected, the tragic moral of the system of Gradgrind is pointed with a sensational obviousness which would be regarded as exaggeration in Dickens.

This very distrust of politics, however, is a part of the rebellious aspect of Dickens. Dickens is almost invariably *against* institutions: in spite of his allegiance to Church and State, in spite of the lip-service he occasionally pays them, whenever he comes to deal with Parliament and its laws, the courts and the public officials, the creeds of Protestant dissenters and of Church of England alike, he makes them either ridiculous or cruel, or both at the same time.

IV

In the work of Dickens' middle period—after the murder in *Martin Chuzzlewit*—the rebel bulks larger than the criminal.

Of all the great Victorian writers, he was probably the most antagonistic to the Victorian Age itself. He had grown up under the Regency and George IV; had been twenty-five at the accession of Victoria. His early novels are freshened by breezes from an England of coaching and village taverns, where the countryside lay just outside London; of an England where jokes and songs and hot brandy were always in order, where every city clerk aimed to dress finely and drink freely, to give an impression of open-handedness and gallantry. The young Dickens of the earliest preserved letters, who invites his friends to partake of "the rosy," sounds not unlike Dick Swiveller. When Little Nell and her grandfather on their wanderings spend a night in an iron foundry, it only has the effect of a sort of Nibelungen interlude, rather like one of those surprise grottoes that you float through when you take the little boat that threads the tunnel of the "Old Mill" in an amusement park—a luridly lighted glimpse on the same level, in Dickens' novel, with the waxworks, the performing dogs, the dwarfs and giants, the village church. From this point it is impossible, as it was impossible for Dickens, to foresee the full-length industrial town depicted in *Hard Times*. In that age the industrial-commercial civilization had not yet got to be the norm; it seemed a disease which had broken out in spots but which a sincere and cheerful treatment would cure. The typical reformers of the period had been Shelley and Robert Owen, the latter so logical a crank, a philanthropist so much all of a piece, that he seems to have been invented by Dickens—who insisted that his Cheeryble brothers, the philanthropic merchants of *Nicholas Nickleby*, had been taken from living originals.

But when Dickens begins to write novels again after his return from his American trip, a new kind of character appears in them, who, starting as an amusing buffoon, grows steadily more unpleasant and more formidable. On the threshold of *Martin Chuzzlewit* (1843–45: the dates of its appearance in monthly numbers), you find Pecksniff, the provincial architect; on the threshold of *Dombey and Son* (1846–48), we find Dombey, the big London merchant; and before you have got very far with the idyllic *David Copperfield* (1849–50), you find Murdstone, of Murdstone and Grimby, wine merchants. All these figures stand for the same thing. Dickens had at first imagined that he was pillorying abstract faults in the manner of the comedy of humors: Selfishness in *Chuzzlewit*, Pride in *Dombey*. But the truth was that he had already begun an indictment against a specific society: the self-important and moralizing middle class who had been making such rapid progress in England and coming down like a damper on the bright fires of English life—that is, on the spontaneity and gaiety, the frankness and independence, the instinctive human virtues, which Dickens admired and trusted. The new age had brought a new kind of virtues to cover up the flourishing vices of cold avarice and harsh exploitation; and Dickens detested these virtues.

The curmudgeons of the early Dickens—Ralph Nickleby and Arthur Gride, Anthony and Jonas Chuzzlewit (for *Martin Chuzzlewit* just marks the transition from the early to the middle Dickens)—are old-fashioned moneylenders and misers of a type that must have been serving for decades in the melodramas of the English stage. In Dickens their wholehearted and outspoken meanness gives them a certain cynical charm. They are the bad uncles in the Christmas pantomime who set off the jolly clowns and the good fairy, and who, as everybody knows from the beginning, are doomed to be exposed and extinguished. But Mr. Pecksniff, in the same novel with the Chuzzlewits, already represents something different. It is to be characteristic of Pecksniff, as it is of Dombey and Murdstone, that he does evil while pretending to do good. As intent on the main chance as Jonas himself, he pretends to be a kindly father, an affectionate relative, a pious churchgoer; he is the pillar of a cathedral town. Yet Pecksniff is still something of a pantomime comic whom it will be easy enough to unmask. Mr. Dombey is a more difficult problem. His virtues, as far as they go, are real: though he is stupid enough to let his business get into the hands of Carker, he does lead an exemplary life of a kind in the interests of the tradition of his house. He makes his wife and his children miserable in his devotion to his mercantile ideal, but that ideal is at least for him serious. With Murdstone the ideal has turned sour: the respectable London merchant now represents something sinister. Murdstone is not funny like Pecksniff; he is not merely a buffoon who masquerades: he is a hypocrite who believes in himself. And where Dombey is made to recognize his error and turn kindly and humble in the end, Mr. Murdstone and his grim sister are allowed to persist in their course of working mischief as a matter of duty.

In such a world of mercenary ruthlessness, always justified by rigorous morality, it is natural that the exploiter of others should wish to dissociate himself from the exploited, and to delegate the face-to-face encounters to someone else who is paid to take the odium. Karl Marx, at that time living in London, was demonstrating through these middle years of the century that this system, with its falsifying of human relations and its wholesale encouragement of cant, was an inherent and irremediable feature of the economic structure itself. In Dickens, the Mr. Spenlow of *David Copperfield*, who is always blaming his mean exactions on his supposedly implacable partner, Mr. Jorkins, develops into the Casby of *Little Dorrit*, the benignant and white-haired patriarch who turns over the rackrenting of Bleeding Heart Yard to his bull-

terrier of an agent, Pancks, while he basks in the admiration of his tenants; and in *Our Mutual Friend*,
into Fledgeby, the moneylender who makes his way
into society while the harmless old Jew Riah is compelled to play the cruel creditor.

With Dickens' mounting dislike and distrust of the
top layers of that middle-class society with which he
had begun by identifying himself, his ideal of middle-
class virtue was driven down to the lower layers. In
his earlier novels, this ideal had been embodied in
such patrons and benefactors as Mr. Pickwick, the
retired business man; the substantial and warm-
hearted Mr. Brownlow, who rescued Oliver Twist;
and the charming old gentleman, Mr. Garland, who
took Kit Nubbles into his service. In *David Copperfield* the lawyer Wickfield, who plays a rôle in relation
to the hero somewhat similar to those of Brownlow
and Garland, becomes demoralized by too much port
and falls a victim to Uriah Heep, the upstart Pecksniff of a lower social level. The ideal—the domestic
unit which preserves the sound values of England—is
located by Dickens through this period in the small
middle-class household: Ruth Pinch and her brother
in *Martin Chuzzlewit*; the bright hearths and holiday
dinners of the *Christmas Books*; the modest home
to which Florence Dombey descends from the great
house near Portland Place, in happy wedlock with the
nephew of Sol Gills, the ships'-instrument-maker.

It is at the end of *Dombey and Son*, when the
house of Dombey goes bankrupt, that Dickens for
the first time expresses himself explicitly on the age
that has come to remain:

"The world was very busy now, in sooth, and had a
deal to say. It was an innocently credulous and a
much ill-used world. It was a world in which there
was no other sort of bankruptcy whatever. There were
no conspicuous people in it, trading far and wide
on rotten banks of religion, patriotism, virtue, honor.
There was no amount worth mentioning of mere
paper in circulation, on which anybody lived pretty

handsomely, promising to pay great sums of goodness with no effects. There were no shortcomings anywhere, in anything but money. The world was very angry indeed; and the people especially who, in a worse world, might have been supposed to be bankrupt traders themselves in shows and pretences, were observed to be mightily indignant."

And now—working always through the observed interrelations between highly individualized human beings rather than through political or economic analysis—Dickens sets out to trace an anatomy of that society. *Dombey* has been the first attempt; *Bleak House* (1852–53) is to realize this intention to perfection; *Hard Times*, on a smaller scale, is to conduct the same kind of inquiry.

For this purpose Dickens invents a new literary *genre* (unless the whole mass of Balzac is to be taken as something of the sort): the novel of the social group. The young Dickens had summed up, developed and finally outgrown the two traditions in English fiction he had found: the picaresque tradition of Defoe, Fielding and Smollett, and the sentimental tradition of Goldsmith and Sterne. People like George Henry Lewes have complained of Dickens' little reading; but no artist has ever absorbed his predecessors— he had read most of them in his early boyhood—more completely than Dickens did. There is something of all these writers in Dickens and, using them, he has gone beyond them all. In the historical novel *Barnaby Rudge*—a detour in Dickens' fiction—he had got out of Scott all that Scott had to give him. He was to profit in *Hard Times* by Mrs. Gaskell's industrial studies. But in the meantime it was Dickens' business to create a new tradition himself.

His novels even through *Martin Chuzzlewit* had had a good deal of the looseness of the picaresque school of *Gil Blas*, where the episodes get their only unity from being hung on the same hero, as well as the multiple parallel plots, purely mechanical com-

binations, that he had acquired from the old plays—
though he seems to have been trying more inten-
sively for a unity of atmosphere and feeling. But now
he is to organize his stories as wholes, to plan all the
characters as symbols, and to invest all the details with
significance. *Dombey and Son* derives a new kind of
coherence from the fact that the whole novel is made
to center around the big London business house: you
have the family of the man who owns it, the manager
and his family, the clerks, the men dependent on the
ships that export its goods, down to Sol Gills and
Captain Cuttle (so *Hard Times* is to get its coherence
from the organism of an industrial town).

In *Bleak House*, the masterpiece of this middle
period, Dickens discovers a new use of plot, which
makes possible a tighter organization. (And we must
remember that he is always working against the difficulties, of which he often complains, of writing for
monthly instalments, where everything has to be
planned beforehand and it is impossible, as he says,
to "try back" and change anything, once it has been
printed.) He creates the detective story which is also
a social fable. It is a *genre* which has lapsed since
Dickens. The detective story—though Dickens' friend
Wilkie Collins preserved a certain amount of social
satire—has dropped out the Dickensian social content; and the continuators of the social novel have
dropped the detective story. These continuators—
Shaw, Galsworthy, Wells—have of course gone further than Dickens in the realistic presentation of emotion; but from the point of view of dramatizing social
issues, they have hardly improved upon *Bleak House*.
In Shaw's case, the Marxist analysis, with which Dickens was not equipped, has helped him to the tighter
organization which Dickens got from his complex
plot. But in the meantime it is one of Dickens' victories in his rapid development as an artist that he
should succeed in transforming his melodramatic in-
trigues of stolen inheritances, lost heirs and ruined
maidens—with their denunciatory confrontations

that always evoke the sound of fiddling in the orchestra—into devices of artistic dignity. Henceforth the solution of the mystery is to be also the moral of the story and the last word of Dickens' social "message."

Bleak House begins in the London fog, and the whole book is permeated with fog and rain. In *Dombey* the railway locomotive—first when Mr. Dombey takes his trip to Leamington, and later when it pulls into the station just at the moment of Dombey's arrival and runs over the fugitive Carker as he steps back to avoid his master—figures as a symbol of that progress of commerce which Dombey himself represents; in *Hard Times* the uncovered coal-pit into which Stephen Blackpool falls is a symbol for the abyss of the industrial system, which swallows up lives in its darkness. In *Bleak House* the fog stands for Chancery, and Chancery stands for the whole web of clotted antiquated institutions in which England stifles and decays. All the principal elements in the story—the young people, the proud Lady Dedlock, the philanthropic gentleman John Jarndyce, and Tom-all-Alone's, the rotting London slum—are involved in the exasperating Chancery suit, which, with the fog-bank of precedent looming behind it like the Great Boyg in *Peer Gynt*, obscures and impedes at every point the attempts of men and women to live natural lives. Old Krook, with his legal junkshop, is Dickens' symbol for the Lord Chancellor himself; the cat that sits on his shoulder watches like the Chancery lawyers the caged birds in Miss Flite's lodging; Krook's death by spontaneous combustion is Dickens' prophecy of the fate of Chancery and all that it represents.

I go over the old ground of the symbolism, up to this point perfectly obvious, of a book which must be still, by the general public, one of the most read of Dickens' novels, because the people who like to talk about the symbols of Kafka and Mann and Joyce have been discouraged from looking for anything of the kind in Dickens, and usually have not read him, at least with mature minds. But even when we think we do know Dickens, we may be surprised to return to him and find in him a symbolism of a more complicated reference and a deeper implication than these metaphors that hang as emblems over the door. The Russians themselves, in this respect, appear to have learned from Dickens.

Thus it is not at first that we recognize all the meaning of the people that thrive or survive in the dense atmosphere of *Bleak House*—an atmosphere so opaque that the somnolent ease at the top cannot see down to the filth at the bottom. And it is an atmosphere where nobody sees clearly what kind of race of beings is flourishing between the bottom and the top. Among the middle ranks of this society we find persons who appear with the pretension of representing Law or Art, Social Elegance, Philanthropy, or Religion—Mr. Kenge and Mr. Vholes, Harold Skimpole, Mr. Turveydrop, Mrs. Pardiggle and Mrs. Jellyby, and Mr. and Mrs. Chadband—side by side with such a sordid nest of goblins as the family of the moneylender Smallweed. But presently we see that all these people are as single-mindedly intent on selfish interests as Grandfather Smallweed himself. This gallery is one of the best things in Dickens. The Smallweeds themselves are artistically an improvement on the similar characters in the early Dickens: they represent, not a theatrical convention, but a real study of the stunted and degraded products of the underworld of commercial London. And the two opposite types of philanthropist: the moony Mrs. Jellyby, who miserably neglects her children in order to dream of doing good in Africa, and Mrs. Pardiggle, who bullies both her children and the poor in order to give herself a feeling of power; Harold Skimpole, with the graceful fancy and the talk about music and art that ripples a shimmering veil over his systematic sponging; and Turveydrop, the Master of Deportment, that parody of the magnificence of the Regency, behind his rouge and his padded coat and his gallantry as cold and as inconsiderate as the Chadbands behind their gaseous preachments. Friedrich Engels, visiting London in the early forties, had written of the people in the streets that they seemed to "crowd by one another as if they had nothing in common, nothing to do with one another, and as if their only agreement were the tacit one that each shall keep to his own side of the pavement, in order not to delay the opposing streams of the crowd, while it never occurs to anyone to honor his fellow with so much as a glance. The brutal indifference, the unfeeling isolation of each in his private interest, becomes the more repellent the more these individuals are herded together within a limited space." This is the world that Dickens is describing.

Here he makes but one important exception: Mr. Rouncewell, the ironmaster. Mr. Rouncewell is an ambitious son of the housekeeper at Chesney Wold, Sir Leicester Dedlock's country house, who has made himself a place in the world which Sir Leicester regards as beyond his station. One of the remarkable scenes of the novel is that in which Rouncewell comes back, quietly compels Sir Leicester to receive him like a gentleman and asks him to release one of the maids from his service so that she may marry Rouncewell's son, a young man whom he has christened Watt. When Lady Dedlock refuses to release the maid, Rouncewell respectfully abandons the project, but goes away and has the insolence to run against Sir Leicester's candidate in the next parliamentary election. (This theme of the intervention of the industrial revolution in the relations between master and servant has already appeared in *Dombey and Son* in the admirable interview between Dombey and Polly Toodles, whom he is employing as a wet-nurse for his motherless child. Polly's husband, who is present, is a locomotive stoker and already represents something anomalous in the hierarchy of British society. When the Dombeys, who cannot accept her real name, suggest calling Polly "Richards," she replies that if she is to be called out of her name, she

ought to be paid extra. Later, when Dombey makes
his railway journey, he runs into Polly's husband, who
is working on the engine. Toodles speaks to him and
engages him in conversation, and Dombey resents
this, feeling that Toodles is somehow intruding outside his own class.)

But in general the magnanimous, the simple of
heart, the amiable, the loving and the honest are
frustrated, subdued, or destroyed. At the bottom of
the whole gloomy edifice is the body of Lady Dedlock's lover and Esther Summerson's father, Captain
Hawdon, the reckless soldier, adored by his men, beloved by women, the image of the old life-loving England, whose epitaph Dickens is now writing. Captain
Hawdon has failed in that world, has perished as a
friendless and penniless man, and has been buried
in the pauper's graveyard in one of the foulest quarters of London, but the loyalties felt for him by the
living will endure and prove so strong after his death
that they will pull that world apart. Esther Summerson has been frightened and made submissive by being treated as the respectable middle class thought it
proper to treat an illegitimate child, by one of those
Puritanical females whom Dickens so roundly detests.
Richard Carstone has been demoralized and ruined;
Miss Flite has been driven insane. George Rouncewell, the brother of the ironmaster, who has escaped
from Sir Leicester's service to become a soldier instead
of a manufacturer and who is treated by Dickens
with the sympathy which he usually feels for his military and nautical characters, the men who are doing
the hard work of the Empire, is helpless in the hands
of moneylenders and lawyers. Caddy Jellyby and her
husband, young Turveydrop, who have struggled for
a decent life in a poverty partly imposed by the necessity of keeping up old Turveydrop's pretenses, can
only produce, in that society where nature is so muti-
lated and thwarted, a sickly defective child. Mr.
Jarndyce himself, the wise and generous, who plays
in *Bleak House* a rôle very similar to that of Captain

Shotover in Bernard Shaw's *Heartbreak House* (which evidently owes a good deal to *Bleak House*), is an eccentric at odds with his environment, who, in his efforts to help the unfortunate, falls a prey to the harpies of philanthropy.

With this indifference and egoism of the middle class, the social structure must buckle in the end. The infection from the poverty of Tom-all-Alone's will ravage the mansions of country gentlemen. Lady Dedlock will inevitably be dragged down from her niche of aristocratic idleness to the graveyard in the slum where her lover lies. The idea that the highest and the lowest in that English society of shocking contrasts are inextricably tied together has already appeared in the early Dickens—in Ralph Nickleby and Smike, for example, and in Sir John Chester and Hugh—as a sort of submerged motif which is never given its full expression. Here it has been chosen deliberately and is handled with immense skill so as to provide the main moral of the fable. And bound up with it is another motif which has already emerged sharply in Dickens. Dickens had evidently in the course of his astonishing rise, found himself up against the blank and chilling loftiness—what the French call *la morgue anglaise*—of the English upper classes: as we shall see, he developed a pride of his own, with which he fought it to his dying day. Pride was to have been the theme of *Dombey*: the pride of Edith Dombey outdoes the pride of Dombey and levels him to the ground. But in *Bleak House*, the pride of Lady Dedlock, who has married Sir Leicester Dedlock for position, ultimately rebounds on herself. Her behavior toward the French maid Hortense is the cause of her own debasement. For where it is a question of pride, a high-tempered girl from the South of France can outplay Lady Dedlock: Hortense will not stop at the murder which is the logical upshot of the course of action dictated by her wounded feelings. Dickens is criticizing here one of the most unassailable moral props of the English hierarchical system.

Between *Dombey and Son* and *Bleak House*, Dickens published *David Copperfield*. It is a departure from the series of his social novels. Setting out to write the autobiography of which the fragments appear in Forster's *Life*, Dickens soon changed his mind and transposed this material into fiction. In the first half of *David Copperfield*, at any rate, Dickens strikes an enchanting vein which he had never quite found before and which he was never to find again. It is the poem of an idealized version of the loves and fears and wonders of childhood; and the confrontation of Betsey Trotwood with the Murdstones is one of Dickens' most successful stagings of the struggle between the human and the anti-human, because it takes place on the plane of comedy rather than on that of melodrama. But *Copperfield* is not one of Dickens' deepest books: it is something in the nature of a holiday. David is too candid and simple to represent Dickens himself; and though the blacking warehouse episode is utilized, all the other bitter circumstances of Dickens' youth were dropped out when he abandoned the autobiography.

v

With *Little Dorrit* (1855–57), Dickens' next novel after *Bleak House* and *Hard Times*, we enter a new phase of his work. To understand it, we must go back to his life.

Dickens at forty had won everything that a writer could expect to obtain through his writings: his genius was universally recognized; he was fêted wherever he went; his books were immensely popular; and they had made him sufficiently rich to have anything that money can procure. He had partly made up for the education he had missed by traveling and living on the Continent and by learning to speak Italian and

French. (Dickens' commentary on the continental countries is usually not remarkably penetrating; but he did profit very much from his travels abroad in his criticism of things in England. Perhaps no other of the great Victorian writers had so much the consciousness that the phenomena he was describing were of a character distinctively English.) Yet from the time of his first summer at Boulogne in 1853, he had shown signs of profound discontent and unappeasable restlessness; he suffered severely from insomnia and, for the first time in his life, apparently, worried seriously about his work. He began to fear that his vein was drying up.

I believe that Forster's diagnosis—though it may not go to the root of the trouble—must here be accepted as correct. There were, he intimates, two things wrong with Dickens: a marriage which exasperated and cramped him and from which he had not been able to find relief, and a social maladjustment which his success had never straightened out.

The opportunities of the young Dickens to meet eligible young women had evidently been rather limited. That he was impatient to get married, nevertheless, is proved by his announcing his serious intentions to three girls in close succession. The second of these was Maria Beadnell, the original of Dora in *David Copperfield* and, one supposes, of Dolly Varden, too, with whom he fell furiously in love, when he was eighteen and she nineteen. Her father worked in a bank and regarded Charles Dickens, the stenographer, as a young man of shabby background and doubtful prospects; Maria, who seems to have been rather frivolous and silly, was persuaded to drop her suitor—with the result for him which may be read in the letters, painful in their wounded pride and their backfiring of a thwarted will, which he wrote her after the break. This was one of the great humiliations of Dickens' early life (he was at that time twenty-one) and, even after he had liquidated it in a sense by depicting the futilities of

David's marriage with Dora, the disappointment still seems to have troubled him and Maria to have remained at the back of his mind as the Ideal of which he had been cheated.

He lost very little time, however, in getting himself a wife. Two years after his rejection by Maria Beadnell, he was engaged to the daughter of George Hogarth, a Scotchman, who, as the law agent of Walter Scott and from having been mentioned in the *Noctes Ambrosianae*, was invested with the prestige of having figured on the fringes of the Edinburgh literary world. He asked Dickens to write for the newspaper which he was editing at that time in London, and invited the young man to his house. There Dickens found two attractive daughters, and he married the elder, Catherine, who was twenty. But the other daughter, Mary, though too young for him to marry—she was only fifteen when he met her—had a strange hold on Dickens' emotions. When, after living with the Dickenses for a year after their marriage, she suddenly died in Dickens' arms, he was so overcome by grief that he stopped writing *Pickwick* for two months and insisted in an obsessed and morbid way on his desire to be buried beside her: "I can't think there ever was love like I bear her. . . . I have never had her ring off my finger day or night, except for an instant at a time, to wash my hands, since she died. I have never had her sweetness and excellence absent from my mind so long." In *The Old Curiosity Shop*, he apotheosized her as Little Nell. What basis this emotion may have had in the fashionable romanticism of the period or in some peculiar psychological pattern of Dickens', it is impossible on the evidence to say. But this passion for an innocent young girl is to recur in Dickens' life; and in the meantime his feeling for Mary Hogarth seems to indicate pretty clearly that even during the early years of his marriage he did not identify the Ideal with Catherine.

Catherine had big blue eyes, a rather receding chin

and a sleepy and languorous look. Beyond this, it is rather difficult to get a definite impression of her. Dickens' terrible gallery of shrews who browbeat their amiable husbands suggests that she may have been a scold; but surely Dickens himself was no Joe Gargery or Gabriel Varden. We do not know much about Dickens' marriage. We know that, with the exception of his sister-in-law Georgina, Dickens grew to loathe the Hogarths, who evidently lived on him to a considerable extent; and we must assume that poor Catherine, in both intellect and energy, was a good deal inferior to her husband. He lived with her, however, twenty years, and, although it becomes clear toward the end that they were no longer particularly welcome, he gave her during that time ten children.

And if Dickens was lonely in his household, he was lonely in society, also. He had, as Forster indicates, attained a pinnacle of affluence and fame which made him one of the most admired and most sought-after persons in Europe without his really ever having created for himself a social position in England, that society *par excellence* where everybody had to have a definite one and where there was no rank reserved for the artist. He had gone straight, at the very first throw, from the poor tenement, the prison, the press table, to a position of imperial supremacy over the imaginations of practically the whole literate world; but in his personal associations, he cultivated the companionship of inferiors rather than—save, perhaps, for Carlyle—of intellectual equals. His behavior toward Society, in the capitalized sense, was rebarbative to the verge of truculence; he refused to learn its patter and its manners; and his satire on the fashionable world comes to figure more and more prominently in his novels. Dickens is one of the very small group of British intellectuals to whom the opportunity has been offered to be taken up by the governing class and who have actually declined that honor.

His attitude—which in the period we have been

discussing was still that of the middle-class "Radical" opposing feudal precedent and privilege: Mr. Rouncewell, the ironmaster, backed against Sir Leicester Dedlock—is illustrated by the curious story of his relations with Queen Victoria. In 1857, Dickens got up a benefit for the family of Douglas Jerrold, in which he and his daughters acted. The Queen was asked to be one of the sponsors; and, since she was obliged to refuse any such request for fear of being obliged to grant them all, she invited Dickens to put on the play at the palace. He replied that he "did not feel easy as to the social position of my daughters, etc., at a Court under those circumstances," and suggested that the Queen might attend a performance which should be given for her alone. She accepted, and sent backstage between the acts asking Dickens to come and speak to her. "I replied that I was in my Farce dress, and must beg to be excused. Whereupon she sent again, saying that the dress 'could not be so ridiculous as that,' and repeating the request. I sent my duty in reply, but again hoped Her Majesty would have the kindness to excuse my presenting myself in a costume and appearance that were not my own. I was mighty glad to think, when I woke this morning, that I had carried the point." The next year he was approached on behalf of the Queen, who wanted to hear him read the *Christmas Carol*; but he expressed his "hope that she would indulge me by making one of some audience or other—for I thought an audience necessary to the effect." It was only in the last year of his life—and then only on what seems to have been the pretext on the Queen's part that she wanted to look at some photographs of the battlefields of the Civil War which Dickens had brought back from America—that an interview was finally arranged. Here the record of Dickens' lecture manager, George Dolby, supplements the account given by Forster. Dickens told Dolby that "Her Majesty had received him most graciously, and that, as Court etiquette requires that no one, in an ordinary interview with the sovereign, should be seated, Her Majesty had remained the whole time leaning over the head of a sofa. There was a little shyness on both sides at the commencement, but this wore away as the conversation proceeded." When Victoria regretted that it had not been possible for her ever to hear Dickens read, he replied that he had made his farewell to the platform; when she said that she understood this, but intimated that it would be gracious on Dickens' part so far to forget his resolve as to give her the pleasure of hearing him, he insisted that this would be impossible. Not impossible, perhaps, said the Queen, but inconsistent, no doubt—and she knew that he was the most consistent of men. Yet they parted on very good terms: she invited him to her next levee and his daughter to the drawing-room that followed. If there is some stickling for his dignity on Dickens' part here, there is evidently also some scruple on the Queen's.

To be caught between two social classes in a society of strict stratifications—like being caught between two civilizations, as James was, or between two racial groups, like Proust—is an excellent thing for a novelist from the point of view of his art, because it enables him to dramatize contrasts and to study inter-relations which the dweller in one world cannot know. Perhaps something of the sort was true even of Shakespeare, between the provincial bourgeoisie and the Court. Dostoevsky, who had a good deal in common with Dickens and whose career somewhat parallels his, is a conspicuous example of a writer who owes his dramatic scope at least partly to a social malad-justment. The elder Dostoevsky was a doctor and his family origins were obscure, so that his social position was poor in a Russia still predominantly feudal; yet he bought a country estate and sent his sons to a school for the children of the nobility. But the family went to pieces after the mother's death: the father took to drink and was murdered by his serfs for his cruelty. Dostoevsky was left with almost nothing, and

he slipped down into that foul and stagnant underworld of the Raskólnikovs and Stavrógins of his
novels. Dickens' case had been equally anomalous:
he had grown up in an uncomfortable position between the upper and the lower middle classes, with
a dip into the proletariat and a glimpse of the aristocracy through their trusted upper servants. But this
position, which had been useful to him as a writer,
was to leave him rather isolated in English society.
In a sense, there was no place for him to go and belong; he had to have people come to him.

And in the long run all that he had achieved could
not make up for what he lacked. *Little Dorrit* and
Great Expectations (1860–61), which follows it after
A Tale of Two Cities, are full of the disillusion and
discomfort of this period of Dickens' life. The treatment of social situations and the treatment of individual psychology have both taken turns distinctly
new.

Dickens now tackles the Marshalsea again, but on
a larger scale and in a more serious way. It is as if he
were determined once for all to get the prison out of
his system. The figure of his father hitherto has always haunted Dickens' novels, but he has never
known quite how to handle it. In Micawber, he made
him comic and lovable; in Skimpole, he made him
comic and unpleasant—for, after all, the vagaries of
Micawber always left somebody out of pocket, and
there is another aspect of Micawber—the Skimpole
aspect he presented to his creditors. But what kind
of person, really, had John Dickens been in himself?
How had the father of Charles Dickens come to be
what he was? Even after it had become possible for
Charles to provide for his father, the old man continued to be a problem up to his death in 1851. He
got himself arrested again, as the result of running up
a wine bill; and he would try to get money out of
his son's publishers without the knowledge of Charles.
Yet Dickens said to Forster, after his father's death:
"The longer I live, the better man I think him"; and

Little Dorrit is something in the nature of a justification of John.

Mr. Dorrit is "a very amiable and very helpless middle-aged gentleman . . . a shy, retiring man, well-looking, though in an effeminate style, with a mild voice, curling hair, and irresolute hands—rings upon the fingers in those days—which nervously wandered to his trembling lip a hundred times in the first half-hour of his acquaintance with the jail." The arrival of the Dorrit family in prison and their gradual habituation to it are done with a restraint and sobriety never displayed by Dickens up to now. The incident in which Mr. Dorrit, after getting used to accepting tips in his rôle of the Father of the Marshalsea, suddenly becomes insulted when he is offered copper halfpence by a workman, has a delicacy which makes up in these later books for the ebb of Dickens' bursting exuberance. If it is complained that the comic characters in these novels, the specifically "Dickens characters," are sometimes mechanical and boring, this is partly, perhaps, for the reason that they stick out in an unnatural relief from a surface that is more quietly realistic. And there are moments when one feels that Dickens might be willing to abandon the "Dickens character" altogether if it were not what the public expected of him. In any case, the story of Dorrit is a closer and more thoughtful study than any that has gone before of what bad institutions make of men.

But there is also in *Little Dorrit* something different from social criticism. Dickens is no longer satisfied to anatomize the organism of society. The main symbol here is the prison (in this connection, Mr. Jackson's chapter is the best thing that has been written on *Little Dorrit*); but this symbol is developed in a way that takes it beyond the satirical application of the symbol of the fog in *Bleak House* and gives it a significance more subjective. In the opening chapter, we are introduced, not to the debtors' prison, but to an ordinary jail for criminals, which, in the case of Rigaud and Cavalletto, will not make the bad man any better or the good man any worse. A little later, we are shown an English business man who has come back from many years in China and who finds himself in a London—the shut-up London of Sunday evening—more frightening, because more oppressive, than the thieves' London of *Oliver Twist*. " 'Heaven forgive me,' said he, 'and those who trained me. How I have hated this day!' There was the dreary Sunday of his childhood, when he sat with his hands before him, scared out of his senses by a horrible tract which commenced business with the poor child by asking him, in its title, why he was going to Perdition?" At last he gets himself to the point of going to see his mother, whom he finds as lacking in affection and as gloomy as he could have expected. She lives in a dark and funereal house with the old offices on the bottom floor, one of the strongholds of that harsh Calvinism plus hard business which made one of the mainstays of the Victorian Age; she lies paralyzed on "a black bier-like sofa," punishing herself and everyone else for some guilt of which he cannot discover the nature. The Clennam house is a jail, and they are in prison, too. So are the people in Bleeding Heart Yard, small tenement-dwelling shopkeepers and artisans, rackrented by the patriarchal Casby; so is Merdle, the great swindler-financier, imprisoned, like Kreuger or Insull, in the vast scaffolding of fraud he has contrived, who wanders about in his expensive house—itself, for all its crimson and gold, as suffocating and dark as the Clennams'—afraid of his servants, unloved by his wife, almost unknown by his guests, till on the eve of the collapse of the edifice he quietly opens his veins in his bath.

At last, after twenty-five years of jail, Mr. Dorrit inherits a fortune and is able to get out of the Marshalsea. He is rich enough to go into Society; but all the Dorrits, with the exception of the youngest, known as "Little Dorrit," who has been born in the

Marshalsea itself and has never made any pretensions, have been demoralized or distorted by the effort to remain genteel while tied to the ignominy of the prison. They cannot behave like the people outside. And yet that outside world is itself insecure. It is dominated by Mr. Merdle, who comes, as the story goes on, to be universally believed and admired—is taken up by the governing class, sent to Parliament, courted by lords. The Dorrits, accepted by Society, still find themselves in prison. The moral is driven home when old Dorrit, at a fashionable dinner, loses control of his wits and slips back into his character at the Marshalsea: "'Born here,' he repeated, shedding tears. 'Bred here. Ladies and gentlemen, my daughter. Child of an unfortunate father, but—ha—always a gentleman. Poor, no doubt, but—hum—proud.'" He asks the company for "Testimonials," which had been what he had used to call his tips. (Dr. Manette, in *A Tale of Two Cities*, repeats this pattern with his amnesic relapses into the shoemaking he has learned in prison.) Arthur Clennam, ruined by the failure of Merdle, finally goes to the Marshalsea himself; and there at last he and Little Dorrit arrive at an understanding. The implication is that, prison for prison, a simple incarceration is an excellent school of character compared to the dungeons of Puritan theology, of modern business, of money-ruled Society, or of the poor people of Bleeding Heart Yard who are swindled and bled by all of these.

The whole book is much gloomier than *Bleak House*, where the fog is external to the characters and represents something removable, the obfuscatory elements of the past. The murk of *Little Dorrit* permeates the souls of the people, and we see more of their souls than in *Bleak House*. Arthur Clennam, with his broodings on his unloving mother, who turns out not to be his real mother (a poor doomed child of natural impulse, like Lady Dedlock's lover), is both more real and more depressing than Lady Dedlock. Old Dorrit has been spoiled beyond repair: he can

never be rehabilitated like Micawber. There is not
even a villain like Tulkinghorn to throw the odium
on a predatory class: the official villain Blandois has
no organic connection with the story save as a caricature of social pretense. (Though the illustrations suggest that he may have been intended as a sort of cartoon of Napoleon III, whose régime Dickens loathed
—in which case the tie-up between Blandois and the
Clennams may figure a close relationship between the
shady financial interests disguised by the flashy façade
of the Second Empire and the respectable business
interests of British merchants, so inhuman behind
their mask of morality. Blandois is crushed in the end
by the collapse of the Clennams' house, as people
were already predicting that Napoleon would be by
that of his own.) The rôle of the Court of Chancery
is more or less played by the Circumlocution Office
and the governing-class family of Barnacles—perhaps
the most brilliant thing of its kind in Dickens: that
great satire on all aristocratic bureaucracies, and indeed on all bureaucracies, with its repertoire of the
variations possible within the bureaucratic type and
its desolating picture of the emotions of a man being
passed on from one door to another. But the Circumlocution Office, after all, only influences the action
in a negative way.

The important thing to note in *Little Dorrit*—
which was originally to have been called *Nobody's
Fault*—is that the fable is here presented from the
point of view of imprisoning states of mind as much
as from that of oppressive institutions. This is illustrated in a startling way by *The History of a Self-
Tormentor*, which we find toward the end of the
book. Here Dickens, with a remarkable pre-Freudian
insight, gives a sort of case history of a woman imprisoned in a neurosis which has condemned her to
the delusion that she can never be loved. There is
still, to be sure, the social implication that her or-
phaned childhood and her sense of being slighted
have been imposed on her by the Victorian attitude

toward her illegitimate birth. But her handicap is now simply a thought-pattern, and from that thought-pattern she is never to be liberated.

Dickens' personal difficulties make themselves felt like an ache at the back of *Little Dorrit*—in which he represents his hero as reflecting: "Who has not thought for a moment, sometimes?—that it might be better to flow away monotonously, like the river, and to compound for its insensibility to happiness with its insensibility to pain." The strain of his situation with his wife had become particularly acute the year that the book was begun. Dickens had been very much excited that February to get a letter from Maria Beadnell, now married. The readiness and warmth of his response shows how the old Ideal had lighted up again. He was on the point of leaving for Paris, and during his absence he looked forward eagerly to seeing her: he arranged to meet her alone. The drop in the tone of his letters after this meeting has taken place is blighting to poor Mrs. Winter. He had found her banal and silly, with the good looks of her girlhood gone. He put her into his new novel as Flora Finching, a sort of Dora Spenlow vulgarized and transmogrified into a kind of Mrs. Nickleby—that is, into another version of Dickens' unforgiven mother. It seems clear that the type of woman that Dickens is chiefly glorifying during the years from *Martin Chuzzlewit* through *Little Dorrit*: the devoted and self-effacing little mouse, who hardly aspires to be loved, derives from Georgina Hogarth, his sister-in-law. Georgina, who had been eight when Dickens was married, had come to womanhood in the Dickens household. Dickens grew fond of her, explaining that his affection was due partly to her resemblance to her dead sister. She gradually took over the care of the children, whom Dickens complained of their mother's neglecting; and became the real head of the household—creating a situation which is reflected in these heroines of the novels. The virtues of Ruth Pinch are brought out mainly through her relation to her brother Tom; Esther Summerson, who keeps house for Mr. Jarndyce but does not suspect that he wants to marry her, is suspended through most of *Bleak House* in a relation to him that is semi-filial; Little Dorrit is shown throughout in a sisterly and filial relation, and Arthur Clennam, before he figures as a lover, plays simply, like Mr. Jarndyce, the rôle of a protective and elderly friend. In the love of Little Dorrit and Clennam, there seems to be little passion, but a sobriety of resignation, almost a note of sadness: they "went down," Dickens says at the end, "into a modest life of usefulness and happiness," one of the objects of which was to be "to give a mother's care . . . to Fanny's [her sister's] neglected children no less than to their own."

These children of Dickens'—he now had nine—were evidently giving him anxiety. He used to grumble about their lack of enterprise; and it would appear from Mrs. Perugini's story, which trails off in a depressing record of their failures and follies and untimely deaths, that in general they did not turn out well. The ill-bred daughter and worthless son of Dorrit probably caricature Dickens' fears. Surely the Dorrits' travels on the Continent caricature the progress of the Dickenses. Old Dorrit's rise in the world is no rescue at the end of a fairy tale, as it would have been in one of the early novels. The point of the story is that this rise can be only a mockery: the Dorrits will always be what the Marshalsea has made them.

The theme of *Little Dorrit* is repeated in *Great Expectations* (1860–61). This second of Dickens novels in which the hero tells his own story is like an attempt to fill in some of the things that have been left out of *David Copperfield*. The story is the reverse of the earlier one. David was a gentleman by birth, who by accident became a wage slave. Pip is a boy out of the blacksmith's shop, who by accident gets a chance to become a gentleman. He straightway turns into a mean little snob.

The formula of *Bleak House* is repeated, too. The solution of the puzzle is again Dickens' moral, here more bitterly, even hatefully, delivered. Pip owes his mysterious income to the convict whom, in his childhood, he befriended on the marshes. Abel Magwitch himself had been a wretched tinker's boy, who had "first become aware of [himself] a-thieving turnips for a living." Later he had been exploited by a gentlemanly rotter turned crook, who had left Magwitch to take the rap when they had both fallen into the hands of the law. The poor rascal had been impressed by the advantage that his companion's social status —he had been to the public school—had given him in the eyes of the court; and when Magwitch later prospered in New South Wales, he decided to make a gentleman of Pip. Thus Pip finds himself in a position very similar to Lady Dedlock's: the money that chains him to Magwitch will not merely associate him with a poverty and ignorance more abject than that from which he has escaped, but will put him under obligations to an individual who represents to him the dregs of the underworld, a man with a price on his head. Not only this; but the proud lady here— who has known Pip in his first phase and scorns him because she thinks him a common village boy—turns out to be the daughter of Magwitch and of a woman who has been tried for murder and who is now employed in the humble capacity of housekeeper by the lawyer who got her off.

The symbol here is the "great expectations" which both Pip and Estella entertain: they figure (Mr. T. A. Jackson has here again put his finger on the point) the Victorian mid-century optimism. Estella and Pip have both believed that they could count upon a wealthy patroness, the heiress of a now disused brewery, to make them secure against vulgarity and hardship. But the patroness vanishes like a phantom, and they are left with their leisure-class habits and no incomes to keep them up. They were originally to lose one another, too: the tragedies in Dickens' novels are coming more and more to seem irremediable. Estella was to marry for his money a brutal country squire, and Pip was never to see her again except for one brief meeting in London. Here is the last sentence of the ending that Dickens first wrote: "I was very glad afterwards to have had the interview; for, in her face, and in her voice, and in her touch, she gave me the assurance that suffering had been stronger than Miss Havisham's teaching, and had given her a heart to understand what my heart used to be."

This was to have been all, and it was perfect in tone and touch. But Bulwer Lytton made Dickens change it to the ending we now have, in which Estella's husband gets killed and Pip and she are united. Dickens was still a public entertainer who felt that he couldn't too far disappoint his audience.

In *Little Dorrit* and *Great Expectations*, there is, therefore, a great deal more psychological interest than in Dickens' previous books. We are told what the characters think and feel, and even something about how they change. And here we must enter into the central question of the psychology of Dickens' characters.

The world of the early Dickens is organized according to a dualism which is based—in its artistic derivation—on the values of melodrama: there are bad people and there are good people, there are comics and there are characters played straight. The only complexity of which Dickens is capable is to make one of his noxious characters become wholesome, one of his clowns turn into a serious person. The most conspicuous example of this process is the reform of Mr. Dombey, who, as Taine says, "turns into the best of fathers and spoils a fine novel." But the reform of Scrooge in *A Christmas Carol* shows the phenomenon in its purest form.

We have come to take Scrooge so much for granted that he seems practically a piece of Christmas folklore; we no more inquire seriously into the mechanics of his transformation than we do into the transformation of the Beast in the fairy tale into the young prince that marries Beauty. Yet Scrooge represents a principle fundamental to the dynamics of Dickens' world and derived from his own emotional constitution. It was not merely that his passion for the theater had given him a taste for melodramatic contrasts; it was rather that the lack of balance between the opposite impulses of his nature had stimulated an appetite for melodrama. For emotionally Dickens *was* unstable. Allowing for the English restraint, which masks what the Russian expressiveness indulges and perhaps over-expresses, and for the pretenses of English biographers, he seems almost as unstable as Dostoevsky. He was capable of great hardness and cruelty, and not merely toward those whom he had cause to resent: people who patronized or intruded on him. On one occasion, in the presence of other guests, he ordered Forster out of his house over some discussion that had arisen at dinner; he was certainly not gentle with Maria Winter; and his treatment of Catherine suggests, as we shall see, the behavior of a Renaissance monarch summarily consigning to a convent the wife who has served her turn. There is more of emotional reality behind Quilp in *The Old Curiosity Shop* than there is behind Little Nell. If Little Nell sounds bathetic today, Quilp has lost none of his fascination. He is ugly, malevolent, perverse; he delights in making mischief for its own sake; yet he exercises over the members of his household a power which is almost an attraction and which resembles what was known in Dickens' day as "malicious animal magnetism." Though Quilp is ceaselessly tormenting his wife and browbeating the boy who works for him, they never attempt to escape: they admire him; in a sense they love him.

So Dickens' daughter, Kate Perugini, who had destroyed a memoir of her father that she had written, because it gave "only half the truth," told Miss Gladys Storey, the author of *Dickens and Daughter*, that the spell which Dickens had been able to cast on his daughters was so strong that, after he and their mother had separated, they had refrained from going to see her, though he never spoke to them about it, because they knew that he did not like it, and would even take music lessons in a house just opposite the one where she was living without daring to pay her a call. "I loved my father," said Mrs. Perugini, "better than any man in the world—in a different way of course. . . . I loved him for his faults." And she added, as she rose and walked to the door: "my father was a wicked man—a very wicked man." But from the memoirs of his other daughter Mamie, who also adored her father and seems to have viewed him uncritically, we hear of his colossal Christmas parties, of the vitality, the imaginative exhilaration, which swept all the guests along. It is Scrooge bursting in on the Cratchits. Shall we ask what Scrooge would actually be like if we were to follow him beyond the frame of the story? Unquestionably he would relapse when the merriment was over—if not while it was still going on—into moroseness, vindictiveness, suspicion. He would, that is to say, reveal himself as the victim of a manic-depressive cycle, and a very uncomfortable person.

This dualism runs all through Dickens. There has always to be a good and a bad of everything: each of the books has its counterbalancing values, and pairs of characters sometimes counterbalance each other from the casts of different books. There has to be a good manufacturer, Mr. Rouncewell, and a bad manufacturer, Mr. Bounderby; a bad old Jew, Fagin, and a good old Jew, Riah; an affable lawyer who is really unscrupulous, Vholes, and a kindly lawyer who pretends to be unfeeling, Jaggers; a malicious dwarf, Quilp, and a beneficent dwarf, Miss Mowcher (though Dickens had originally intended her to be bad); an embittered and perverse illegitimate daughter, Miss Wade, the Self-Tormentor, and a sweet and submissive illegitimate daughter, Esther Summerson. Another example of this tendency is Dickens' habit, noted by Mr. Kingsmill, of making the comic side of his novels a kind of parody on the sentimental side. Pecksniff is a satire on that domestic sentiment which wells up so profusely in Dickens himself when it is a question of a story for the Christmas trade; the performances of the Vincent Crummleses provide a burlesque of the stagy plot upon which *Nicholas Nickleby* is based.

Dickens' difficulty in his middle period, and indeed more or less to the end, is to get good and bad together in one character. He had intended in *Dombey and Son* to make Walter Gay turn out badly, but hadn't been able to bring himself to put it through. In *Bleak House*, however, he had had Richard Carstone undergo a progressive demoralization. But the real beginnings of a psychological interest may be said to appear in *Hard Times*, which, though parts of it have the crudity of a cartoon, is the first novel in which Dickens tries to trace with any degree of plausibility the processes by which people become what they are. We are given a certain sympathetic insight into what has happened to the Gradgrind children; and the conversion of Mr. Gradgrind is very much better prepared for than that of Mr. Dombey. In *Great Expectations* we see Pip pass through a whole psychological cycle. At first, he is sympathetic, then by a more or less natural process he turns into something unsympathetic, then he becomes sympathetic again. Here the effects of both poverty and riches are seen from the inside in one person. This is for Dickens a great advance; and it is a development which, if carried far enough, would end by eliminating the familiar Dickens of the lively but limited stage characters, with their tag lines and their unvarying makeups.

The crisis of Dickens' later life had already come

before *Great Expectations*. That "old unhappy loss or
want of something" which he makes David Copperfield feel after his marriage to Dora had driven him
into a dream of retreating to the monastery of the
Great St. Bernard, where it had been his original idea
to have the whole of *Little Dorrit* take place. But he
had ended by resorting to another order which, in
mimicking the life of men, may remain almost as
impenetrably cut off from it as the monks of the St.
Bernard themselves. Dickens embarked upon a series
of theatricals, which, though undertaken originally
as benefits, took on a semi-professional character and
came to look more and more like pretexts for Dickens
to indulge his appetite for acting.

He had written Forster of "the so happy and yet
so unhappy existence which seeks its realities in unrealities, and finds its dangerous comfort in a per-
petual escape from the disappointment of heart
around it." But now the pressure of this disappointment was to drive him into a deeper addiction to that
dangerous comfort of unrealities. It was as if he had
actually to embody, to act out in his own person, the
life of his imagination. He had always loved acting:
as a child, he had projected himself with intensity into
the characters of the plays he had seen. He had always
loved amateur theatricals and charades. He used to
say that it relieved him, if only in a game, to throw
himself into the personality of someone else. His
whole art had been a kind of impersonation, in which
he had exploited this or that of his impulses by in-
corporating it in an imaginary person rather than—
up to this point, at any rate—exploring his own personality. The endings of his early novels, in which
the villain was smashingly confounded and the young
juvenile got the leading woman, had been the conventional dénouements of Drury Lane. Whole scenes
of *Barnaby Rudge* had been high-flown declamations
in a blank verse which connects Dickens almost as
closely with the dramatic tradition of Shakespeare as
with the fictional tradition of Fielding. Dickens ad-

mitted that he found it difficult, whenever he became
particularly serious, to refrain from falling into blank
verse; and though his prose, like everything else in
his art, underwent a remarkable development, tight-
ening up and becoming cleaner, he never quite got
rid of this tendency. The scene in which Edith Dombey turns upon and unmasks Mr. Carker, with its
doors arranged for exits and entrances, its suspense
engineered through the presence of the servants, its
set speeches, its highfalutin language, its hair-raising
reversal of rôles, its interruption at the climactic moment by the sudden sound of the bell that announces
the outraged husband—this scene, which is one of the
worst in Dickens, must be one of the passages in fiction most completely conceived in terms of the stage.
In *Bleak House*, he is still theatrical, but he has found
out how to make this instinct contribute to the effectiveness of a novel: the theatrical present tense
of the episodes which alternate with Esther Summerson's diary does heighten the excitement of the narrative, and the theatrical Lady Dedlock is an improvement on Edith Dombey. Yet in the novels that follow
Bleak House, this theatricalism recurs as something
never either quite eliminated from or quite assimi-
lated by Dickens' more serious art, an element which
remains unreal if it is not precisely insincere and on
which his stories sometimes run aground. Later, when
he was giving his public readings, he wrote a whole
series of stories—*Somebody's Luggage, Mrs. Lirriper,
Doctor Marigold*—which were primarily designed for
public performance and in which excellent character
monologues lead up to silly little episodes in the bad
sentimental taste of the period which Dickens had
done so much to popularize. Dickens had a strain of
the ham in him, and, in the desperation of his later
life, he gave in to the old ham and let him rip.

That this satisfied the deeper needs of Dickens as
little as it does those of his readers seems to be proved
by what followed. He met behind the scenes of the
theater sometime in '57 or '58 a young girl named

Ellen Ternan, the daughter of a well-known actress.
When Dickens first saw her, she was hiding behind
one of the properties and crying because she had to
go on in a costume that offended her sense of modesty. Dickens reassured her. She was eighteen, and
she evidently appealed to that compassionate interest
in young women which had made him apotheosize
Mary Hogarth. He saw her again and became infatu-
ated. He had been complaining to Forster that "a
sense comes always crashing on me now, when I fall
into low spirits, as of one happiness I have missed in
life, and one friend and companion I have never
made"; and it must have seemed to him that now he
had found her.

He had made an agreement with Catherine in the
early days of their marriage that if either should fall
in love with anyone else, he should frankly explain to
the other. He now told her that he was in love with
Miss Ternan and compelled her to call on the girl.
Dickens conducted the whole affair with what appears to us the worst possible taste, though I shall
show in a moment that there were special reasons why
his behavior seemed natural to him. He arranged to
have Ellen Ternan take part in his benefit performances, and, whether by design or not, gave her rôles
which ran close enough to the real situation to offend
Mrs. Dickens. Mr. Wright, who first made this whole
episode public in 1934, believes, probably rightly, that
Sydney Carton is Dickens' dramatization of the first
hopeless phase of his love. In the spring of '58, however, Dickens arranged a separation from Catherine
and left her with one of their sons in London while
he removed with the rest of the children and Georgina to the new place he had bought at Gadshill.
He published a statement in *Household Words* and
circulated a singular letter which was not long in getting into print, in which he explained that he and
Catherine had nothing whatever in common and
should never have got married; defended, without
naming her, Ellen Ternan; and denounced, without

naming them, as "two wicked persons" his mother-in-law and his sister-in-law Helen for having intimated that there could be "on this earth a more virtuous and spotless creature" than Ellen. It was true that he and Ellen had not been lovers; but he now induced Ellen to be his mistress and set her up in an establishment of her own. He wrote her name into his last three novels as Estella Provis, Bella Wilfer, and finally Helena Landless—her full name was Ellen Lawless Ternan.

In order to understand what is likely to seem to us on Dickens' part a strange and disagreeable exhibitionism, we must remember his relation to his public. Perhaps no other kind of writer depends so much on his audience as the novelist. If the novelist is extremely popular, he may even substitute his relation to his public for the ordinary human relations. And for this reason he responds to his sales in a way which may seem ridiculous to a writer in a different field; yet to the novelist the rise or the drop in the number of the people who buy his books may be felt in very much the same way as the coolness or the passion of a loved one. In Dickens' case, a falling-off in the popularity of his monthly instalments would plunge him into anxiety and depression. He had played up Sam Weller in *Pickwick* because he saw that the character was going well, and he sent Martin Chuzzlewit to America because he found that interest in the story was flagging. And now it had come to be true in a sense that his only companion in his fictional world was the public who saw him act and read his novels. When he began, as he did that same spring, to give regular public readings—which enabled him to live these novels, as it were, in his own person, and to feel the direct impact on his audience—the relation became more intimate still. For Dickens, the public he addressed in this statement about his marriage was probably closer than the wife by whom he had had ten children; and now that he had fallen in love with Ellen, instead of finding in her a real escape from the

eternal masquerade of his fiction, his first impulse was
to transport her to dwell with him in that imaginary
world itself, to make her a character in a novel or
play, and to pay court to her in the presence of his
public.

But the old sense of "loss or want" does not seem to
have been cured by all this. "My father was like a madman," says Mrs. Perugini, "when my mother left
home. This affair brought out all that was worst—all
that was weakest in him. He did not care a damn what
happened to any of us. Nothing could surpass the misery and unhappiness of our home." And this misery
still hung over the household, in spite of Dickens' fes-
tive hospitality, even after the separation had been arranged. Poor Mrs. Dickens in her exile was wretched
—"Do you think he is sorry for me?" she asked Kate
on one of the only two occasions when she ever heard
her mother mention her father—and there was always
at the back of their consciousness this sense of something deeply wrong. Kate Dickens, with more independence than Mamie, does not seem much to have
liked having Miss Ternan come to Gadshill; and she
finally married a brother of Wilkie Collins, without
really caring about him, in order to get away from
home. After the wedding, which Mrs. Dickens had not
attended, Mamie found her father weeping in Kate's
bedroom, with his face in her wedding dress: "But for
me," he said to her, "Katy would not have left home."

This episode of Ellen Ternan has been hushed up
so systematically, and the information about it is still
so meager, that it is difficult to get an impression of
Ellen. We do, however, know something about what
Dickens thought of her from the heroines in his last
books who are derived from her. Estella is frigid and
indifferent: it amuses her to torture Pip, who loves
her "against reason, against promise, against peace,
against hope, against happiness, against all discour-
agement that could be"; she marries a man she does
not love for his money. Bella Wilfer up to her conversion by Mr. Boffin is equally intent upon money—

which was certainly one of the things that Ellen got
out of her liaison with Dickens. Both Estella and
Bella are petulant, spoiled and proud. They represent,
as it were, the qualities of the Edith Dombey-Lady
Dedlock great lady combined with the capriciousness
of Dora Spenlow—the old elements of Dickens'
women simply mixed in a new way. And these novels
of Dickens in which Ellen figures show perhaps more
real desperation than *Little Dorrit* itself, with its clos-
ing note of modest resignation. It seems to be the general opinion that Ellen was neither so fascinating nor
so gifted as Dickens thought her. After his death, she
married a clergyman, and she confided to Canon Ben-
ham that she had loathed her relationship with Dickens and deeply regretted the whole affair. She had
borne Dickens a child, which did not live. It may be
—though we have no date—that Dickens' short story,
Doctor Marigold (1865), which became one of his
favorite readings, the monologue of a traveling
"cheap jack," who keeps an audience entertained with
his patter while his child is dying in his arms, is a reflection of this event.

In spite of the energy of a *diable au corps* which
enabled him to put on his plays and to perform prodigies of walking and mountain-climbing at the same
time that he was composing his complicated novels,
the creative strain of a lifetime was beginning to tell
heavily on Dickens. He had always felt under an obligation to maintain a standard of living conspicu-
ously lavish for a literary man: in his statement about
his separation from his wife, he boasts that he has provided for her as generously "as if Mrs. Dickens were
a lady of distinction and I a man of fortune." And
now he was compelled both by the demon that drove
him and by the necessity of earning money in order to
keep up the three establishments for which he had
made himself responsible and to launch his sons and
daughters on the world, to work frantically at his public readings. His nervous disorders persisted: he was
troubled while he was writing *Great Expectations*

with acute pains in the face; and he developed a lameness in his left foot, which, though he blamed it on taking walks in heavy snowstorms, was also evidently due to the burning-out of his nerves. He was maimed by it all the rest of his life. "Twice last week," he writes in '66, "I was seized in a most distressing manner—apparently in the heart; but, I am persuaded, only in the nervous system."

Three years had passed since *Great Expectations* before Dickens began another novel; he worked at it with what was for him extreme slowness, hesitation and difficulty; and the book shows the weariness, the fears and the definitive disappointments of this period.

This story, *Our Mutual Friend* (1864-65), like all these later books of Dickens, is more interesting to us today than it was to Dickens' public. It is a next number in the Dickens sequence quite worthy of its predecessors, a development out of what has gone before that is in certain ways quite different from the others. It may be said Dickens never really repeats himself: his thought makes a consistent progress, and his art, through the whole thirty-five years of his career, keeps going on to new materials and effects; so that his work has an interest and a meaning as a whole. The difficulty that Dickens found in writing *Our Mutual Friend* does not make itself felt as anything in the nature of an intellectual disintegration. On the contrary, the book compensates for its shortcomings by the display of an intellectual force which, though present in Dickens' work from the first, here appears in a phase of high tension and a condition of fine muscular training. The Dickens of the old eccentric "Dickens characters" has here, as has often been noted, become pretty mechanical and sterile. It is a pity that the creator of Quilp and of Mrs. Jarley's waxworks should have felt himself under the necessity of fabricating Silas Wegg and the stuffed animals of Mr. Venus. Also, the complex Dickens plot has come to seem rather tiresome and childish. But Dickens has here distilled the mood of his later years, dramatized the tragic discrepancies of his character, delivered his final judgment on the whole Victorian exploit, in a fashion so impressive that we realize how little the distractions of this period had the power to direct him from the prime purpose of his life: the serious exercise of his art.

As the fog is the symbol for *Bleak House* and the prison for *Little Dorrit*, so the dust-pile is the symbol for *Our Mutual Friend*. It dominates even the landscape of London, which has already been presented by Dickens under such a variety of aspects, but which now appears—though with Newgate looming over it as it did in *Barnaby Rudge*—under an aspect that is new: "A gray dusty withered evening in London city has not a hopeful aspect," he writes of the day when Bradley Headstone goes to pay his hopeless court to Lizzie Hexam. "The closed warehouses and offices have an air of death about them, and the national dread of color has an air of mourning. The towers and steeples of the many house-encompassed churches, dark and dingy as the sky that seems descending on them, are no relief to the general gloom; a sun-dial on a church-wall has the look, in its useless black shade, of having failed in its business enterprise and stopped payment for ever; melancholy waifs and strays of housekeepers and porters sweep melancholy waifs and strays of papers and pins into the kennels, and other more melancholy waifs and strays explore them, searching and stooping and poking for everything to sell. The set of humanity outward from the City is as a set of prisoners departing from gaol, and dismal Newgate seems quite as fit a stronghold for the mighty Lord Mayor as his own state-dwelling."

The actual dust-pile in question has been amassed by a dust-removal contractor, who has made out of it a considerable fortune. The collection of refuse at that time was still in private hands, and was profitable because the bones, rags and cinders, and even the dust itself, were valuable for various kinds of manufacture. The plot of *Our Mutual Friend* has to do with the struggle of a number of persons to get possession of or some share in this money. (The other principal industry which figures in *Our Mutual Friend* is the robbing of the dead bodies in the Thames.) But the real meaning of the dust-pile is not in doubt: "My lords and gentlemen and honorable lords," writes Dickens, when the heap is being carted away, "when you in the course of your dust-shoveling and cinder-raking have piled up a mountain of pretentious failure, you must off with your honorable coats for the removal of it, and fall to the work with the power of all the queen's horses and all the queen's men, or it will come rushing down and bury us alive."

Dickens' line in his criticism of society is very clear in *Our Mutual Friend*, and it marks a new position on Dickens' part, as it results from a later phase of the century. Dickens has come at last to despair utterly of the prospering middle class. We have seen how he judged the morality of the merchants. In *Bleak House*, the ironmaster is a progressive and self-sustaining figure who is played off against parasites of various sorts; but in *Hard Times*, written immediately afterward, the later development of Rouncewell is dramatized in the exploiter Bounderby, a new kind of Victorian hypocrite, who pretends to be a self-made man. In *Little Dorrit*, the one set of characters who are comparatively healthy and cheerful still represent that middle-class home which has remained Dickens' touchstone of virtue; but even here there is a distinct change in Dickens' attitude. Mr. Meagles, the retired banker, with his wife and his beloved only daughter, become the prey of Henry Gowan, a well-connected young man of no fortune who manages to lead a futile life (the type has been well observed) between the social and artistic worlds without ever making anything of either. But the smugness and insularity, even the vulgarity, of the Meagleses is felt by Dickens as he has never felt it in connection with such people before. After all, in taking in Tattycoram, the foundling, the Meagleses could not help making her feel her position of inferiority. A little more emphasis in this direction by Dickens and the Meagleses might seem to the reader as odious as they recurrently do to her. Tattycoram herself, with her painful alternations between the extremes of affection and resentment, probably reflects the oscillations of Dickens himself at this period.

But the resentment is to get the upper hand. The Meagleses turn up now as the Podsnaps, that horrendous middle-class family, exponents of all the soundest British virtues, who, however, are quite at home in a social circle of sordid adventurers and phony *nouveaux riches*, and on whom Dickens visits a satire as brutal as themselves. Gone are the high spirits that made of Pecksniff an exhilarating figure of fun—gone with the Yoho! of the stagecoach on which Tom Pinch traveled to London. The Podsnaps, the Lammles, the Veneerings, the Fledgebys, are unpleasant as are no other characters in Dickens. It comes to us as a disturbing realization that Dickens is now *afraid* of Podsnap (who, with his talk about the paramount importance of not bringing the blush to the young person's cheek, would of course have been the loudest among those who disapproved of Dickens' affair with Miss Ternan). And Fledgeby, the young moneylender of the second generation, with his peachy cheeks and slender figure, who lives in the Albany and dines out —Grandfather Smallweed is a man beside him! It is startling to find that Dickens has here even hit upon a principle which another group of commercial-patriotic rotters were later to exploit on a large scale. One of the ugliest scenes in Dickens is that in which Fledgeby ascribes his own characteristics to the gentle old Jew Riah and makes him the agent of his meanness and sharp-dealing. And not content with making Fledgeby a cur, Dickens himself shows a certain cruelty in having him ultimately thrashed by Lammle under circumstances of peculiar ignominy and then having the little dolls' dressmaker apply plasters with pepper on them to his wounds. This incident betrays a kind of sadism which we never felt in Dickens' early work—when Nicholas Nickleby beat Squeers, for example—but which breaks out now and then in these later books in a disagreeable fashion.

If the middle class has here become a monster, the gentry have taken on an aspect more attractive than we have ever known them to wear as a class in any previous novel of Dickens. If an increase of satiric emphasis turns the Meagleses into the Podsnaps, so a shift from the satirical to the straight turns the frivolous and idle young man of good family, who has hitherto always been exhibited as more or less of a scoundrel—James Harthouse or Henry Gowan—into the sympathetic Eugene Wrayburn. Eugene and his friend Mortimer Lightwood, the little old dinerout named Twemlow, the only gentleman in the Veneerings' circle, and the Reverend Frank Milvey, "expensively educated and wretchedly paid," the Christian turned social worker, are the only representatives of the upper strata who are shown as having decent values; and they are all the remnants of an impoverished gentry. Outside these, you find the decent values—or what Dickens intends to be such—in an impoverished proletariat and lower middle class: the modest clerk, the old Jew, the dolls' dressmaker, the dust-contractor's foreman, the old woman who minds children for a living. And the chief heroine is not Bella Wilfer, who has to be cured of her middle-class ideals, but Lizzie Hexam, the illiterate daughter of a Thames-side water-rat. Dickens has here, for the first time in his novels, taken his leading woman from the lowest class; and it will be the principal moral of *Our Mutual Friend* that Wrayburn will have the courage to marry Lizzie. The inevitable conjunction of the high with the low is not here to result in a tragedy but to figure as a fortunate affair. Nor does it involve the whole structure of society in the same way as in the earlier novels: the mechanics are somewhat different. The point is made that the Podsnap-Veneering upper scum of the successful middle class remain unaffected by what has happened and do not seriously affect anyone else. Such people, in Dickens' view, have by this time become completely dissociated from anything that is admirable in English life. Simply, Eugene Wrayburn no longer appears at the Veneerings' parties. When they sneer at the unseemliness of his marriage, Mr. Twemlow suddenly flares up and declares with an authority which makes everyone uncomfortable that Eugene has behaved like a gentleman; and that is the end of the book.

Dickens has aligned himself in *Our Mutual Friend* with a new combination of forces. Shrinking from Podsnap and Veneering, he falls back on that aristocracy he had so savagely attacked in his youth, but to which, through his origins, he had always been closer than he had to the commercial classes. After all, Sir John Chester had had qualities of coolness, grace and ease which, when they appear in an excellent fellow like Eugene, are infinitely preferable to Podsnap. The Chartist movement in England had run into the sands in the fifties; but during the sixties the trade union movement had been making remarkable progress. Dickens had begun *Our Mutual Friend* in the autumn of 1863, and the first number appeared the following May. In July definite steps were taken at a meeting of French and English workers for an "international working men's alliance," and the Workers' International, under the guidance of Karl Marx, was founded at the end of September. This trend may have influenced Dickens, for the final implication of his story is—to state it in the Marxist language—that the declassed representatives of the old professional upper classes may unite with the proletariat against the commercial middle class.

There is, however, another element that plays an important rôle in the story: the proletarian who has educated himself to be a member of this middle class. Lizzie Hexam has a brother, whom she has induced to get an education and who, as soon as he has qualified himself to teach, drops his family even more callously than Pip did his; and the schoolmaster of Charley Hexam's school, another poor man who has advanced himself, is the villain of *Our Mutual Friend*. We are a long way here from the days when the villains and bad characters in Dickens, the Quilps and the Mrs. Gamps, could be so fascinating through their resourcefulness and vitality that, as G. K. Chesterton says, the reader is sorry at the end when they are finally banished from the scene and hopes that the discredited scoundrel will still open the door and stick his head in and make one more atrocious remark. Such figures are so much all of a piece of evil that they have almost a kind of innocence. But here Bradley Headstone has no innocence: he is perverted, tormented, confused. He represents a type which begins to appear in these latest novels of Dickens and which originally derives perhaps from those early theatrical villains, of the type of the elder Rudge or Monks in *Oliver Twist*, skulking figures with black looks and ravaged faces: a literary convention of which one would suppose it would be impossible to make anything plausible. Yet Dickens does finally succeed in giving these dark figures reality.

In Bradley Headstone's case, it is his very aspirations which have gone bad and turned the stiff and anxious schoolmaster into a murderer. He wants to marry Lizzie Hexam and he is wounded by her preference for Eugene, whose nonchalance and grace infuriate him because he knows he can never achieve them. In order to make himself a place in society, he has had rigorously to repress his passions; and now that they finally break out, it is more horrible than Bill Sikes or Jonas Chuzzlewit, because we understand Bradley as a human being. Bradley is the first murderer in Dickens who exhibits any complexity of character. And he is the first to present himself as a member of respectable Victorian society. There is a dreadful and convincing picture of the double life led by Headstone as he goes about his duties as a schoolmaster after he has decided to murder Eugene. In *Great Expectations*, the Ellen Ternan character, Estella, rejects the love of the hero. In *Our Mutual Friend*, Bella Wilfer rejects Rokesmith in much the same way—though less cruelly, and though she later marries him. But Rokesmith is a colorless character, and the real agonies of frustrated passion appear in *Our Mutual Friend* in the scene between Bradley and Lizzie. This is the kind of thing—the Carker and Edith Dombey kind of thing—that is likely to be bad in Dickens; but here it has a certain reality and a certain unpleasant power. Who can forget the top-hatted schoolmaster striking his fist against the stone wall of the church?

The inference is, of course, that Bradley, if he had not been shipwrecked in this way, would have approximated as closely as possible to some sort of Murdstone or Gradgrind. But his death has a tragic symbolism which suggests a different kind of moral. In order to escape detection, he has disguised himself at the time of the murder as a disreputable water-side character who is known to have a grievance against Eugene. When the man finds out what has happened, he makes capital of it by blackmailing Bradley. Headstone finally tackles him on the edge of the deep lock of a canal, drags him into the water, and holds him under until he is drowned; but in doing so, he drowns himself. It is as if the illiterate ruffian whom he would now never be able to shake off has come to represent the brutish part of Bradley's own nature. Having failed to destroy Eugene, he destroys himself with the brute.

VI

In *The Mystery of Edwin Drood*, the motif of Bradley Headstone is, with certain variations, repeated. This novel, written five years later, Dickens never lived to finish, and it is supposed to have been left an

enigma. We must first try to solve this enigma; and
to do so we must proceed with a consciousness of the
real meaning of Dickens' work. For though it is true
that *Edwin Drood* has been enormously written
about, it has been always from the point of view of
trying to find out what Dickens intended to do with
the plot. None of the more serious critics of Dickens
has ever been able to take the novel very seriously.
They persist in dismissing it as a detective story with
good touches and promising characters, but of no
interest in the development of Dickens' genius. Bernard Shaw, who is interested in the social side of
Dickens, declares that it is "only a gesture by a man
three quarters dead"; and it is true, as Forster remarked, that *The Mystery of Edwin Drood* seems
quite free from the social criticism which had grown
more biting as Dickens grew older; but what Forster
and Shaw do not see is that the psychological interest
which had been a feature of Dickens' later period is
carried farther in *Edwin Drood*. Like all the books
that Dickens wrote under the strain of his later years,
it has behind it bitter judgments and desperate emotions. Here as elsewhere the solution of the mystery
was to have said something that Dickens wanted to
say.

It did not, it is true, become possible to gauge the
full significance of the novel until certain key discoveries had been made in regard to the plot itself;
but the creation of such a character as John Jasper at
this point in Dickens' development should have had
its significance for any student of Dickens and should
have led to a more careful consideration, in the light
of certain hints supplied by Forster, of the psychological possibilities of the character. It has remained
for two American scholars to hit upon the cardinal
secrets that explain the personality of Jasper. Since
both these discoveries have been made since the publication in 1912 of W. Robertson Nicoll's otherwise
comprehensive book, *The Problem of Edwin Drood*,
they have not received attention there; they are not

included by Thomas Wright in the bibliography of
Edwin Drood in his *Life of Charles Dickens*, published in 1936; and so far as I know, up to the present
time, nobody who has written about Dickens has
been in a position to combine these ideas. Yet what
happens when one puts them together is startling:
the old novel acquires a sudden new value. Just as
one can revive invisible ink by holding it over a lamp
or bring out three dimensions in a photograph by
looking at it through certain lenses, so it is possible
to recall to life the character of John Jasper as he
must have been conceived by Dickens.

The most important revelation about *Edwin
Drood* has been made by Mr. Howard Duffield, who
published an article called *John Jasper—Strangler* in
The American Bookman of February, 1930. Mr.
Duffield has here shown conclusively that Jasper is
supposed to be a member of the Indian sect of
Thugs, who made a profession of ingratiating themselves with travelers and then strangling them with a
handkerchief and robbing them. This brotherhood,
which had been operating for centuries pretty much
all over India and which had given the British government a great deal of trouble before it succeeded
in putting them down during the thirties, had already
attracted attention in the West. Two of the British
officers who had been engaged in the suppression of
the Thugs had written books about them—one of
them in the form of a story, Meadows Taylor's *Con-
fessions of a Thug*, supposed to be narrated by the
Thug himself. Eugène Sue had introduced into *The
Wandering Jew* a Thug strangler practicing in Europe; and an American novelist, James de Mille, was
publishing a novel called *Cord and Creese*, which exploited the situation of an Englishman affiliated with
the Thugs, in the same year, 1869, that Dickens began
Edwin Drood. We know that Dickens' friend,
Bulwer Lytton, had already thought of using this
theme. Dickens himself had mentioned the Thugs
in 1857 in connection with a garrotting epidemic

in London. The publication in 1868 of Wilkie Collins' detective story, *The Moonstone*, in which a band of Hindu devotees commit a secret murder in England, seems to have inspired Dickens with the idea of outdoing his friend the next year with a story of a similar kind.

Now, we know from the statement of Sir Luke Fildes, Dickens' illustrator in *Edwin Drood*, that Dickens intended to have Jasper strangle Drood with the long scarf which he (Jasper) wears around his neck; and we know from many circumstances and certain hints that the story is to have its roots in the East. Neville and Helena Landless are supposed to come from Ceylon; and Mr. Jasper, who smokes opium and sees elephants in his trances, is described as having "thick, lustrous, well-arranged black hair and whiskers" and a voice that sometimes sounds "womanish"—in short, as something very much like a Hindu. Furthermore, as Mr. Duffield has established, John Jasper—and this explains a good deal that has never been understood—has been trying to fulfill the ritualistic requirements for a sanctified and successful Thug murder. The Thugs were worshipers of Kali, the Hindu goddess of destruction, and their methods had been prescribed by the goddess. They had to commit their crimes with the fold of cloth which was a fragment of the gown of Kali. Kali's gown was supposed to be black, and Jasper's scarf is black. This cloth had to be worn, as Jasper's scarf is. A secret burial place had to be selected, as Jasper selects Mrs. Sapsea's tomb, before the murder took place. The omens had to be observed, as is done by Mr. Jasper when he makes his nocturnal trip to the top of the cathedral tower; the call of a rook in sight of a river was regarded as a favorable sign, the approving word of the goddess, and that, one finds, is precisely what Jasper hears. The significance of the birds is planted plainly at the beginning of Chapter II, when the Cloisterham rooks are first mentioned: "Whosoever has observed that sedate and clerical bird, the rook, may perhaps have noticed that when he wings his way homeward toward nightfall, in a sedate and clerical company, two rooks will suddenly detach themselves from the rest, will retrace their flight for some distance, and will there poise and linger; conveying to mere men the fancy that it is of some occult importance to the body politic, that this artful couple should pretend to have renounced connection with it." The Thug preys exclusively on travelers: Edwin Drood is going on a journey; and when Jasper, in his second opium dream, is heard talking to himself about the murder, it is all in terms of a journey and a fellow traveler. The Thug is to use exaggerated words of endearment, as Jasper does with Drood. He is to persuade his victim to leave his lodging a little after midnight, as Jasper has done Drood, and to stupefy him with a drug in his food or drink, as Jasper has obviously done, first to Edwin and Neville, and afterwards to Durdles.

Since Jasper is eventually to be caught, he is evidently to have slipped up in the ritual. Mr. Duffield suggests that Jasper's mistake has been to commit the murder without an assistant; but he has overlooked the Thug superstition (recorded by Edward Thornton in *Illustrations of the History and Practices of the Thugs,* published in 1837) that nothing but evil could come of murdering a man with any gold in his possession. Now Drood, unknown to Jasper, is carrying the gold ring which Grewgious has given him for Rosa; and we have it on Dickens' own testimony to Forster that the body of Edwin Drood is to be identified by means of this ring, which has survived the effects of the quicklime. True, Edwin had also been wearing the stickpin and the gold watch; but since Jasper knew about these and took care to leave them in the weir, he may have made a point of removing them after Edwin was drugged and before he committed the murder.

Supplementing this interesting discovery we find a paper by Mr. Aubrey Boyd in the series of *Human-*

istic Studies (Volume IX) published by Washington University, in which he shows that Jasper is also a hypnotist. Dickens had always been interested in hypnotism. Forster speaks of his first seriously studying it in 1841. He even found that he himself, with that extraordinarily magnetic personality which made it possible for him so to fascinate his audiences and which exerted, as Mrs. Perugini testifies, so irresistible a power over his family, had the ability to hypnotize. His first experiment was performed on his wife in the course of his earlier trip to America. He had, he wrote Forster, been "holding forth upon the subject rather luminously, and asserting that I thought I could exercise the influence, but had never tried." "Kate sat down, laughing, for me to try my hand upon her. . . . In six minutes, I magnetized her into hysterics, and then into the magnetic sleep. I tried again next night, and she fell into the slumber in little more than two minutes. . . . I can wake her with perfect ease; but I confess (not being prepared for anything so sudden and complete) I was on the first occasion rather alarmed." Later, we hear of his hypnotizing John Leech in order to relieve his pain during an illness.

In the meantime, he had a strange experience, reported by Mrs. Perugini, with an Englishwoman he had met in Genoa in 1844. This lady, who was married to a Swiss printer, was afflicted with delusions that "took the form of a phantom which spoke to her, and other illusionary figures of the most hideous shapes and gory appearance, which came in a crowd, chattering one to the other as they pursued her, and after a time faded, veiling their loathsome faces as they disappeared into space." Dickens, who at the time was suffering from a recurrence of the spasms of pain in his side which had afflicted him as a child in the blacking warehouse, hypnotized her once or twice every day and found that he could control the delusions. He seems to have become obsessed with the case: the treatment went on for months. On one occasion, "he was in such a fever of anxiety to receive a letter from his friend concerning the state of his wife that he watched through a telescope the arrival of the mailbags into port." He mesmerized her "in the open country and at wayside inns where . . . they would halt for refreshment or stay the night. He mesmerized her in railway carriages—anywhere, if the moment was opportune. By degrees she became better and more serene in her mind and body." The delusions were apparently dispelled.

It was obviously on the cards that Dickens would do something with this subject in his novels; and it ought to have given the Drood experts a lead when they encountered a reference to it in the third chapter of *Edwin Drood*. W. Robertson Nicoll, disregarding this key passage, mentions the matter in another connection: he sees that Jasper has "willed" Crisparkle to go to the weir, where he will find the watch and stickpin of Edwin; but he does not inquire farther. It remained for Mr. Boyd, who has some special knowledge of Mesmer and his writings, to recognize that Dickens has introduced the whole repertory of the supposed feats of mesmerism—called also "animal magnetism" at the time—just as he has reproduced the practices of the Thugs. Mr. Jasper is clearly exercising "animal magnetism," in this case the kind known as "malicious," on Rosa Budd in the scene in which he accompanies her at the piano; he is exercising it on Edwin and Neville when he causes them to quarrel in his rooms. It was supposed in Dickens' time that this influence could be projected through the agency of mere sound: hence the insistent keynote in the piano scene and the swelling note of the organ that frightens Rosa in the garden. And it was also supposed to penetrate matter: hence Rosa's remark to Helena that she feels as if Jasper could reach her through a wall. It could be made to impregnate objects in such a way as to remain effective after the master of the magnetic fluid was no longer himself on the scene: Jasper has put a spell on the water in which Edwin's watch and stickpin are to be found.

And it is possible, though Mr. Boyd does not suggest it, that the transmission of Jasper's influence from a distance may also explain the behavior, of which the implausible character has been noted, of the men who pursue and waylay Landless.

The revealing hint here, however, is the passage in the third chapter, of which Boyd has understood the significance and which has led him to a brilliant conjecture: "As, in some cases of drunkenness," writes Dickens, "and in others of animal magnetism, there are two states of consciousness that never clash, but each of which pursues its separate course as though it were continuous instead of broken (thus, if I hide my watch when I am drunk, I must be drunk again before I can remember where), so Miss Twinkleton has two distinct and separate phases of being." Dickens had told Forster that the originality of his idea for *Drood*, "a very strong one, though difficult to work" (Dickens' words in a letter), was to consist (Forster's words in recounting a conversation with Dickens) "in the review of the murderer's career by himself at the close, when its temptations were to be dwelt upon as if, not he the culprit, but some other man, were the tempted. The last chapters were to be written in the condemned cell, to which his wickedness, all elaborately elicited from him as if told of another, had brought him."

John Jasper has then "two states of consciousness"; he is, in short, what we have come to call a dual personality. On the principle that "if I hide my watch when I am drunk, I must be drunk again before I can remember where," it will be necessary, in order to extort his confession, to induce in him that state of consciousness, evidently not the one with which he meets the cathedral world, which has driven him to commit the murder. The possibility of opium, suggested by Robertson Nicoll, ought surely to be excluded, since Wilkie Collins, in *The Moonstone*, had just made use of this device: the man who has taken the Moonstone under the influence of laudanum, administered to him without his knowing it, is made to repeat his action under the influence of a second dose. The drunkenness in which Jasper will betray himself will not, then, be produced by a drug. Dickens must go Collins one better. Mr. Boyd has evidently solved the puzzle in guessing that Helena Landless is eventually to hypnotize Jasper. In the scene at the piano, in which Jasper is made to work upon Rosa with the effect of her becoming hysterical, Helena maintains an attitude of defiance and announces that she is not afraid of him. It had already been established by J. Cuming Walters—it was the first of the important discoveries about *Drood*—that Datchery, the mysterious character who comes to Cloisterham to spy on Jasper, is Helena in disguise. We have been told, in Chapter VII, that Helena had several times "dressed as a boy, and shown the daring of a man," in running away from her brutal stepfather; and Dickens' alterations in his text, both the amplifications of the written copy and the later excisions from the proofs, indicate very clearly that he was aiming— in dealing with such details as Helena's wig and her attempts to conceal her feminine hands—to insinuate evidences of her real identity without allowing the reader to find it out too soon. Helena is to get the goods on Jasper, and in the end, having no doubt acquired in India the same secret which he has been exploiting (there may be also, as so often in Dickens, some question of a family relationship), she will put him in a trance and make him speak.

What Mr. Boyd, however, was not in a position to do was combine this idea with the Thug theme. The Thugs were all in a sense divided personalities. Colonel James L. Sleeman, in his book on the subject, emphasizes what he calls this "Jekyll-and-Hyde" aspect of their activities. The Thugs were devoted husbands and loving fathers; they made a point—again like Mr. Jasper—of holding positions of honor in the community. And in their own eyes they were virtuous persons: they were serving the cult of the goddess.

In their case, the Jekyll-and-Hyde aspect of their careers was exceptional only from the point of view of persons outside the cult. When caught, they would proudly confess to the number of lives they had taken. But in the case of Mr. Jasper, there is a respectable and cultivated Christian gentleman living in the same soul and body with a worshiper of the goddess Kali. The murder has been rehearsed in his opium dreams: he has evidently gone to the opium den for that purpose. He has kept himself under the influence of the drug all the time he has been plotting the murder. But it will not be possible to make him confess by compelling him to take opium. Helena, with her stronger will, will achieve this through hypnotism.

And now what has all this to do with the Dickens we already know? Why should he have occupied the last years of his life in concocting this sinister detective story?

Let us return to his situation at this period. He is still living between Gadshill and the house of Ellen Lawless Ternan, who appears now in *Edwin Drood* identified even more plainly than before under the name of Helena Landless. The motif of the disagreeable scene between Bradley Headstone and Lizzie Hexam is repeated in the even more unpleasant, though theatrical and unconvincing, interview between Jasper and Rosa Budd—Jasper presenting, like Headstone, a ghastly travesty of the respectable Victorian. The Ellen Ternan heroine is here frankly made an actress: Helena Landless is an impersonator so accomplished that she can successfully play a male character in real life; and she is even more formidable than Estella because she is to stand up to and unmask Jasper. Her strength is to be contrasted not only with the fatal duplicity of Jasper, but with the weakness of Drood and Neville. All of these three men are to perish, and Helena is to marry Mr. Tartar, the foursquare young ex-Navy man, bursting with good spirits, agility and a perhaps rather overdone good health.

Dickens had just finished his public appearances and had said his farewell to the platform. The great feature of his last series of readings had been the murder of Nancy by Sikes, a performance which he had previously tried on his friends and from which Forster and others had tried to dissuade him. He was warned by a woman's doctor of his acquaintance that "if only one woman cries out when you murder the girl, there will be a contagion of hysteria all over the place." But Dickens obviously derived from thus horrifying his hearers some sort of satisfaction. The scene was perhaps a symbolical representation of his behavior in banishing his wife. Certainly the murder of Nancy had taken on something of the nature of an obsessive hallucination. Dickens' imagination had always been subject to a tendency of this kind. It had been pointed out by Taine that the fantasies and monomanias of his lunatics only heighten characteristics that are apparent in Dickens' whole work—the concentration on and reiteration of some isolated aspect or detail of a person or a place, as when Mr. Dick in *David Copperfield* is haunted by King Charles's head. In one of the sketches of *The Uncommercial Traveller*, written during these later years, Dickens tells of having been obsessed by the image of a drowned and bloated corpse that he had seen in the Paris morgue, which for days kept popping up among the people and things he encountered and sometimes compelled him to leave public places, though it eventually drove him back to the morgue. In the case of the woman in Italy whose delusions he attempted to dispel, one gets the impression that these bloody visions were almost as real to him as they were to her. And now, at the time of these readings, he jokes about his "murderous instincts" and says that he goes about the street feeling as if he were "wanted" by the police.

He threw himself at any rate into the murder scene

with a passion that became quite hysterical, as if reading it had become at this point in his life a real means of self-expression. At Clifton, he wrote Forster, "we had a contagion of fainting; and yet the place was not hot. I should think we had from a dozen to twenty ladies taken out stiff and rigid, at various times!" At Leeds, whether to intensify the effect or to avert the possible objections of the audience, he hired a man to rise from the stalls and protest in the middle of the murder scene against daring to read such a thing before ladies—with the result that the people hissed him and put him out. It was the opinion of Dickens' doctor that the excitement and strain of acting this episode were the immediate cause of Dickens' death. It always took him a long time to calm himself after he had played this scene, and the doctor who noted his pulse at the end of each selection saw that it always ran higher then than it did after any of the other scenes. When Dolby, the manager of Dickens' tours, tried to persuade him to cut down on the murder, reserving it for the larger towns, Dickens had a paroxysm of rage: "Bounding up from his chair, and throwing his knife and fork on his plate (which he smashed to atoms), he exclaimed: 'Dolby! your infernal caution will be your ruin one of these days!'" Immediately afterwards, he began to weep and told Dolby that he knew he was right. The doctors eventually compelled him to interrupt his tour and take a rest.

His son, Sir Henry Dickens, who speaks in his memoir of his father of the latter's "heavy moods of deep depression, of intense nervous irritability, when he was silent and oppressed," tells of an incident that occurred at a Christmas party the winter before Dickens died: "He had been ailing very much and greatly troubled with his leg, which had been giving him much pain; so he was lying on a sofa one evening after dinner, while the rest of the family were playing games." Dickens participated in one of these games, in which you had to remember long strings of words, contributed by the players in rotation. When it came around to Dickens, he gave a name which meant nothing to anybody: "Warren's Blacking, 30, Strand." He did this, says his son, who knew nothing at that time of this episode in his father's childhood, "with an odd twinkle and strange inflection in his voice which at once forcibly arrested my attention and left a vivid impression on my mind for some time afterwards. Why, I could not, for the life of me, understand. . . . At that time, when the stroke that killed him was gradually overpowering him, his mind reverted to the struggles and degradation of his childhood, which had caused him such intense agony of mind, and which he had never been able entirely to cast from him."

Two weeks before his death, he went to a dinner arranged by Lord and Lady Houghton in order that the Prince of Wales and the King of Belgium might meet him. Lady Houghton was a granddaughter of that Lord Crewe in whose house Dickens' grandfather had been butler. She well remembered going as a child to the housekeeper's room to hear his grandmother tell wonderful stories. Dickens' neuritic foot was giving him such trouble at this time that up till almost an hour before dinner he could not be sure of going. He did finally decide to go; but when he got to the Houghton house, he found that he could not mount the stairs, and the Prince and the Belgian king had to come down to meet him.

But now the Dickens who has been cut off from society has discarded the theme of the rebel and is carrying the theme of the criminal, which has haunted him all his life, to its logical development in his fiction. He is to explore the deep entanglement and conflict of the bad and the good in one man. The subject of *Edwin Drood* is the subject of Poe's *William Wilson*, the subject of *Dr. Jekyll and Mr. Hyde*, the subject of *Dorian Gray*. It is also the subject of

that greater work than any of these, Dostoevsky's
Crime and Punishment. Dostoevsky, who owed so
much to Dickens and who was probably influenced
by the murder in *Chuzzlewit*, had produced in 1866
a masterpiece on the theme at which Dickens is only
just arriving in 1869. Raskólnikov—*raskólnik* means
dissenter—combines in his single person the two
antisocial types of the deliberate criminal and the
rebel, which, since Hugh in *Barnaby Rudge*, Dickens
has been keeping distinct. Dostoevsky, with the courage of his insight, has studied the states of mind which
are the results of a secession from society: the contemptuous will to spurn and to crush confused with
the impulse toward human brotherhood, the desire to be loved twisted tragically with the desire to
destroy and to kill. But the English Dickens, with his
middle-class audience, would not be able to tell such
a story even if he dared to imagine it. In order to
stage the "war in the members," he must contrive a
whole machinery of mystification: of drugs, of tele-
pathic powers, of remote oriental cults.

How far he has come and to how strange a goal we
recognize when we note that he has returned to that
Rochester he had so loved in his boyhood—the
Rochester where he had made Mr. Pickwick put up
at the Bull Inn and picnic on good wine and cold
fowl out of the hampers of the Wardles' barouche.
Gadshill was next door to Rochester, and the Cloisterham of the novel is Rochester; but what Dickens
finds in Rochester today is the nightmare of John
Jasper. There is plenty of brightness in *Edwin Drood*
and something of the good things of life: Mrs. Crisparkle's spices, jams and jellies, Mr. Tartar's shipshape
rooms; but this brightness has a quality new and
queer. The vivid colors of *Edwin Drood* make
upon us an impression more disturbing than the
dustiness, the weariness, the dreariness, that set the
tone for *Our Mutual Friend*. In this new novel, which
is to be his last, Dickens has found a new intensity.
The descriptions of Cloisterham are among the best

written in all his fiction: they have a nervous concentration and economy (nervous in the old-fashioned sense) that produce a rather different effect from anything one remembers in the work of his previous phases. We are far from the prodigal improvisation of the poetical early Dickens: here every descriptive phrase is loaded with implication. It is as if Dickens' art, which in *Our Mutual Friend* had come to seem to him so sorely fatigued, has now rested and found a revival. Dickens at last, here, has abandoned the task of analyzing society—British imperialism in the East is evidently to play some part in the story, but it is impossible to tell whether this is to have any moral implications. (A writer in the Princeton undergraduate publication, the *Nassau Literary Magazine*, of May, 1882, who complains of the little interest that has been shown in *Edwin Drood*, suggests that the opium traffic may be the social problem here.) Here, so far as we can see, the novelist is exclusively concerned with a psychological problem. The duality of high and low, rich and poor, has here given place completely to the duality of good and evil. The remarkable opening pages in which the Victorian choirmaster, with his side whiskers and tall hat, mixes, in his opium-vision, the picture of the English cathedral with memories of the Orient and comes to in the squalid den to stagger out, short of breath, to his services, is for its time, from the psychological point of view, a very complex piece of writing. But the characters that are healthy, bright and good—Rosa Budd, for example, with her baby name—seem almost as two-dimensional as colored paper dolls. We have got back to the fairy tale again. Yet this fairy tale contains no Pickwick: its most convincing figure is Jasper; and its most powerful artistic effect is procured by an instillation into the greenery, the cathedral, the winter sun, the sober and tranquil old town, of the suggestion of moral insecurity, of evil. Even the English rooks, which in *The Old Curiosity Shop* had figured simply as a pleasant feature of the old English countryside in which Nell and her grandfather wandered, have here become the omens of a terror that comes from outside that English world. The Christmas season itself, of which Dickens has been the laureate, which he has celebrated so often with warm charity, candid hopes and hearty cheer, is now the appointed moment for the murder by an uncle of his nephew.

Mr. Jasper is, like Dickens, an artist: he is a musician, he possesses a magical voice. He smokes opium, and so, like Dickens, leads a life of the imagination apart from the common life. Like Dickens, he is a skilful magician, whose power over his fellows may be dangerous. Like Dickens, he is an alien from another world; yet, like Dickens, he has made himself respected in the conventional English community. Is he a villain? From the point of view of the cathedral congregation of Cloisterham, who have admired his ability as an artist, he will be seen to have been playing a diabolic rôle. All that sentiment, all those edifying high spirits, which Dickens has been dispensing so long, which he is still making the effort to dispense—have they now grown as false as those hymns to the glory of the Christian God which are performed by the worshiper of Kali? And yet in another land there exists another point of view from which Jasper is seen to figure as a good and faithful servant. It has been driven by his *alter ego* and acting in the name of his goddess that Jasper has committed his crime.

None the less, he is a damned soul here and now. All this bright and pious foreground of England is to open or fade away, and to show a man condemned to death. But it will not be the innocent Pickwick, the innocent Micawber, the innocent Dorrit, whom we are now to meet in jail: nor yet the wicked Fagin, the wicked Dennis, the wicked elder Rudge. It will be a man who is both innocent and wicked. The protest against the age has turned into a protest against self. In this last moment, the old hierarchy of England does enjoy a sort of triumph over the weary and debilitated Dickens, because it has made him accept its ruling that he is a creature irretrievably tainted; and the mercantile middle-class England has had its triumph, too. For the Victorian hypocrite—developing from Pecksniff, through Murdstone, through Headstone, to his final transformation in Jasper—has finally come to present an insoluble moral problem which is identified with Dickens' own. As Headstone makes his own knuckles bleed in striking them against the church and drowns himself in order to drown Riderhood, so Jasper is eventually to destroy himself. When he announces in the language of the Thugs that he "devotes" himself to the "destruction" of the murderer, he is preparing his own execution. (He is evidently quite sincere in making this entry in his diary, for he has now sobered up from the opium and resumed his Cloisterham personality. It is exclusively of this personality that the diary is a record.) So Dickens, in putting his nerves to the torture by enacting the murder of Nancy, has been invoking his own death.

In this last condemned cell of Dickens, the respectable half of the divided John Jasper was to be brought face to face with the other half. But this confrontation—"difficult to work," as Dickens had told Forster—was never, in fact, to take place. For Dickens, in his moral confusion, was never completely to dramatize himself, was not, even in this final phase, to succeed in coming quite clear. He was to leave *Edwin Drood* half-finished, with Jasper's confession just around the corner.

He had put in a long day on *Drood* when (June 9, 1870) he had a stroke while he was eating dinner. He got up from the table in his stunned condition and said he must go to London; then he fell to the floor and never recovered consciousness. He died the next afternoon.

1941

HEMINGWAY: GAUGE OF MORALE

Ernest Hemingway's *In Our Time* was an odd and original book. It had the appearance of a miscellany of stories and fragments; but actually the parts hung together and produced a definite effect. There were two distinct series of pieces which alternated with one another: one a set of brief and brutal sketches of police shootings, bullfight crises, hangings of criminals, and incidents of the war; and the other a set of short stories dealing in its principal sequence with the growing-up of an American boy against a landscape of idyllic Michigan, but interspersed also with glimpses of American soldiers returning home. It seems to have been Hemingway's intention—"*In Our Time*"—that the war should set the key for the whole. The cold-bloodedness of the battles and executions strikes a discord with the sensitiveness and candor of the boy at home in the States; and presently the boy turns up in Europe in one of the intermediate vignettes as a soldier in the Italian army, hit in the spine by machine-gun fire and trying to talk to a dying Italian: "*Senta*, Rinaldi. *Senta*," he says, "you and me, we've made a separate peace."

But there is a more fundamental relationship between the pieces of the two series. The shooting of Nick in the war does not really connect two different worlds: has he not found in the butchery abroad the same world that he knew back in Michigan? Was not life in the Michigan woods equally destructive and cruel? He had gone once with his father, the doctor, when he had performed a Caesarean operation on an Indian squaw with a jacknife and no anaesthetic and had sewed her up with fishing leaders, while the Indian hadn't been able to bear it and had cut his throat in his bunk. Another time, when the doctor had saved the life of a squaw, her Indian had picked a quarrel with him rather than pay him in work. And Nick himself had sent his girl about her business when he had found out how terrible her mother was. Even fishing in Big Two-Hearted River—away and free in the woods—he had been conscious in a curious way of the cruelty inflicted on the fish, even of the silent agonies endured by the live bait, the grasshoppers kicking on the hook.

Not that life isn't enjoyable. Talking and drinking with one's friends is great fun; fishing in Big Two-Hearted River is a tranquil exhilaration. But the brutality of life is always there, and it is somehow bound up with the enjoyment. Bullfights are especially enjoyable. It is even exhilarating to build a simply priceless barricade and pot the enemy as they are trying to get over it. The condition of life is pain; and the joys of the most innocent surface are somehow tied to its stifled pangs.

The resolution of this dissonance in art made the beauty of Hemingway's stories. He had in the process tuned a marvelous prose. Out of the colloquial American speech, with its simple declarative sentences and its strings of Nordic monosyllables, he got effects of the utmost subtlety. F. M. Ford has found the perfect simile for the impression produced by this writing: "Hemingway's words strike you, each one, as if they were pebbles fetched fresh from a brook. They live and shine, each in its place. So one of his pages has the effect of a brook-bottom into which you look down through the flowing water. The words form a tessellation, each in order beside the other."

Looking back, we can see how this style was already being refined and developed at a time—fifty years before—when it was regarded in most literary quarters as hopelessly non-literary and vulgar. Had there not been the nineteenth chapter of *Huckleberry Finn?*—"Two or three nights went by; I reckon I might say they swum by; they slid along so quick and smooth and lovely. Here is the way we put in the time. It was a monstrous big river down there—sometimes a mile and a half wide," and so forth. These pages, when we happen to meet them in Carl Van Doren's anthology of world literature, stand up in a striking way beside a passage of description from Turgenev; and the pages which Hemingway was later to write about American wood and water are equivalents to the transcriptions by Turgenev—the *Sportsman's Notebook* is much admired by Hemingway—of Russian forests and fields. Each has brought to an immense and wild country the freshness of a new speech and a sensibility not yet conventionalized by literary associations. Yet it *is* the European sensibility which has come to Big Two-Hearted River, where the Indians are now obsolescent; in those solitudes it feels for the first time the cold current, the hot morning sun, sees the pine stumps, smells the sweet fern. And along with the mottled trout, with its "clear water-over-gravel color," the boy from the American Middle West fishes up a nice little masterpiece.

In the meantime there had been also Ring Lardner, Sherwood Anderson, Gertrude Stein, using this American language for irony, lyric poetry or psychological insight. Hemingway seems to have learned from them all. But he is now able to charge this naïve accent with a new complexity of emotion, a new shade of emotion: a malaise. The wholesale shattering of human beings in which he has taken part has given the boy a touch of panic.

II

The next fishing trip is strikingly different. Perhaps the first had been an idealization. Is it possible to attain to such sensuous bliss merely through going alone into the woods: smoking, fishing, and eating, with no thought about anyone else or about anything one has ever done or will ever be obliged to do? At any rate, today, in *The Sun Also Rises,* all the things that are wrong with human life are there on the holiday, too—though one tries to keep them back out of the foreground and to occupy one's mind with the trout, caught now in a stream of the Pyrenees, and with the kidding of the friend from the States. The feeling of insecurity has deepened. The young American now appears in a seriously damaged condition: he has somehow been incapacitated sexually through wounds received in the war. He is in love with one of those international sirens who flourished in the cafés of the post-war period and whose ruthless and uncontrollable infidelities, in such a circle as that depicted by Hemingway, have made any sort of security impossible for the relations between women and men. The lovers of such a woman turn upon and rend one another because they are powerless to make themselves felt by *her.*

The casualties of the bullfight at Pamplona, to which these young people have gone for the *fiesta,* only reflect the blows and betrayals of demoralized human beings out of hand. What is the tiresome lover with whom the lady has just been off on a casual escapade, and who is unable to understand that he has been discarded, but the man who, on his way to the bull ring, has been accidentally gored by the bull? The young American who tells the story is the only character who keeps up standards of conduct, and he is prevented by his disability from dominating and directing the woman, who otherwise, it is intimated, might love him. Here the membrane of the style has been stretched taut to convey the vibrations of these qualms. The dry sunlight and the green summer landscapes have been invested with a sinister quality which must be new in literature. One enjoys the sun and the green as one enjoys suckling pigs and Spanish wine, but the uneasiness and apprehension are undruggable.

Yet one can catch hold of a code in all the drunkenness and the social chaos. "Perhaps as you went along you did learn something," Jake, the hero, reflects at one point. "I did not care what it was all about. All I wanted to know was how to live in it. Maybe if you found out how to live in it you learned from that what it was all about." "Everybody behaves badly. Give them the proper chance," he says later to Lady Brett.

"'You wouldn't behave badly.' Brett looked at me." In the end, she sends for Jake, who finds her alone in a hotel. She has left her regular lover for a young bullfighter, and this boy has for the first time inspired her with a respect which has restrained her from "ruining" him: "You know it makes one feel rather good deciding not to be a bitch." We suffer and we make suffer, and everybody loses out in the long run; but in the meantime we can lose with honor.

This code still markedly figures, still supplies a dependable moral backbone, in Hemingway's next book of short stories, *Men Without Women*. Here Hemingway has mastered his method of economy in apparent casualness and relevance in apparent indirection, and has turned his sense of what happens and the way in which it happens into something as hard and clear as a crystal but as disturbing as a great lyric. Yet it is usually some principle of courage, of honor, of pity—that is, some principle of sportsmanship in its largest human sense—upon which the drama hinges. The old bullfighter in *The Undefeated* is defeated in everything except the spirit which will not accept defeat. You get the bull or he gets you: if you die, you can die game; there are certain things you cannot do. The burlesque show manager in *A Pursuit Race* refrains from waking his advance publicity agent when he overtakes him and realizes that the man has just lost a long struggle against whatever anguish it is that has driven him to drink and dope. "They got a cure for that," the manager had said to him before he went to sleep; " 'No,' William Campbell said, 'they haven't got a cure for anything.' " The burned major in *A Simple Enquiry*—that strange picture of the bedrock stoicism compatible with the abasement of war —has the decency not to dismiss the orderly who has rejected his proposition. The brutalized Alpine peasant who has been in the habit of hanging a lantern in the jaws of the stiffened corpse of his wife, stood in the corner of the woodshed till the spring will make it possible to bury her, is ashamed to drink with the sexton after the latter has found out what he has done. And there is a little sketch of Roman soldiers just after the Crucifixion: "You see me slip the old spear into him?—You'll get into trouble doing that some day.—It was the least I could do for him. I'll tell you he looked pretty good to me in there today."

This Hemingway of the middle twenties—*The Sun Also Rises* came out in '26—expressed the romantic disillusion and set the favorite pose for the period. It was the moment of gallantry in heartbreak, grim and nonchalant banter, and heroic dissipation. The great watchword was "Have a drink"; and in the bars of New York and Paris the young people were getting to talk like Hemingway.

III

The novel, *A Farewell to Arms*, which followed *Men Without Women*, is in a sense not so serious an affair. Beautifully written and quite moving of course it is. Probably no other book has caught so well the strangeness of life in the army for an American in Europe during the war. The new places to which one

was sent of which one had never heard, and the things
that turned out to be in them; the ordinary people of
foreign countries as one saw them when one was quar-
tered among them or obliged to perform some common work with them; the pleasures of which one managed to cheat the war, intensified by the uncertainty
and horror—and the uncertainty, nevertheless, almost
become a constant, the horror almost taken for
granted; the love affairs, always subject to being suddenly broken up and yet carried on while they lasted
in a spirit of irresponsible freedom which derived
from one's having forfeited control of all one's other
actions—this Hemingway got into his book, written
long enough after the events for them to present
themselves under an aspect fully idyllic.

But *A Farewell to Arms* is a tragedy, and the lovers
are shown as innocent victims with no relation to the
forces that torment them. They themselves are not
tormented within by that dissonance between personal satisfaction and the suffering one shares with
others which it has been Hemingway's triumph to
handle. *A Farewell to Arms,* as the author once said,
is a *Romeo and Juliet.* And when Catherine and
her lover emerge from the stream of action—the account of the Caporetto retreat is Hemingway's best
sustained piece of narrative—when they escape from
the alien necessities of which their romance has
been merely an accident, which have been writing
their story for them, then we see that they are not in
themselves convincing as human personalities. And
we are confronted with the paradox that Hemingway,
who possesses so remarkable a mimetic gift in getting
the tone of social and national types and in making
his people talk appropriately, has not shown any very
solid sense of character, or, indeed, any real interest
in it. The people in his short stories are satisfactory
because he has only to hit them off: the point of
the story does not lie in personalities, but in the emotion to which a situation gives rise. This is true even
in *The Sun Also Rises,* where the characters are

sketched with wonderful cleverness. But in A *Farewell to Arms*, as soon as we are brought into real intimacy with the lovers, as soon as the author is obliged to see them through a searching personal experience, we find merely an idealized relationship, the abstractions of a lyric emotion.

With *Death in the Afternoon*, three years later, a new development for Hemingway commences. He writes a book not merely in the first person, but in the first person in his own character as Hemingway, and the results are unexpected and disconcerting. *Death in the Afternoon* has its value as an exposition of bullfighting; and Hemingway is able to use the subject as a text for an explicit statement of his conception of man eternally pitting himself—he thinks the bullfight a ritual of this—against animal force and the odds of death. But the book is partly infected by a queer kind of maudlin emotion, which sounds at once neurotic and drunken. He overdoes his glorification of the bravery and martyrdom of the bullfighter. No doubt the professional expert at risking his life single-handed is impressive in contrast to the flatness and unreality of much of the business of the modern world; but this admirable miniaturist in prose has already made the point perhaps more tellingly in the little prose poem called *Banal Story*. Now he offsets the virility of the bullfighters by anecdotes of the male homosexuals that frequent the Paris cafés, at the same time that he puts his chief celebration of the voluptuous excitement of the spectacle into the mouth of an imaginary old lady. The whole thing becomes a little hysterical.

The master of that precise and clean style now indulges in purple patches which go on spreading for pages. I am not one of those who admire the last chapter of *Death in the Afternoon*, with its rich, all too rich, unrollings of memories of good times in Spain, and with its what seem to me irrelevant reminiscences of the soliloquy of Mrs. Bloom in *Ulysses*. Also, there are interludes of kidding of a kind which

Hemingway handles with skill when he assigns them to characters in his stories, but in connection with which he seems to become incapable of exercising good sense or good taste as soon as he undertakes them in his own person (the burlesque *Torrents of Spring* was an early omen of this). In short, we are compelled to recognize that, as soon as Hemingway drops the burning-glass of the disciplined and objective art with which he has learned to concentrate in a story the light of the emotions that flood in on him, he straightway becomes befuddled, slops over.

This befuddlement is later to go further, but in the meantime he publishes another volume of stories—*Winner Take Nothing*—which is almost up to its predecessor. In this collection he deals much more effectively than in *Death in the Afternoon* with that theme of contemporary decadence which is implied in his panegyric of the bullfighter. The first of these stories, *After the Storm*, is another of his variations—and one of the finest—on the theme of keeping up a code of decency among the hazards and pains of life. A fisherman goes out to plunder a wreck: he dives down to break in through a porthole, but inside he sees a woman with rings on her hands and her hair floating loose in the water, and he thinks about the passengers and crew being suddenly plunged to their deaths (he has almost been killed himself in a drunken fight the night before). He sees the cloud of sea birds screaming around, and he finds that he is unable to break the glass with his wrench and that he loses the anchor grapple with which he next tries to attack it. So he finally goes away and leaves the job to the Greeks, who blow the boat open and clean her out.

But in general the emotions of insecurity here obtrude themselves and dominate the book. Two of the stories deal with the hysteria of soldiers falling off the brink of their nerves under the strain of the experiences of the war, which here no longer presents an idyllic aspect; another deals with a group of patients in a hospital, at the same time crippled and hopeless; still another (a five-page masterpiece) with a waiter, who, both on his own and on his customers' account, is reluctant to go home at night, because he feels the importance of a "clean well-lighted cafe" as a refuge from the "nothing" that people fear. *God Rest You Merry, Gentlemen* repeats the theme of castration of *The Sun Also Rises*; and four of the stories are concerned more or less with male or female homosexuality. In the last story, *Fathers and Sons*, Hemingway reverts to the Michigan forest, as if to take the curse off the rest: young Nick had once enjoyed a nice Indian girl with plump legs and hard little breasts on the needles of the hemlock woods.

These stories and the interludes in *Death in the Afternoon* must have been written during the years that followed the stock-market crash. They are full of the apprehension of losing control of oneself which is aroused by the getting out of hand of a social-economic system, as well as of the fear of impotence which seems to accompany the loss of social mastery. And there is in such a story as *A Clean Well-Lighted Place* the feeling of having got to the end of everything, of having given up heroic attitudes and wanting only the illusion of peace.

IV

And now, in proportion as the characters in his stories run out of fortitude and bravado, he passes into a phase where he is occupied with building up his public personality. He has already now become a legend, as Mencken was in the twenties; he is the Hemingway of the handsome photographs with the sportsmen's tan and the outdoor grin, with the ominous resemblance to Clark Gable, who poses with giant marlin which he has just hauled in off Key West. And unluckily—but for an American inevitably—the opportunity soon presents itself to exploit this personality for profit: he turns up delivering Hemingway

monologues in well-paying and trashy magazines; and
the Hemingway of these loose disquisitions, arrogant,
belligerent and boastful, is certainly the worst-in-
vented character to be found in the author's work. If
he is obnoxious, the effect is somewhat mitigated by
the fact that he is intrinsically incredible.

There would be no point in mentioning this journalism at all, if it did not seem somewhat to have contributed to the writing of certain unsatisfactory books.
Green Hills of Africa (1935) owes its failure to falling
between the two *genres* of personal exhibitionism
and fiction. "The writer has attempted," says Hemingway, "to write an absolutely true book to see
whether the shape of a country and the pattern of a
month's action can, if truly presented, compete with
a work of the imagination." He does try to present his
own rôle objectively, and there is a genuine Hemingway theme—the connection between success at big-
game hunting and sexual self-respect—involved in his
adventures as he presents them. But the sophisticated
technique of the fiction writer comes to look artificial
when it is applied to a series of real happenings; and
the necessity of sticking to what really happened
makes impossible the typical characters and incidents
which give point to a work of fiction. The monologues by the false, the publicity, Hemingway with
which the narrative is interspersed are almost as bad
as the ones that he has been writing for the magazines. He inveighs with much scorn against the literary life and against the professional literary man of
the cities; and then manages to give the impression
that he himself is a professional literary man of the
touchiest and most self-conscious kind. He delivers a
self-confident lecture on the high possibilities of
prose writing; and then produces such a sentence as
the following: "Going downhill steeply made these
Spanish shooting boots too short in the toe and there
was an old argument, about this length of boot and
whether the bootmaker, whose part I had taken, un-
wittingly first, only as interpreter, and finally em-

braced his theory patriotically as a whole and, I believed, by logic, had overcome it by adding onto the
heel." As soon as Hemingway begins speaking in the
first person, he seems to lose his bearings, not merely
as a critic of life, but even as a craftsman.

In another and significant way, *Green Hills of
Africa* is disappointing. *Death in the Afternoon* did
provide a lot of data on bullfighting and build up for
us the bullfighting world; but its successor tells us
little about Africa. Hemingway keeps affirming—as if
in accents of defiance against those who would en-
gage his attention for social problems—his passionate
enthusiasm for the African country and his perfect
satisfaction with the hunter's life; but he has produced what must be one of the only books ever
written which make Africa and its animals seem dull.
Almost the only thing we learn about the animals is
that Hemingway wants to kill them. And as for the
natives, though there is one fine description of a tribe
of marvelous trained runners, the principal impression we get of them is that they were simple and inferior people who enormously admired Hemingway.

It is not only that, as his critics of the Left had been
complaining, he shows no interest in political issues,
but that his interest in his fellow beings seems actually
to be drying up. It is as if he were throwing himself
on African hunting as something to live for and believe in, as something through which to realize himself; and as if, expecting of it too much, he had got
out of it abnormally little, less than he is willing to
admit. The disquiet of the Hemingway of the twenties had been, as I have said, undruggable—that is, in
his books themselves, he had tried to express it, not
drug it, had given it an appeasement in art; but now
there sets in, in the Hemingway of the thirties, what
seems to be a deliberate self-drugging. The situation
is indicated objectively in *The Gambler, the Nun and
the Radio*, one of the short stories of 1933, in which
everything from daily bread to "a belief in any new
form of government" is characterized as "the opium

of the people" by an empty-hearted patient in a hospital.

But at last there did rush into this vacuum the blast of the social issue, which had been roaring in the wind like a forest fire.

Out of a series of short stories that Hemingway had written about a Florida waterside character he decided to make a little epic. The result was *To Have and Have Not*, which seems to me the poorest of all his stories. Certainly some deep agitation is working upon Hemingway the artist. Craftsmanship and style, taste and sense, have all alike gone by the board. The negative attitude toward human beings has here become definitely malignant: the hero is like a wooden-headed Punch, always knocking people on the head (inferiors—Chinamen or Cubans); or, rather, he combines the characteristics of Punch with those of Popeye the Sailor in the animated cartoon in the movies. As the climax to a series of prodigies, this stupendous pirate-smuggler named Harry Morgan succeeds, alone, unarmed, and with only a hook for one hand—though at the cost of a mortal wound—in outwitting and destroying with their own weapons four men carrying revolvers and a machine gun, by whom he has been shanghaied in a launch. The only way in which Hemingway's outlaw suffers by comparison with Popeye is that his creator has not tried to make him plausible by explaining that he does it all on spinach.

The impotence of a decadent society has here been exploited deliberately, but less successfully than in the earlier short stories. Against a background of homosexuality, impotence and masturbation among the wealthy holiday-makers in Florida, Popeye-Morgan is shown gratifying his wife with the same indefatigable dexterity which he has displayed in his other feats; and there is a choral refrain of praise of his *cojones*, which wells up in the last pages of the book when the abandoned Mrs. Popeye regurgitates Molly Bloom's soliloquy.

To be a man in such a world of maggots is noble, but it is not enough. Besides the maggots, there are double-crossing rats, who will get you if they are given the slightest chance. What is most valid in *To Have and Have Not* is the idea—conveyed better, perhaps, in the first of the series of episodes than in the final scenes of massacre and agony—that in an atmosphere (here revolutionary Cuba) in which man has been set against man, in which it is always a question whether your companion is not preparing to cut your throat, the most sturdy and straightforward American will turn suspicious and cruel. Harry Morgan is made to realize as he dies that to fight this bad world alone is hopeless. Again Hemingway, with his barometric accuracy, has rendered a moral atmosphere that was prevalent at the moment he was writing—a moment when social relations were subjected to severe tensions, when they seemed sometimes already disintegrating. But the heroic Hemingway legend has at this point invaded his fiction and, inflaming and inflating his symbols, has produced an implausible hybrid, half Hemingway character, half nature myth.

Hemingway had not himself particularly labored this moral of individualism *versus* solidarity, but the critics of the Left labored it for him and received his least creditable piece of fiction as the delivery of a new revelation. The progress of the Communist faith among our writers since the beginning of the depression has followed a peculiar course. That the aims and beliefs of Marx and Lenin should have come through to the minds of intellectuals who had been educated in the bourgeois tradition as great awakeners of conscience, a great light, was quite natural and entirely desirable. But the conception of the dynamic Marxist will, the exaltation of the Marxist religion, seized the members of the professional classes like a capricious contagion or hurricane, which shakes one and leaves his neighbor standing, then returns to lay hold on the second after the first has become quiet again. In the moment of seizure, each one of them saw a scroll un-

rolled from the heavens, on which Marx and Lenin
and Stalin, the Bolsheviks of 1917, the Soviets of the
Five-Year Plan, and the GPU of the Moscow trials
were all a part of the same great purpose. Later the
convert, if he were capable of it, would get over his
first phase of snow blindness and learn to see real
people and conditions, would study the development
of Marxism in terms of nations, periods, personalities,
instead of logical deductions from abstract proposi-
tions or—as in the case of the more naïve or dishonest
—of simple incantatory slogans. But for many there
was at least a moment when the key to all the
mysteries of human history seemed suddenly to have
been placed in their hands, when an infallible guide
to thought and behavior seemed to have been given
them in a few easy formulas.

Hemingway was hit pretty late. He was still in
Death in the Afternoon telling the "world-savers,"
sensibly enough, that they should "get to see" the
world "clear and as a whole. Then any part you make
will represent the whole, if it's made truly. The thing
to do is work and learn to make it." Later he jibed at
the literary radicals, who talked but couldn't take it;
and one finds even in *To Have and Have Not* a crack
about a "highly paid Hollywood director, whose brain
is in the process of outlasting his liver so that he will
end up calling himself a Communist, to save his soul."
Then the challenge of the fight itself—Hemingway
never could resist a physical challenge—the natural
impulse to dedicate oneself to something bigger than
big-game hunting and bullfighting, and the fact that
the class war had broken out in a country to which he
was romantically attached, seem to have combined to
make him align himself with the Communists as well
as the Spanish Loyalists at a time when the Marxist
philosophy had been pretty completely shelved by the
Kremlin, now reactionary as well as corrupt, and
when the Russians were lending the Loyalists only
help enough to preserve, as they imagined would be
possible, the balance of power against Fascism while

they acted at the same time as a police force to beat
down the real social revolution.

Hemingway raised money for the Loyalists, reported the battle fronts. He even went so far as to
make a speech at a congress of the League of American Writers, an organization rigged by the supporters
of the Stalinist régime in Russia and full of precisely
the type of literary revolutionists that he had been
ridiculing a little while before. Soon the Stalinists had
taken him in tow, and he was feverishly denouncing
as Fascists other writers who criticized the Kremlin.
It has been one of the expedients of the Stalin administration in maintaining its power and covering up
its crimes to condemn on trumped-up charges of
Fascist conspiracy, and even to kidnap and murder,
its political opponents of the Left; and, along with
the food and munitions, the Russians had brought to
the war in Spain what the Austrian journalist Willi
Schlamm called that diversion of doubtful value for
the working class: "Herr Vyshinsky's Grand
Guignol."

The result of this was a play, *The Fifth Column*,
which, though it is good reading for the way the
characters talk, is an exceedingly silly production. The
hero, though an Anglo-American, is an agent of the
Communist secret police, engaged in catching Fascist
spies in Spain; and his principal exploit in the course
of the play is clearing out, with the aid of a single
Communist, an artillery post manned by seven Fascists. The scene is like a pushover and getaway from
one of the cruder Hollywood Westerns. It is in the
nature of a small boy's fantasy, and would probably
be considered extravagant by most writers of books
for boys.

The tendency on Hemingway's part to indulge
himself in these boyish day-dreams seems to begin to
get the better of his realism at the end of *A Farewell
to Arms*, where the hero, after many adventures of
fighting, escaping, love-making and drinking, rows his
lady thirty-five kilometers on a cold and rainy night;

and we have seen what it could do for Harry Morgan. Now, as if with the conviction that the cause and the efficiency of the GPU have added several cubits to his stature, he has let this tendency loose; and he has also found in the GPU's grim duty a pretext to give rein to the appetite for describing scenes of killing which has always been a feature of his work. He has progressed from grasshoppers and trout through bulls and lions and kudus to Chinamen and Cubans, and now to Fascists. Hitherto the act of destruction has given rise for him to complex emotions: he has identified himself not merely with the injurer but also with the injured; there has been a masochistic complement to the sadism. But now this paradox which splits our natures, and which has instigated some of Hemingway's best stories, need no longer present perplexities to his mind. The Fascists are dirty bastards, and to kill them is a righteous act. He who had made a separate peace, who had said farewell to arms, has found a reason for taking them up again in a spirit of rabietic fury unpleasantly reminiscent of the spy mania and the sacred anti-German rage which took possession of so many civilians and staff officers under the stimulus of the last war.

Not that the compensatory trauma of the typical Hemingway protagonist is totally absent even here. The main episode is the hero's brief love affair and voluntary breaking off with a beautiful and adoring girl whose acquaintance he has made in Spain. As a member of the Junior League and a graduate of Vassar, she represents for him—it seems a little hard on her—that leisure-class playworld from which he is trying to get away. But in view of the fact that from the very first scenes he treats her with more or less open contempt, the action is rather lacking in suspense as the sacrifice is rather feeble in moral value. One takes no stock at all in the intimation that Mr. Philip may later be sent to mortify himself in a camp for training Young Pioneers. And in the meantime he has fun killing Fascists.

In *The Fifth Column*, the drugging process has been carried further still: the hero, who has become finally indistinguishable from the false or publicity Hemingway, has here dosed himself not only with whiskey, but with a seductive and desirous woman, for whom he has the most admirable reasons for not taking any responsibility, with sacred rage, with the excitement of a bombardment, and with indulgence in that headiest of sports, for which he has now the same excellent reasons: the bagging of human beings.

v

You may fear, after reading *The Fifth Column*, that Hemingway will never sober up; but as you go on to his short stories of this period, you find that your apprehensions were unfounded. Three of these stories have a great deal more body—they are longer and more complex—than the comparatively meager anecdotes collected in *Winner Take Nothing*. And here are his real artistic successes with the material of his adventures in Africa, which make up for the miscarried *Green Hills*: *The Short Happy Life of Francis Macomber* and *The Snows of Kilimanjaro*, which disengage, by dramatizing them objectively, the themes he had attempted in the earlier book but that had never really got themselves presented. And here is at least a beginning of a real artistic utilization of Hemingway's experience in Spain: an incident of the war in two pages which outweighs the whole of *The Fifth Column* and all his Spanish dispatches, a glimpse of an old man, "without politics," who has so far occupied his life in taking care of eight pigeons, two goats and a cat, but who has now been dislodged and separated from his pets by the advance of the Fascist armies. It is a story which takes its place among the war prints of Callot and Goya, artists whose union of elegance with sharpness has already been recalled by Hemingway in his earlier battle pieces: a story which might have been written about almost any war.

And here—what is very remarkable—is a story, *The Capital of the World*, which finds an objective symbol for, precisely, what is wrong with *The Fifth Column*. A young boy who has come up from the country and waits on table in a pension in Madrid gets accidentally stabbed with a meat knife while playing at bullfighting with the dishwasher. This is the simple anecdote, but Hemingway has built in behind it all the life of the pension and the city: the priesthood, the working-class movement, the grown-up bullfighters who have broken down or missed out. "The boy Paco," Hemingway concludes, "had never known about any of this nor about what all these people would be doing on the next day and on other days to come. He had no idea how they really lived nor how they ended. He did not realize they ended. He died, as the Spanish phrase has it, full of illusions. He had not had time in his life to lose any of them, or even, at the end, to complete an act of contrition." So he registers in this very fine piece the discrepancy between the fantasies of boyhood and the realities of the grown-up world. Hemingway the artist, who feels things truly and cannot help recording what he feels, has actually said good-bye to these fantasies at a time when the war correspondent is making himself ridiculous by attempting to hang on to them still.

The emotion which principally comes through in *Francis Macomber* and *The Snows of Kilimanjaro*—as it figures also in *The Fifth Column*—is a growing antagonism to women. Looking back, one can see at this point that the tendency has been there all along. In *The Doctor and the Doctor's Wife*, the boy Nick goes out squirrel-hunting with his father instead of obeying the summons of his mother; in *Cross Country Snow*, he regretfully says farewell to male companionship on a skiing expedition in Switzerland, when he is obliged to go back to the States so that his wife can have her baby. The young man in *Hills Like White Elephants* compels his girl to have an abortion contrary to her wish; another story, *A Canary for One*, bites almost unbearably but exquisitely on the loneliness to be endured by a wife after she and her husband shall have separated; the peasant of *An Alpine Idyll* abuses the corpse of his wife (these last three appear under the general title *Men Without Women*). Brett in *The Sun Also Rises* is an exclusively destructive force: she might be a better woman if she were mated with Jake, the American; but actually he is protected against her and is in a sense revenging his own sex through being unable to do anything for her sexually. Even the hero of *A Farewell to Arms* eventually destroys Catherine—after enjoying her abject devotion—by giving her a baby, itself born dead. The only women with whom Nick Adams' relations are perfectly satisfactory are the little Indian girls of his boyhood who are in a position of hopeless social disadvantage and have no power over the behavior of the white male—so that he can get rid of them the moment he has done with them. Thus in *The Fifth Column* Mr. Philip brutally breaks off with Dorothy—he has been rescued from her demoralizing influence by his enlistment in the Communist crusade, just as the hero of *The Sun Also Rises* has been saved by his physical disability—to revert to a little Moorish whore. Even Harry Morgan, who is represented as satisfying his wife on the scale of a Paul Bunyan, deserts her in the end by dying and leaves her racked by the cruelest desire.[1]

[1] There would probably be a chapter to write on the relation between Hemingway and Kipling, and certain assumptions about society which they share. They have much the same split attitude toward women. Kipling anticipates Hemingway in his beliefs that "he travels the fastest that travels alone" and that "the female of the species is more deadly than the male"; and Hemingway seems to reflect Kipling in the submissive infra-Anglo-Saxon women that make his heroes such perfect mistresses. The most striking example of this is the amoeba-like little Spanish girl, Maria, in *For Whom the Bell Tolls*. Like the docile native "wives" of English officials in the early stories of Kipling, she lives only to serve her lord and to merge her identity with his; and this love

And now this instinct to get the woman down presents itself frankly as a fear that the woman will get the man down. The men in both these African stories are married to American bitches of the most soul-destroying sort. The hero of *The Snows of Kilimanjaro* loses his soul and dies of futility on a hunting expedition in Africa, out of which he has failed to get what he had hoped. The story is not quite stripped clean of the trashy moral attitudes which have been coming to disfigure the author's work: the hero, a seriously intentioned and apparently promising writer, goes on a little sloppily over the dear early days in Paris when he was earnest, happy and poor, and blames a little hysterically the rich woman whom he has married and who has debased him. Yet it is one of Hemingway's remarkable stories. There is a wonderful piece of writing at the end when the reader is made to realize that what has seemed to be an escape by plane, with the sick man looking down on Africa, is only the dream of a dying man. The other story, *Francis Macomber*, perfectly realizes its purpose. Here the male saves his soul at the last minute, and then is actually shot down by his woman, who does not want him to have a soul. Here Hemingway has at last got what Thurber calls the war between men and women right out into the open and has written a terrific fable of the impossible civilized woman who despises the civilized man for his failure in initiative and nerve and then jealously tries to break him down as soon as he begins to exhibit any. (It ought to be noted, also, that whereas in *Green Hills of Africa* the descriptions tended to weigh down the narrative with their excessive circumstantiality, the landscapes and

affair with a woman in a sleeping-bag, lacking completely the kind of give and take that goes on between real men and women, has the all-too-perfect felicity of a youthful erotic dream. One suspects that *Without Benefit of Clergy* was read very early by Hemingway and that it made on him a lasting impression. The pathetic conclusion of this story of Kipling's seems unmistakably to be echoed at the end of *A Farewell to Arms*.

animals of *Francis Macomber* are alive and unfalteringly proportioned.)

Going back over Hemingway's books today, we can see clearly what an error of the politicos it was to accuse him of an indifference to society. His whole work is a criticism of society: he has responded to every pressure of the moral atmosphere of the time, as it is felt at the roots of human relations, with a sensitivity almost unrivaled. Even his preoccupation with licking the gang in the next block and being known as the best basketball player in high school has its meaning in the present epoch. After all, whatever is done in the world, political as well as athletic, depends on personal courage and strength. With Hemingway, courage and strength are always thought of in physical terms, so that he tends to give the impression that the bullfighter who can take it and dish it out is more of a man than any other kind of man, and that the sole duty of the revolutionary socialist is to get the counter-revolutionary gang before they get him.

But ideas, however correct, will never prevail by themselves: there must be people who are prepared to stand or fall with them, and the ability to act on principle is still subject to the same competitive laws which operate in sporting contests and sexual relations. Hemingway has expressed with genius the terrors of the modern man at the danger of losing control of his world, and he has also, within his scope, provided his own kind of antidote. This antidote, paradoxically, is almost entirely moral. Despite Hemingway's preoccupation with physical contests, his heroes are almost always defeated physically, nervously, practically: their victories are moral ones. He himself, when he trained himself stubbornly in his unconventional unmarketable art in a Paris which had other fashions, gave the prime example of such a victory; and if he has sometimes, under the menace of the general panic, seemed on the point of going to pieces as an artist, he has always pulled himself together the next moment. The principle of the Bourdon gauge, which is used to measure the pressure of liquids, is that a tube which has been curved into a coil will tend to straighten out in proportion as the liquid inside it is subjected to an increasing pressure.

The appearance of *For Whom the Bell Tolls* since this essay was written in 1939 carries the straightening process further. Here Hemingway has largely sloughed off his Stalinism and has reverted to seeing events in terms of individuals pitted against specific odds. His hero, an American teacher of Spanish who has enlisted on the side of the Loyalists, gives his life to what he regards as the cause of human liberation; but he is frustrated in the task that has been assigned him by the confusion of forces at cross-purposes that are throttling the Loyalist campaign. By the time that he comes to die, he has little to sustain him but the memory of his grandfather's record as a soldier in the American Civil War. The psychology of this young man is presented with a certain sobriety and detachment in comparison with Hemingway's other fulllength heroes; and the author has here succeeded as in none of his earlier books in externalizing in plausible characters the elements of his own complex personality. With all this, there is an historical point of view which he has learned from his political adventures: he has aimed to reflect in this episode the whole course of the Spanish War and the tangle of tendencies involved in it.

The weaknesses of the book are its diffuseness—a shape that lacks the concision of his short stories, that sometimes sags and sometimes bulges; and a sort of exploitation of the material, an infusion of the operatic, that lends itself all too readily to the movies.

1941

A. E. HOUSMAN

The voice, sent forth, can never be recalled.

When A. E. Housman's *Introductory Lecture* delivered in 1892 "Before the Faculties of Arts and Laws and of Science in University College, London" was reprinted in 1933, Housman characteristically wrote of it as follows: "The Council of University College, not I, had the lecture printed." He described it as "rhetorical and not wholly sincere" and put upon the title page, *Nescit vox missa reverti.*

The little essay is curious in largely evading the questions it raises and taking the direction of a piece of special pleading for the author's own pursuits. Both the sciences and the arts, says Housman, are ordinarily defended by arguments which make their interests appear mutually antagonistic. But the arguments on both sides are mistaken. Science is said to be useful; but what is the use, for example, of a great deal of astronomical research? And the businessmen who make practical use of the results of scientific study are usually not scientists at all. (They do make use of them, nevertheless; and the results of the most gratuitous researches are always likely to turn out to be useful.) The Humanities, on the other hand, are supposed to "transform and beautify our inner nature by culture." Yet the proportion of the human race capable of being benefited by classical studies is certainly very small, and these "can attain the desired end without that minute and accurate study of the classical tongues which affords Latin professors their only excuse for existing." Not even the great critics of the classics are genuine classical scholars: "When it comes to literary criticism, heap up in one scale all the literary criticism that the whole nation of professed scholars ever wrote, and drop into the other the thin green volume of Matthew Arnold's *Lectures on Translating Homer*, which has long been out of print because the British public does not care to read it, and the first scale, as Milton says, will straight fly up and kick the beam." (We shall look into the assumptions here in a moment.)

The arts and the sciences alike are only to be defended, says Housman, on the ground that the desire for knowledge is one of the normal human appetites, and that men suffer if they do not have it gratified. And "once we have recognized that knowledge in itself is good for man, we shall need to invent no pretexts for studying this subject or that; we shall import no extraneous considerations of use or ornament to justify us in learning one thing rather than another. If a certain department of knowledge specially attracts a man, let him study that, and study it because it attracts him; and let him not fabricate excuses for that which requires no excuse, but rest assured that the reason why it most attracts him is that it is best for him."

This is certainly true in so far as it means that we should follow the direction of our aptitudes; but it seems to imply that there is no difference in value between one department of learning and another or between the different points of view from which the various kinds of research can be conducted. There is no conception in Housman's mind, as there would have been in Whitehead's, for example, of relating the part to the whole, understanding the organism through the cell. Knowledge seems to be regarded by Housman as a superior sort of pastime—"good for man" because it gives him pleasure and at most be-

cause "it must in the long run be better for a man to
see things as they are than to be ignorant of them;
just as there is less fear of stumbling or of striking
against corners in the daylight than in the dark."
(*The thoughts of others Were light and fleeting, Of
lovers' meeting Or luck or fame; Mine were of trouble
And mine were steady, So I was ready When Trouble
came.*) The disillusionment of western man in regard to his place in the universe, finding "that he has
been deceived alike as to his origin and his expectations, that he neither springs of the high lineage he
fancied, nor will inherit the vast estate he looked for,"
is described in an eloquent passage; and the activities
of the "Arts and Laws and Science" are finally characterized as "the rivalry of fellow soldiers in striving
which can most victoriously achieve the common end
of all, to set back the frontier of darkness."

In other words, there is no role for creation in
Housman's scheme of things. Indeed, if one had read
only his poetry, one might be surprised to find that
he even believed that it was possible or of any importance to set back the frontier of darkness. In this
poetry, we find only the realization of man's smallness
on his turning globe among the other revolving
planets and of his own basic wrongness to himself,
his own inescapable anguish. No one, it seems, can
do anything about this universe which "ails from its
prime foundation": we can only, like Mithridates,
render ourselves immune to its poisons by compelling
ourselves to absorb them in small quantities in order
that we may not succumb to the larger doses reserved
for us by our fellows, or face the world with the hard
mask of stoicism, "manful like the man of stone." For
the rest, "let us endure an hour and see injustice
done." And now we learn that for Housman knowledge itself meant at most the discovery of things that
were already there—of those sharp corners which it
was just as well not to bump into, of facts that were as
invariable and as inert as the astronomical phenomena which are always turning up in his poems and

form the subject of the poem of Manilius to which
he devoted so much of his life. He does not look
to the sciences and arts for the births of new worlds
of thought, of new possibilities for men themselves. It is characteristic of him that he should speak,
in this essay, of Milton as a greater artist than Shakespeare, of Shakespeare, in fact, as not "a great artist"
—as if the completeness and richness of Shakespeare's
dramatic imagination, a kind of genius which Milton,
by comparison, seems hardly to possess at all, were not
important enough to be taken into account in esti-
mating his greatness as an artist—as if those stretches
of *Paradise Lost* where everything is dead but the
language were not the result of artistic deficiency.
Again, the creation of life has no place in the universe
of Housman.

Housman's practice in his own field of scholarship
is an astonishing proof of this. The modern English
classical scholar of the type of A. W. Verrall or Gilbert Murray is a critic not merely of texts but of the
classics in their quality as literature and of literature
in its bearing on history. This school on one of its
sides sometimes merges with the anthropology of J.
G. Frazer; and it deals with ancient Greece and Rome
in relation to the life of its own time, restates them
in terms of its own time. The danger, of course, with
a Verrall or a Murray is that, with something of the
poet's imagination himself, he may give way, in the
case of Greek drama, for example, to inventing new
plays of his own and trying to foist them on Euripides
or Aeschylus. With Housman we do not run this
danger. Housman is the opposite kind of scholar; he
is preoccupied with the emendation of texts. He
could never have been guilty of the extravagances of
a Gilbert Murray or a Verrall, but he was not capable
of their kind of illumination. Note his assumption,
in the passage quoted above, that "the minute and
accurate study of the classical tongues," with which
he himself is exclusively preoccupied, "affords Latin

professors their only excuse for existing." Have those
classical scholars who write history, who write criticism, who make translations—Gibbon and Renan
and Verrall and Murray and Jowett and Mackail (to
take in the whole field of the classics)—no excuse for
existing, then? Is it so certain that, if their literary
criticism were put into the scales with Matthew
Arnold on Homer, the scholars would kick the beam?
Or are such persons not scholars at all? In either case,
it is plain that, for Housman, their activities lie outside the periphery of the sphere which he has chosen
for himself.

Not, however, that Housman in this limited sphere
has left the poet of *The Shropshire Lad* behind him.
On the contrary, the peculiar genius which won him
a place beside Porson and Bentley, which established
him in his own time as almost supreme, with, apparently, only Wilamowitz as a rival, was derived from
his ability to combine with the most "minute and
accurate" mastery of language a first-hand knowledge
of how poets express themselves. "The task of editing
the classics," he wrote in his preface to Juvenal, "is
continually attempted by scholars who have neither
enough intellect nor enough literature. Unless a false
reading chances to be unmetrical or ungrammatical
they have no means of knowing that it is false." And
he himself seemed able with a miraculous sureness to
give the authors back their lines as they had written
them. So, for example, despite a unanimity of manuscripts which read "Omnis ab hac cura mens relavata
mea est," Housman restored to Ovid from an inscrip-
tion one of the latter's characteristic turns of style:
"Omnis ab hac cura cura levata mea est." ("*And set
you at your threshold down, Townsman of a stiller
town*"; "*Runners whom renown outran And the name
died before the man*"; "*By Sestos tower, in Hero's
town, On Hero's heart Leander lies.*") So, slightly
emending the text, he turned a meaningless accepted
reading of Juvenal, "Perditus ac vilis sacci mercator
olentis," into a characteristically vivid satiric stroke:

"Perditus ac similis sacci mercator olentis"—the
money-chasing merchant, on a stormy voyage, turns
as yellow as his bag of saffron. (*They shook, they
stared as white's their shirt: Them it was their poison
hurt.*) So, without even an emendation and simply
by indicating a new relation between three words of
Virgil's, he was able to save Virgil's style in a phrase
—*fallax herba veneni*—which had always up to then
been read as if it had been written with neither style
nor grammar: substituting for "the deceitful plant of
poison," "the plant that dissimulates its venom."
(*And bear from hill and valley The daffodil away
That dies on Easter day*"; "*Lie long, high snowdrifts
in the hedge That will not shower on me*"; "*Snap not
from the bitter yew His leaves that live November
through.*") Several of his readings, I understand, have
been confirmed by the subsequent discovery of manuscripts which Housman had never seen.

To this rescue of the Greek and Roman poets from
the negligence of the Middle Ages, from the incom-
petence and insensitivity of the scholars, A. E. Housman brought an unremitting zeal which may almost
be described as a passion. It has been said of the
theorems of Newton that they cause the pulse to beat
faster as one follows them. But the excitement and
satisfaction afforded by the classical commentary of
Housman must be unique in the history of scholarship. Even the scraping of the rust from an old coin
is too tame an image to convey the experience of
pursuing one of his arguments to its climax. It is as
if, from the ancient author, so long dumb with his
language itself, his very identity blurred or obliterated,
the modern classicist were striking a new spark of life
—as if the poet could only find his tongue at the touch
across Time of the poet. So far is Housman the
scholar a giver of life—yet it is only as re-creator. He
is only, after all, again, discovering things that were
already there. His findings do not imply a new vision.

It was a queer destiny, and one that cramped him

—if one should not say rather that he had cramped himself. (Not to dispute, however, with Housman, who thought that human beings were all but helpless, the problem of natural fate and free will.)

The great work of A. E. Housman's life in the field of classical scholarship was his edition of the five books of Manilius, the publication of which alone extended from 1903 to 1930. We are told in a memoir of Housman by his colleague, Professor A. S. F. Gow of Cambridge, that Housman regarded Manilius as "a facile and frivolous poet, the brightest facet of whose genius was an eminent aptitude for doing sums in verse." And the layman may be disposed to assume that by Housman's time the principal Latin poets had already been covered so completely that there was nobody left except third-rate ones like Manilius. But it turns out from Professor Gow that Housman's real favorite was Propertius, and that he had done a great deal of valuable work on him and had at one time contemplated a complete edition. Professor Gow says that presumably Housman saw in Manilius and Lucan (Lucan he seems also to have despised) "more opportunity than in Propertius of displaying his special gifts, and more hope of approaching finality in the solution of the problems presented," but adds that he "cannot help regretting that he [Housman] abandoned a great and congenial poet on whom so much time had already been lavished."

The elegist of *The Shropshire Lad*, then, deliberately and grimly chose Manilius when his real interest was in Propertius. There is an element of perversity, of self-mortification, in Housman's career all along. (Gow tells how up to the time of his death "he would be found reading every word of books whose insignificance must have been apparent in ten pages, and making remorseless catalogues of their shortcomings.") And his scholarship, great as it is in its way, is poisoned in revenge by the instincts which it seems to be attempting to destroy, so that it radiates more ha-

tred for his opponents than love for the great literature of antiquity. Housman's papers on classical
subjects, which shocked the sense of decorum of his
colleagues, are painful to the admirers of his poetry.
The bitterness here *is* indecent as in his poetry it
never is. In a prose, old-fashioned and elaborate,
which somewhat resembles Pope's, he will attack the
German professors who have committed the unpar-
donable sin of editing the Latin authors inade-
quately with sentences that coil and strike like rattle-
snakes, or that wrap themselves around their victims
and squeeze them to death like boa constrictors.
When English fails, he takes to scurrilous Latin. And
the whole thing is likely at any moment to give way
to some morose observation on the plight of the human race: "To believe that wherever a best *ms* gives
possible readings it gives true readings, and that only
when it gives impossible readings does it give false
readings, is to believe that an incompetent editor is
the darling of Providence, which has given its angels
charge over him lest at any time his sloth and folly
should produce their natural results and incur their
appropriate penalty . . . How the world is managed,
and why it was created, I cannot tell; but it is no
feather-bed for the repose of sluggards." And not only,
he continues, has the notion been imposed that "inert adhesion to one authority is methodical criticism,"
but "rational criticism has been branded with a term
of formal reprobation." "But still there is a hitch.
Competent editors exist; and side by side with those
who have embraced 'the principles of criticism,' there
are those who follow the practice of critics: who possess intellects, and employ them on their work. Consequently their work is better done, and the contrast
is mortifying. This is not as it should be. As the wise
man dieth, so dieth the fool: why then should we
allow them to edit the classics differently? If nature,
with flagitious partiality, has given judgment and industry to some men and left other men without them,
it is our evident duty to amend her blind caprice; and

those who are able and willing to think must be deprived of their unfair advantage by stringent prohibitions. In Association football you must not use your hands, and similarly in textual criticism you must not use your brains. Since we cannot make fools behave like wise men, we will insist that wise men should behave like fools: by these means only can we redress the injustice of nature and anticipate the equality of the grave."

And here is the somber and threatening, the almost Isaian, utterance to which he is moved by the failure of one of the compilers of a German-Latin dictionary to include in the article on *aelurus*, the Latinized Greek word for *cat*, any mention of an instance of its occurrence arrived at by an emendation in Juvenal and believed by Housman to be the first extant: "Everyone can figure to himself the mild inward glow of pleasure and pride which the author of this unlucky article felt while he was writing it and the peace of mind with which he said to himself, when he went to bed that night, 'Well done, thou good and faithful servant.' This is the felicity of the house of bondage, and of the soul which is so fast in prison that it cannot go forth; which commands no outlook on the past or the future, but believes that the fashion of the present, unlike all fashions heretofore, will endure perpetually and that its own flimsy tabernacle of second-hand opinions is a habitation for everlasting."

Even when Housman is saying something positive the emotion is out of proportion to its object: he speaks feverishly, seems unnaturally exalted. Here is a passage on Bentley from the preface to the first volume of his Manilius: "*Lucida tela diei:* these are the words that come into one's mind when one has halted at some stubborn perplexity of reading or interpretation, has witnessed Scaliger and Gronovius and Huetius fumble at it one after another, and then turns to Bentley and sees Bentley strike his finger on the place and say *thou ailest here, and here . . .* The

firm strength and piercing edge and arrowy swiftness
of his intellect, his matchless facility and adroitness
and resource, were never so triumphant as where defeat seemed sure; and yet it is other virtues that one
most admires and welcomes as one turns from the
smoky fire of Scaliger's genius to the sky and air of
Bentley's: his lucidity, his sanity, his great and simple
and straightforward fashion of thought." Transferring
Arnold's words for Goethe to Bentley is not perhaps
comparing great things with small, but in the sub-
stitution for the "physician of the Iron Age" of the
physician of mangled texts, there is a narrowing of
scope almost comic. The preface to the first book of
Manilius, from which the above passage has been
quoted, magnificent as it is in its way, has also something monstrous about it.

Yet some acquaintance with the classical work of
Housman greatly increases one's estimate of his stature. One encounters an intellectual pride almost
Dantesque or Swiftian. "You would be welcome to
praise me," he writes, "if you did not praise one another"; and "the reader whose good opinion I desire
and have done my utmost to secure is the next Bentley or Scaliger who may chance to occupy himself
with Manilius." His arrogance is perhaps never more
ferocious than when he is judging himself severely:
when a friend who had ventured to suggest the publication of a paper on Swinburne which Housman
had read before a college literary society had been
told by Housman that he was leaving directions to
have it destroyed after his death and had retorted that
if the writer really thought it so bad, he would already
himself have destroyed it, Housman replied: "I do
not think it bad: I think it not good enough for me."
And he put on the title page of his edition of Juvenal,
editorum in usum edidit, to indicate that this feat of
erudition—according to his own announcement, un-
precedented—was merely intended as a hint to future
scholars who might tackle the subject as to how they

might accomplish their task in a thoroughgoing fashion.

Is this the spectacle of a great mind crippled? Certainly it is the spectacle of a mind of remarkable penetration and vigor, of uncommon sensibility and intensity, condemning itself to duties which prevent it from rising to its full height. Perhaps it is the case of a man of genius who has never been allowed to come to growth. Housman's anger is tragic like Swift's. He is perhaps more pitiable than Swift, because he has been compelled to suppress himself more completely. Even when Swift had been exiled to Ireland, he was able to take out his fury in crusading against the English. But A. E. Housman, giving up Greek in order to specialize in Latin because he "could not attain to excellence in both," giving up Propertius, who wrote about love, for Manilius, who did not even deal with human beings, turning away from the lives of the Romans to rivet his attention to the difficulties of their texts, can only flatten out small German professors with weapons which would have found fit employment in the hands of a great reformer or a great satirist. He is the hero of *The Grammarian's Funeral*—the man of learning who makes himself impressive through the magnitude, not the importance, of his achievement. After all, there was no need for another Bentley.

It is only in the Latin verses—said to have been called by Murray the best since the ancient world—which Housman prefixed to his Manilius, in his few translations from Latin and Greek, and in his occasional literary essays, that the voice of the Shropshire Lad comes through—that voice which, once sped on its way, so quickly pierced to the hearts and the minds of the whole English-speaking world and which went on vibrating for decades, disburdening hearts with its music that made loss and death and disgrace seem so beautiful, while poor Housman, burdened sorely forever, sat grinding and snarling at his texts. Would he have called back that voice if he could, as he recalled, or tried to recall, so much else? There are moments when his ill humor and his pedantry, his humility which is a perverse kind of pride, almost make us think that he would.

At this point Professor Gow is able to throw some further light on his friend. It seems that Housman had marked the following passage from Colonel Lawrence's *Seven Pillars of Wisdom*, which he had come across in a review:

"There was my craving to be liked—so strong and nervous that never could I open myself friendly to another. The terror of failure in an effort so important made me shrink from trying; besides, there was the standard; for intimacy seemed shameful unless the other could make the perfect reply, in the same language, after the same method, for the same reasons.

"There was a craving to be famous; and a horror of being known to like being known. Contempt for my passion for distinction made me refuse every offered honor. I cherished my independence almost as did a Beduin, but my impotence of vision showed me my shape best in painted pictures, and the oblique overheard remarks of others best taught me my created impression. The eagerness to overhear and oversee myself was my assault upon my own inviolate citadel."

Housman had written in the margin, "This is me." Both had been compelled by their extreme sensibility to assume in the presence of their fellows eccentric or repellent masks. Both had been led by extreme ambition to perform exploits which did not do them justice, exploits which their hearts were but half in: Professor Gow says that Housman's prime motive in undertaking his edition of Manilius was the ambition to "build" himself "a monument." And just as Lawrence was always losing the manuscripts of his books, limiting their circulation, making the pretense of suppressing them altogether, so Housman kept his poems out of anthologies, made the gestures of a negative attitude in regard to the reprinting of his other writings, and left instructions that his classical papers, of which Gow says there are something like a hundred, should never be collected in a volume (instructions which it is to be hoped will be disobeyed).

Both were products of the English universities; and it would take an Englishman properly to account for them. But their almost insane attempts to conceal their blazing lights under bushels are recognizable as exaggerations of the Englishman's code of understatement in connection with his achievements and conquests. And both obviously belong to the monastic order of English university ascetics. The company to which Housman refers himself is that of Walter Pater, Lewis Carroll, Edward Fitzgerald and Gerard Manley Hopkins—and, earlier, Thomas Gray. Hopkins, converted at Oxford, entered the Jesuit order; Pater and Dodgson stayed on there as dons; Fitzgerald and Gray, when they had finished at Cambridge, continued to haunt the place: they remained men of the monastery all their lives. Are their humility, which seems imposed by moral principles, their shyness in relation to the extra-collegiate world, derived from the ages when learning was the possession of pious brotherhoods and shut away between the walls of foundations?

Certainly their failure to develop emotionally is due to that semi-monastic training. All seem checked at some early stage of growth, beyond which the sensibility and the intellect—even, in Lawrence's case, the ability to manage men—may crystallize in marvelous forms, but after which there is no natural progress in the experience of human relationships. Their works are among the jewels of English literature rather than among its great springs of life; and Alice and the Shropshire Lad and Marius the Epicurean are all the beings of a looking-glass world, either sexless or with an unreal sex which turns only

toward itself in the mirror of art. Isn't the state of
mind indicated by Lawrence in the first of the para-
graphs quoted above essentially an adolescent one?
We are told, in a recent memoir, that Housman used
to rail against marriage and child-bearing. "My father
and my mother," he makes one of his hanged heroes
say, "They had a likely son, And I have none."

It would not be true to say of Housman, as it would
be of Fitzgerald or Gray, that his achievement has
been merely to state memorably certain melancholy
commonplaces of human existence without any real
presentation of that existence as we live it through.
There *is* immediate emotional experience in Housman of the same kind that there is in Heine, whom
he imitated and to whom he has been compared. But
Heine, for all his misfortunes, moves at ease in a larger
world. There is in his work an exhilaration of adventure—in travel, in love, in philosophy, in literature,
in politics. Doleful though his accents may sometimes be, he always lets in air and light to the mind.
But Housman is closed from the beginning. His world
has no opening horizons; it is a prison that one can
only endure. One can only come the same painful
cropper over and over again and draw from it the
same bitter moral.

And Housman has managed to grow old without
in a sense ever knowing maturity. He has somehow
never arrived at the age when the young man decides
at last to summon all his resources and try to make
something out of this world he has never made.

                                                   1938

BERNARD SHAW AT EIGHTY

Time has shifted our point of view on Bernard Shaw, yet he is still worth our contemplation. Let us cast a look back over his career.

George Bernard Shaw was born in Dublin, July 26, 1856, the son of shabby-genteel parents who had connections with the Irish nobility. The elder Shaw became an alcoholic, and the boy had to go to work as a clerk at the age of fifteen. Mrs. Shaw finally left her husband and went to London, where she made a living by teaching music. Her son came to live with her when he was twenty and wrote novels which he was unable to sell and picked up through journalism such money as he could. He remained with his mother till he was forty-two.

In the fall of 1882 he happened to attend a lecture on land nationalization delivered by Henry George in London. The result was a revelation: "It flashed on me," he writes, "that 'the conflict between religion and science' . . . the overthrow of the Bible, the higher education of women, Mill on Liberty and all the rest of the storm that raged around Darwin, Tyndall, Huxley, Spencer and the rest, on which I had brought myself up intellectually, was a mere middle-class business . . . The importance of the economic basis dawned on me.' He read George's *Progress and*

Poverty—then someone told him to read *Das Kapital*. "Karl Marx," he once said, "made a man of me."

The result of the depression of the eighties was a revival of socialist agitation. Bernard Shaw became a socialist and spoke in halls, on street corners, in Hyde Park. The "insurrectionism" of the period reached a climax in the "Bloody Sunday" of November 1887, when the socialists, at the head of a working-class demonstration, invaded Trafalgar Square and were routed by the police. After this, business revived and took up the slack of unemployment, and the agitation quieted down.

In the meantime, Shaw had attached himself to the socialist statistician, Sidney Webb, and with others they had founded the Fabian Society, which had "agreed to give up the delightful ease of revolutionary heroics and take to the hard work of practical reform on ordinary parliamentary lines." Webb was a civil servant with a post in the colonial office and later a member of the London County Council; Shaw became a vestryman, then a borough councilor. The Fabians continued to treat Marx with respect, but the polite and reasonable criticism to which they subjected him was designed to discredit some of his main assumptions. Marx had asserted that the value of commodities was derived from the labor which had gone to produce them; and the Fabians, by elaborating a counter-theory that made value depend on demand, shifted the emphasis from the working class to the "consumer." They also repudiated the class war, showed that it would never occur. Socialist nationalization was to be accomplished by a corps of experts who should "permeate" government and business, quietly invading Whitehall and setting up state departments which, unassisted by the action of the masses, should put socialist ideas into effect. Shaw boasted that the Fabians had made socialism respectable.

This variation of Marxism in England was natural to the place and time. A period of prosperity during the seventies had deflated the Chartist agitation (I am indebted to Mr. Mark Starr for a Marxist analysis of Fabian Marxism); and it was not until the eighties, when British commercial domination was being challenged by the United States and Germany, that the dangers of the capitalist system began to become generally plain. But now attention was principally directed toward the evils of competition. The development of large-scale industry was eliminating competition and making municipal ownership seem desirable, not only to the lower layers of the middle class, but even to private enterprise itself, which benefited from good housing and cheap tram-lines. The professional middle class were in a position to see the value of nationalization, and the working class had not yet discovered that for them there was not very much difference between being exploited by a private employer and being exploited by a government that was controlled by the propertied classes. The Fabians looked no further than their reforms.

In Bernard Shaw's case, this compromise Marxism played in with the elements of his character and influenced its subsequent development. Coming to London, as he has recently told us, with a conviction of his own superiority and a snobbish family tradition, but with no money and no social experience, Shaw was himself one of the dispossessed, and the socialist criticism of the class system based on property strongly recommended itself to him. Yet at the same time that in all good faith he was working to destroy that system, there is apparent in his career a tendency in the inverse direction to this. At the same time that he was spurred by a moral need to work for a future society consistent with his sense of justice, he was spurred, also, by a social need to vindicate his rightful position in the society in which he lived. He has told us that his father's bad habits had caused his family to be dropped socially in Dublin and that when he first came to London he was so shy that he would not accept dinner invitations and would "sometimes walk up and down the Embankment for twenty minutes or more before venturing to knock at the door" of a house to which he had been asked. He goes on to say, "The house and its artistic atmosphere were most congenial to me; and I liked all the Lawsons; but I had not mastered the art of society at that time and could not bear making an inartistic exhibition of myself; so I soon ceased to plague them." There has always been thus in Shaw a certain amount of social snobbery mixed up with his intellectual snobbery.

The confusion produced in his thought by these two conflicting tendencies is curiously illustrated in a passage from his autobiographical preface to the collected edition of his works: "Finding one's place may be made very puzzling," he writes, "by the fact that there is no place in ordinary society for extraordinary individuals. For the worldly wiseman, with common ambitions, the matter is simple enough: money, title, precedence, a seat in parliament, a portfolio in the cabinet, will mean success both to him and to his circle. But what about people like St. Francis and St. Clare? Of what use to them are the means to live the life of the country house and the West End mansion? They have literally no business in them, and must necessarily cut an unhappy and ridiculous figure there. They have to make a society of Franciscans and Poor Clares for themselves before they can work or live socially. It is true that those who are called saints are not saintly all the time and in everything. In eating and drinking, lodging and sleeping, chatting and playing: in short, in everything but working out their destiny as saints, what is good enough for a plowman is good enough for a poet, a philosopher, a saint or a higher mathematician. But Hodge's work is not good enough for Newton, nor Falstaff's conversation holy enough for Shelley. Christ adapted himself so amicably to the fashionable life of his time in his leisure that he was reproached for being a gluttonous man and a winebibber, and for frequenting frivolous and worthless sets. But he did not work where he feasted, nor flatter the Pharisees, nor ask the Romans to buy him with a sinecure. He knew when he was being entertained, well treated, lionized: not an unpleasant adventure for once in a way; and he did not quarrel with the people who were so nice to him. Besides, to sample society is part of a prophet's business: he must sample the governing class above all, because his inborn knowledge of human nature will not explain the anomalies produced in it by Capitalism and Sacerdotalism. But he can never feel at home in it."

But which is true: that the St. Francis or the St. Clare can't "live socially" till they have "made a society of Franciscans and Poor Clares" or that "in eating and drinking, lodging and sleeping, chatting and playing," "what is good enough for a plowman is good enough for a saint"? And as for Shaw's description of Christ, it evokes an incongruous picture: what one sees is the preacher of the Sermon on the Mount very much pleased with himself on the beach at the Riviera or playing Santa Claus at Lady Astor's Christmas party.

And other influences, from his early education, came to deflect the straight line of his socialism.

The escapades of the romantic hero, from Childe Harold through Don César de Bazan, with his *"Tant pis! C'est moi!,"* to Siegfried, had been a protest against the meanness and dullness of the commercial bourgeois world; but this revolt was itself merely a further phase of the tradition of individual assertion which, deriving from the Protestant conscience, had produced the anarchic individualism of the competitive commercial system. The romantic, like the old-fashioned capitalist, proclaimed the power of the personal will in defiance of society and God.

William Archer tells us that the first time he ever saw Shaw, the latter was sitting in the British Museum studying alternately the French translation of *Das Kapital* and the score of *Tristan und Isolde*.

When Shaw first came before the public, he fell instinctively into dramatizing himself as a semi-romantic character—and this in spite of the fact that he was managing to figure at the same time as the arch-enemy and blasphemer of romanticism. The impulse to satirize romanticism implies, as in the case of Flaubert, a strong predisposition toward it; and the exploded romantic, Captain Brassbound, is offset by the Devil's Disciple. It is true that Shaw's conscious intention was to ridicule and shame his audience out of exclusive preoccupation with the emotions of their personal lives—especially, with romantic love—and to interest them in the problems of society. Here is the fine and well-known passage from *Man and Superman,* in which he defends what he calls the "artist-philosophers" against the "mere artists": "This is the true joy in life, the being used for a purpose recognized by yourself as a mighty one; the being thoroughly worn out before you are thrown on the scrap heap; the being a force of Nature instead of a feverish selfish little clod of ailments and grievances complaining that the world will not devote itself to making you happy." Yet is this not, too, a kind of romanticism—romanticism *par excellence?* The ego has now, to be sure, identified itself with a force of Nature, but this simply makes the ego seem godlike. There is nothing to guarantee that it will respect either the feelings or the interests of others. The ideal artist-philosopher of Bernard Shaw has always a strong social conscience, and his heroes are likely to be philosopher-statesmen or social prophets or saviors of society; but there is nothing to guarantee that they shall be, in the socialist sense, genuine popular leaders, deriving their power from, as well as guiding, the dispossessed: they may be simply despot-heroes— as Shaw's Julius Caesar actually is—acting in the right of their own superiority and giving people what they know to be good for them.

And finally, of course, Bernard Shaw was not only a political prophet struggling for socialist ideas, but an artist trying to realize himself through art. There was a poet in Shaw, still partly suppressed, or at any rate terribly overtaxed, by the round of political meetings, the functions of vestryman and borough councilor, and the years of theatergoing and weekly article-writing about the theater, which he had come to judge almost exclusively in terms of the sort of thing that he wanted to do himself. His own plays he had been writing in note-books while traveling on the tops of buses between one engagement and another. Now in 1898, when he was forty-two, he had what seems to have been a general collapse as the result of a bad fall and a serious injury to his foot. When he recovered, he married an Irish lady, well-to-do but belonging like Shaw to the general "advanced" movement, who gave him for apparently the first time in his life a comfortable place to live and took the most excellent care of him. Thereafter, he was able to give up the journalism on which he had depended for a living and to devote all his best energies to his plays. He remained a public man, but he spoke no more at dockers' strikes.

By 1905 he was writing *Major Barbara*, in which the type of Christian sainthood, an aristocratic Salvation Army worker, is confronted with a self-made munitions manufacturer, the type of successful capitalism; and ending the play with an alliance between them. In his preface, he made out a ringing case for the man who recognizes poverty as the worst of all the evils and consequently the worst of all the sins, and who saves himself from it at any cost. *Major Barbara* contains one of the best expositions of the capitalist point of view ever written. Bernard Shaw, like his hero, Andrew Undershaft, had come by that time to know what it was to make one's way in capitalist society and to occupy a position of power. He had himself become the type of the critic, who, by scolding the bourgeoisie, makes good with it and becomes one of its idols. He was gradually, for all the scandal of his début, turning into a dependable

member of the British propertied classes; and he was
to end as an esteemed public figure in a country
where an aristocratic governing class was still able to
contribute to public life a certain distinction and
glamor.

II

The real Shaw has thus never been the single-
minded crusader that people at one time used to think
him. Except for a limited period during the eighties
and early nineties—when he wrote his only straight
socialist plays, *Widowers' Houses* and *Mrs. Warren's
Profession*—he has never really been a practicing
socialist. And I am inclined to believe that the future
will exactly reverse the opinion which his contemporaries have usually had of him. It used always to be
said of Shaw that he was primarily not an artist, but a
promulgator of certain ideas. The truth is, I think,
that he is a considerable artist, but that his ideas—that
is, his social philosophy proper—have always been
confused and uncertain. As he has grown older and
as the world has been shaken out of the pattern to
which he had adapted his attitudes, the inadequacy
of those attitudes has been exposed.

One is struck, as one goes through the volumes of
the collected edition of Shaw, which includes a good
deal of his journalism, by the fact that, though his
writing on musical and theatrical and literary subjects
remains remarkably fresh, the pieces on public affairs
and on social questions in general prove very much
less satisfactory than one had remembered their seem-
ing when they first came out. There are passages of
admirable exposition and passages of wonderful
eloquence—some of which, such as the peroration to
*The Intelligent Woman's Guide to Socialism and
Capitalism*, will probably always stand among the
classics of socialist literature. But the political writing
of Shaw does not drive you into taking up a position
as the greatest socialist writing does: indeed, before he

has finished—and he is likely to go on talking too long —he has often seemed to compromise the points which you had imagined he was trying to make, and has produced, with much earnestness and emphasis, an impression rather blurred by rhetoric. Both his intelligence and his sense of justice have prevented him from assailing the capitalist system with such intolerant resentment and unscrupulous methods as Voltaire trained on the Church. With Voltaire, it *is* the crusader that counts; with Shaw, it is the dramatic poet.

The volume which covers the wartime exposes Bernard Shaw's contradictions in a particularly striking manner. Though he was perfectly familiar with the Marxist theory of capitalist expansion and aggression, and had expounded it on many occasions, he had always been liable to fits of admiration for the exploits of the British Empire. Irishman though he was, he had never been an Irish patriot; and, critical though he was of the English, he had in *John Bull's Other Island*—which was written for but declined by the Abbey Theater—backed them against the Irish on account of what he regarded as their superior enterprise and practicality. And though he denounced the Denshawai massacre in Egypt, he supported the British against the Boers at the time of the South African war, because the Boers represented for him a backward civilization and the British a progressive one. When the civilizing forces of the various nations had finally collided in 1914, it was Lenin, the revolutionary exile, not Shaw, the successful British citizen, who wrote *Imperialism: The Last Stage of Capitalism.*

What Bernard Shaw did write was *Common Sense About the War*, which, although it raised a terrible outcry in the fall of 1914 on the part of certain elements of the British public who thought that Shaw ought to be put in the Tower, seems today rather a double-facing document. Shaw, to be sure, makes a certain amount of effort still to keep before the minds of his readers the socialist interpretation of the War. "Will you," he writes, "now at last believe, O stupid British, German and French patriots, what the Socialists have been telling you for so many years: that your Union Jacks and tricolors and Imperial Eagles ('where the carcase is, there will the eagles be gathered') are only toys to keep you amused, and that there are only two real flags in the world henceforth: the red flag of Democratic Socialism and the black flag of Capitalism, the flag of God and the flag of Mammon? What earthly or heavenly good is done when Tom Fool shoots Hans Narr? The plain fact is that if we leave our capital to be dealt with according to the selfishness of the private man he will send it where wages are low and workers enslaved and docile: that is, as many thousand miles as possible from the Trade Unions and Trade Union rates and parliamentary Labour parties of civilization; and Germany, at his sordid behest, will plunge the world into war for the sake of disgracing herself with a few rubber plantations, poetically described by her orators and journalists as 'a place in the sun.' When you do what the Socialists tell you by keeping your capital jealously under national control and reserving your shrapnel for the wasters who not only shirk their share of the industrial service of their country, but intend that their children and children's children shall be idle wasters like themselves, you will find that not a farthing of our capital will go abroad as long as there is a British slum to be cleared and rebuilt or a hungry, ragged and ignorant British child to be fed, clothed and educated."

This sounds spirited enough by itself, yet the burden of *Common Sense About the War* is that the war must be supported and vigorously prosecuted. Shaw afterwards visited and wrote about the front at the invitation of Sir Douglas Haig and even did some work for the propaganda department of the government. In his discussion of compulsory military service in *Common Sense About the War*, he defends his position as follows: "In my own case, the question of conscientious objection did not arise: I was past military age. I did not counsel others to object, and should not have objected myself if I had been liable to serve: for intensely as I loathed the war, and free as I was from any illusion as to its character, and from the patriotic urge (patriotism in my native country taking the form of an implacable hostility to England), I knew that when war is once let loose, and it becomes a question of kill or be killed, there is no stopping to argue about it: one must just stand by one's neighbors and take a hand with the rest. If England had adopted me, as some of my critics alleged in their attempts to convict me of gross ingratitude, I could have pleaded that she must take the consequences without claiming any return; but as I had practically adopted England by thrusting myself and my opinions on her in the face of every possible rebuff, it was for me to take the consequences, which certainly included an obligation to help my reluctant ward in her extremity as far as my means allowed."

Frank Harris, in his book about Shaw, reproached him for supporting the war; and Shaw retorted in a postscript that Harris "could not stop to ask himself the first question . . . of the intellectually honest judicious critic, 'What else could I have done had it been my own case?'" Yet surely there were other courses open to a man of Shaw's opinions. He could have expressed his disapproval and shut up, as John Morley and others did. But it is impossible for Shaw to shut up, and he went on talking incessantly through the whole four years of slaughter. Much of what he had to say was intelligent, and it required some courage to say it. Compared with most of the British writers, he seemed at the time to an American remarkably cool and sagacious. The atmosphere was feverish with panic and stupefying with the fumes of propaganda, and Shaw did do something to clear the air for a discussion of the origin and aims of the war. But when we reread what he wrote today, he looks a

little foolish. The old socialist has gone down into
the mêlée and sacrificed something of his moral dignity: we hear him remonstrating, scolding, exhorting,
making fun of the politicians and at the same time
lending a hand to the government, pleading for the
conscientious objectors and at the same time "joy-rid-
ing at the front"—and doing everything with equal
cocksureness.

Before the Peace Conference, he had great hopes
of Wilson. Before the Washington Disarmament
Conference, he was cynical. Later, he spoke a kind
word for the League of Nations. And in the meantime the Russian Revolution had set him off on a
different tack. He would alternately lecture Lenin
and Trotsky on the futility of what they were trying
to do and applaud them for succeeding in doing it: he
was alternately a middle-class socialist using Fabianism against the Marxists and a Marxist using Lenin
and Trotsky against the British governing class. (It
is interesting to note that Lenin characterized him as
"a good man fallen among Fabians," and that
Trotsky, of whom Shaw wrote enthusiastically as "the
Prince of Pamphleteers," expressed the wish,
apropos of his own exclusion from England, that "the
Fabian fluid that ran in [Bernard Shaw's] veins"
might have "been strengthened by even so much as
five per cent of the blood of Jonathan Swift." It is
amusing to see Trotsky's indignation in his *Where Is
Britain Going?* over Shaw's cavalier suggestion that
Marx had been superseded by H. G. Wells's *Outline
of History*: Trotsky had gone to the trouble of pro-
curing and looking into Wells.)

In his political utterances since the war, it is hardly
too much to say that Bernard Shaw has behaved like
a jackass. In the autumn of 1927, he was staying in
Italy on the Lago Maggiore and throwing bouquets
at Mussolini. It was his old admiration for the romantic hero, his old idealization—which was as likely
to be set off by an imperialist as a Marxist theme—of
the practical Caesarean statesman who makes people

stand around. Mussolini had, according to Shaw, "achieved a dictatorship in a great modern state without a single advantage, social, official or academic, to assist him, after marching to Rome with a force of Black Shirts which a single disciplined regiment backed by a competent government could have routed at any moment . . . After the war the government of Italy" had been "so feeble that silly Syndicalists were seizing factories, and fanatical devotees of that curious attempt at a new Catholic church called the Third International were preaching a *coup d'état* and a Crusade in all directions, and imagining that this sort of thing was Socialism and Communism. Mussolini, without any of Napoleon's prestige, has done for Italy what Napoleon did for France, except that for the Duc d'Enghien you must read Matteotti." When Gaetano Salvemini reminded Shaw that, so far from being "without a single advantage," Mussolini had had behind him "the money of the banks, the big industrialists and the landowners," and that his Black Shirts had been "equipped with rifles, bombs, machine-guns, and motor-lorries by the military authorities, and assured of impunity by the police and the magistracy, while their adversaries were disarmed and severely punished if they attempted resistance," Shaw's rebuttal was almost unbelievable: Why, he demanded, had Mussolini been able to command the support of the army officers and capitalists "instead of Signors Salvemini, Giolitti, Turati, Matteotti and their friends, in spite of the fact that he was farther to the Left in his political opinions than any of them? The answer, as it seems to me, is that he combined with extreme opinions the knowledge that the first duty of any Government, no matter what its opinions are, is to carry on, and make its citizens carry on, liberty or no liberty, democracy or no democracy, socialism or no socialism, capitalism or no capitalism. Until Salvemini and his friends convince Italy that they understand this necessity as well as Mussolini does they will never shake his hold

on the situation. To rail at him as Shelley railed at
Castlereagh and Eldon, Marx at Napoleon III and
Thiers, Kautsky at Lenin, is to play the amusing but
inglorious part of Thersites." Now a dramatist in his
capacity of dramatist may make out a very interesting
case for a Castlereagh or a Napoleon III; but why
should Shaw in his capacity as a political writer take
the part of such politicians against their philosophical
opponents? He is himself of the company of Shelley
and Marx—the company of the poets and prophets;
and railing at the Castlereaghs and Napoleons—of
which Shaw himself has done plenty on occasion—is
by no means the least valuable of their functions. The
analogy between these other cases and Kautsky complaining of Lenin is certainly a silly and dishonest
one.

That spring he had finished a long treatise—*The
Intelligent Woman's Guide*—in which he had made
a more comprehensive effort than he had ever done
in his socialist days in the eighties to analyze capitalist
society and to argue the case for socialism. Perhaps
the book should have been written in the eighties.
Ramsay Macdonald and Sidney Webb had come to
power with the Labour Government in 1924, and
Macdonald had not yet definitely sold out; and the
whole story is repeated in general in the familiar
Fabian terms—to which Shaw, without Fabian sanction, had added equality of income as a prime item
of his socialist program. Through many pages of swift
exposition, perhaps Shaw's most precise and limpid
writing, which, together with the magnificent close,
give the book an enduring value, he makes his way
to conclusions that perplex us in proportion as the
reasoning becomes more fine-spun and that do not
seem finally to land us in any very realistic relation
to the England of after the war. "A series of properly
prepared nationalizations may not only be understood and voted for by people who would be quite
shocked if they were called Socialists, but would fit
in perfectly with the habits of the masses who take

their bread as it comes and never think about anything of a public nature." And in the meantime the road to socialism remains for a good part of the way —through "nationalizations, expropriative taxation and all the constructive political machinery"—identical with the road to state capitalism. So that Lenin, says Shaw, had been quite in the wrong when he had denounced the methods of the Fabians as state capitalism.

But Lenin had been aware of the psychological pitfalls in the approach of the Fabians toward socialism —pitfalls which no amount of lucid explanation was able to get them over and which Shaw continued to stumble into himself. From the moment that you propose to benefit people from the point of view of imposing upon them what is best for them rather than of showing them the way to what they ought to have and awaiting the moment when they will know that they must have it, what is to prevent your slipping— the post-Lenin period in Russia has proved it as much as the Ramsay Macdonald Labour Government—into imposing upon the people something which will benefit you yourself?

I shall not here pursue the story of the subsequent career of the Fabians, as I want to show further on how it was reflected in Bernard Shaw's later plays. But I will note here that in 1931 he visited Soviet Russia in company with the Tory Lady Astor and with the liberal Marquess of Lothian, had an audience with Stalin, at which, as he said, they treated Stalin like "a friendly emperor," and, on his return, began loudly endorsing Russia and especially scolding the United States for not following the Soviet example. Later, in his *Preface on Bosses* in his volume of plays of 1936, he was back praising Mussolini again and even throwing a few kind words to Hitler, whom he described as "not a stupid German" (did Bernard Shaw prefer a crazy Austrian?) and whose persecution of the Jews he characterized considerately as "a craze, a complex, a bee in his bonnet, a hole in his

armor, a hitch in his statesmanship, one of those
lesions which sometimes prove fatal." Of the systematic persecution by the Nazis of Communists, Socialists, and Pacifists, of everybody—including critics and
artists—who belonged to Bernard Shaw's own camp,
he had nothing whatever to say save to mention it
and minimize it in passing as "plundering raids and
coups d'état against inconvenient Liberals or Marxists." At the time of the Ethiopian War, he came out
strongly for Mussolini on the same grounds on which
he had formerly defended the behavior of the British
in South Africa, and insisted that the League of Nations, on behalf of which in 1928 he had written a
Fabian pamphlet, should never have tried to inter-
fere.

Thus in this period of disastrous dictatorships,
when it was very important for a socialist to keep
clear in the eyes of the public the difference between
the backing and aims of Lenin and the backing and
aims of Mussolini, Bernard Shaw has done a good deal
to confuse them and, parliamentary socialist though
he claims to be, to exalt the ideal of the dictator.
When the socialist dictatorship of Lenin gave way
to the despotism of Stalin, Shaw did not seem to know
the difference, but applauded the suppression of the
old Leninists, on the ground that most professional
revolutionists ought to be shot the morning after the
revolution, and, on the principle that the socially
harmful had to be got out of the way, gave his blessing to the Russian concentration camps, with their
millions of political prisoners.

All this he has handled, of course, with his marvelous cleverness and style. Analyzing everybody perpetually, he is a great master of the smoke-screen
against criticism. It is done partly by sheer personal
hypnotism and Irish gift of gab. Before you arrive
at any book of Bernard Shaw's—from *What I Really
Wrote About the War* to his correspondence with
Ellen Terry—you have almost invariably been told
what to think of it in a preface by which Shaw has

protected himself against your possible perception of his weakness. If you submit to his spell, you will allow him to manipulate the lights in such a way that, by the time the curtain goes up, you find Shaw looking noble in the center of the stage with everything else left in semi-obscurity, and yourself with your discriminatory powers in a temporary state of suspension, under the illusion that you must either accept or reject him. (Of late the exhibitionistic vanity which seemed dashing in his early days when he was assailing the philistines with such spirit has come to be tiresome and even repellent—as, for example, when his comment on the death of one of his distinguished contemporaries takes the form of the irrelevant reflection, "I'll be dead very soon myself!")

But there has been also an odd kind of trickery involved in the whole of Bernard Shaw's career. It depends on a technique which he has mastered of functioning on three distinct planes and of shifting from one to another. His air of certainty, his moralist's tone, his well-drilled sentences, his regular emphasis, all go to create an impression of straightforwardness. But actually the mind of Shaw is always fluctuating between various emotions which give rise to various points of view.

The mechanics seem to be somewhat as follows: At the bottom of Shaw is a commonsense sphere of practical considerations; above this is a plane of socialism, of the anticipated reorganization of society in the interest of ideal values; and above this, a poet-philosopher's ether from which he commands a longer view of life *sub specie aeternitatis* and where the poet allows himself many doubts which neither the socialist nor the bourgeois citizen can admit. Shaw has never really taken up his residence for any great length of time on any one of these three planes of thinking. The socialist, for example, denounces war; but when England actually goes to war, the respectable householder backs her. The moralist denounces marriage; but the conventional married man always

advises young people to get married. The socialist
takes sword in hand to battle for a sounder society
based on a redistribution of income; and the long-
view philosopher-poet comes to sap the socialist's faith
with misgivings as to the capacity for intellect and
virtue of the material of common humanity as contrasted with philosopher-poets. The poet gets a good
way above the earth in the ecstasy of imaginative vision; but the socialist reminds him that it is the duty
of art to teach a useful social lesson, and the householder damps the fires of both by admonishing them
that the young people in the audience oughtn't to
be told anything that will get them into trouble.
The result is that reading Shaw is like looking through
a pair of field glasses of which the focus is always
equally sharp and clear but the range may be changed
without warning.

So adroit are Shaw's transitions that we are usually
unaware of what has happened; and when we have
come to be conscious of them, we wonder how much
Shaw is aware. It is curious to go back over his work
and see him juggling with his various impersonations:
the socialist, the fascist, the saint, the shrewd businessman, the world genius, the human being, the clever
journalist who knows how to be politic, the popular
speaker who knows how to be tactful. It is quite as
if they were the characters in a comedy, each of whom
he can pick up where he has dropped him and have
him go on with his part.

III

But comedies are best presented in the theater; and
in the theater Shaw's conflicts of impulse, his intellectual flexibility and his genius for legerdemain—all
the qualities that have had the effect of weakening his
work as a publicist—have contributed to his success as
an artist.

One of the prime errors of recent radical criticism
has been the assumption that great novels and plays

must necessarily be written by people who have everything clear in their minds. People who have everything clear in their minds, who are not capable of identifying themselves imaginatively with, who do not actually embody in themselves, contrary emotions and points of view, do not write novels or plays at all—do not, at any rate, write good ones. And—given genius—the more violent the contraries, the greater the works of art.

Let us consider Shaw as an artist.

Bernard Shaw's great rôle in the theater has been to exploit the full possibilities of a type of English comedy which had first been given its characteristic form during the seventies of the nineteenth century in the comedies of W. S. Gilbert. The comedy of the Restoration, which had culminated in Congreve, had been the product of an aristocratic society, which depended for its ironic effects on the contrast between artificial social conventions and natural animal instincts, between fine manners and fine intelligence, on the one hand, and the crudest carnal appetites, on the other. The comedy of the nineteenth century—setting aside Oscar Wilde—depended on the contrast between the respectable conventions of a pious middle-class society and the mean practical realities behind them, between the pretension to high moral principles and the cold complacency which underlay it. As with the dramatists of the Restoration, it was always the pursuit of pleasure that emerged from behind the formalities, so, in the comedies of Gilbert which preceded his Savoy operas and of which the most famous and successful was *Engaged* (1877), it is always the greed for money that extrudes from behind the screen of noble words and discreet behavior. "Dear papa," says the Victorian young lady in one of the scenes of *Engaged*, when she has just heard of the failure of a bank in which the fortune of her fiancé was invested, "I am very sorry to disappoint you, but unless your tom-tit is very much mistaken, the Indestructible was registered under the Joint Stock

Companies Act of '62 and in that case the stockholders are jointly and severally liable to the whole extent of their available capital. Poor little Minnie don't pretend to have a business head; but she is not quite such a little donkey as that, dear papa!" The characters of Gilbert's comedies, who talk the language of Victorian fiction, are never for a moment betrayed by emotion into allowing themselves to be diverted from the main chance; and the young men are perfectly ready, not from appetite but from sheer indifference, to make equally passionate professions to any number of young ladies at the same time. It is not far from the Symperson family and Cheviot Hill of *Engaged* to Shaw's *The Philanderer* and *Widowers' Houses*.

But neither Gilbert nor Dickens nor Samuel Butler —those two other great satirists of the money-minded English, to whom, also, Shaw is indebted—could teach him to analyze society in terms of economic motivation or to understand and criticize the profit system. This he learned to do from Karl Marx, whose work during his English residence, the period when *Das Kapital* was written, was itself of course a product of and an ironical protest against English nineteenth-century civilization. Bernard Shaw thus brought something quite new into English imaginative literature. His study of economics had served him, as he said, for his plays as the study of anatomy had served Michael Angelo. And with economic insight and training he joined literary qualities of a kind that had never yet appeared in combination with them—qualities, in fact, that, since the century before, had been absent from English literature entirely.

The Irish of Bernard Shaw's period enjoyed, in the field of literature, certain special advantages over the English, due to the fact that, since Irish society was still mainly in the pre-industrial stage, they were closer to eighteenth-century standards. If we compare Shaw, Yeats and Joyce to, say, Galsworthy, Wells and Bennett, we are struck at once by the extent to which these latter writers have suffered from their submergence in the commercial world. In their worst phases of sentimentality and philistinism, there is almost nothing to choose between them and the frankly trashy popular novelist; whereas the Irish have preserved for English literature classical qualities of hardness and elegance.

Bernard Shaw has had the further advantage of a musical education. "Do not suppose for a moment," he writes, "that I learnt my art from English men of letters. True, they showed me how to handle English words; but if I had known no more than that, my works would never have crossed the Channel. My masters were the masters of a universal language; they were, to go from summit to summit, Bach, Handel, Haydn, Mozart, Beethoven and Wagner . . . For their sakes, Germany stands consecrated as the Holy Land of the capitalistic age." Einstein has said that Shaw's plays remind him of Mozart's music: every word has its place in the development. And if we allow for some nineteenth-century prolixity, we can see in Shaw's dramatic work a logic and grace, a formal precision, like that of the eighteenth-century composers.

Take *The Apple Cart*, for example. The fact that Shaw is here working exclusively with economic and political materials has caused its art to be insufficiently appreciated. If it had been a sentimental comedy by Molnar, the critics would have applauded its deftness; yet Shaw is a finer artist than any of the Molnars or Schnitzlers. The first act of *The Apple Cart* is an exercise in the scoring for small orchestra at which Shaw is particularly skillful. After what he has himself called the overture before the curtain of the conversation between the two secretaries, in which the music of King Magnus is foreshadowed, the urbane and intelligent King and the "bull-roarer Boanerges" play a duet against one another. Then the King plays a single instrument against the whole nine of the cabinet. The themes emerge: the King's disinterestedness and the labor government's sordid self-interest. The development is lively: the music is tossed from one instrument to another, with, to use the old cliché, a combination of inevitableness and surprise. Finally, the King's theme gets a full and splendid statement in the long speech in which he declares his principles: "I stand for the great abstractions: for conscience and virtue; for the eternal against the expedient; for the evolutionary appetite against the day's gluttony," etc. This silver voice of the King lifts the movement to a poignant climax; and now a dramatic reversal carries the climax further and rounds out and balances the harmony. Unexpectedly, one of the brasses of the ministry takes up the theme of the King and repeats it more passionately and loudly: "Just so! . . . Listen to me, sir," bursts out the Powermistress, "and judge whether I have not reason to feel everything you have just said to the very marrow of my bones. Here am I, the Powermistress Royal. I have to organize and administer all the motor power in the country for the good of the country. I have to harness the winds and the tides, the oils and the coal seams." And she launches into an extraordinary tirade in which the idea of political disinterestedness is taken out of the realm of elegant abstraction in which it has hitherto remained with the King and reiterated in terms of engineering: "every little sewing machine in the Hebrides, every dentist's drill in Shetland, every carpet sweeper in Margate," etc. This ends on crashing chords, but immediately the music of the cabinet snarlingly reasserts itself. The act ends on the light note of the secretaries.

This music is a music of ideas—or rather, perhaps, it is a music of moralities. Bernard Shaw is a writer of the same kind as Plato. There are not many such writers in literature—the *Drames philosophiques* of Renan would supply another example—and they are likely to puzzle the critics. Shaw, like Plato, repudiates as a dangerous form of drunkenness the indulgence in literature for its own sake; but, like Plato, he then proceeds, not simply to expound a useful morality, but himself to indulge in an art in which moralities are used as the motifs. It is partly on this account, certainly, that Bernard Shaw has been underrated as an artist. Whether people admire or dislike him, whether they find his plays didactically boring or morally stimulating, they fail to take account of the fact that it is the enchantment of a highly accomplished art which has brought them to and kept them in the playhouse. It is an art that has even had the power to preserve such pieces as *Getting Married*, of which the 1908 heresies already seemed out of date twenty or thirty years later but of which the symphonic development still remains brilliant and fresh. So far from being relentlessly didactic, Shaw's mind has reflected in all its complexity the intellectual life of his time; and his great achievement is to have reflected it with remarkable fidelity. He has *not* imposed a cogent system, but he has worked out a vivid picture. It is, to be sure, not a passive picture, like that of Santayana or Proust: it is a picture in which action plays a prominent part. But it does not play a consistent part: the dynamic principle in Shaw is made to animate a variety of forces.

Let us see what these forces are and to what purpose they interact.

IV

What are the real themes of Bernard Shaw's plays?

He has not been a socialist dramatist in the sense that, say, Upton Sinclair has been a socialist novelist. His economics have served him, it is true, as anatomy served Michael Angelo; but to say that is to give as little idea of what kind of characters he creates and what his plays are about as it would of the figures of the sculptor to say that they were produced by an artist who understood the skeleton and the muscles. It is quite wrong to assume, as has sometimes been done, that the possession of the social-economic intelligence must imply that the writer who has it writes tracts for social reform.

Shaw is himself partly responsible for this assumption. In his early days, when he *was* a social reformer, he wrote books about Wagner and Ibsen which introduced them to the English-speaking public as primarily social reformers, too. There is of course a social revolutionist, a man of 1848, in Wagner, and a critic of bourgeois institutions in Ibsen. But Bernard Shaw, in his brilliant little books, by emphasizing these aspects of their work at the expense of everything else, seriously misrepresents them. He appreciates Siegfried and Brunhilde in their heroic and rebellious phases; but Wagner's tragedies of love he pooh-poohs; and it is sometimes just when Ibsen is at his strongest—as in *Brand* or *Rosmersholm*—that Bernard Shaw is least satisfactory on him, because the tragic spirit of Ibsen does not fit into Shaw's preconception. In Ibsen's case, Shaw is particularly misleading, because Ibsen disclaimed again and again any social-reforming intentions. His great theme, characteristic though it is of nineteenth-century society, is not a doctrine of social salvation: it is the conflict between one's duty to society as a unit in the social organism and the individual's duty to himself. Ibsen treats this theme over and over but in a number of different ways, sometimes emphasizing the validity of social claims as opposed to the will of the individual (*Little Eyolf*), sometimes showing them as unjustified and oppressive (*Ghosts*); sometimes showing the individual undone by self-indulgence or perverse self-assertion (*Peer Gynt* and *Brand*), sometimes showing him as noble and sympathetic (the hero and heroine of *Rosmersholm*); sometimes dramatizing the two poles of conduct in the career of a single individual, like Dr. Stockman in *An Enemy of the People*, who begins by trying to save society but who later, when society turns against him, is driven back into an individualistic vindication of the social conscience itself with the realization that "the strongest man is he who stands most alone." But the conflict is always serious; and it usually ends in disaster. Rarely—*A Doll's House* is the principal example—does it result in a liberation. Ibsen is hardly ever a social philosopher: he goes no further than the conflict itself.

Now is there any such basic theme in Bernard Shaw? Has he been creating a false impression not only about Ibsen but also about himself? Certainly the prefaces he prefixes to his plays do not really explain them any more than *The Quintessence of Ibsenism* really explains Ibsen.

The principal pattern which recurs in Bernard Shaw—aside from the duel between male and female, which seems to me of much less importance—is the polar opposition between the type of the saint and the type of the successful practical man. This conflict, when it is present in his other writing, has a blurring, a demoralizing effect, as in the passage on Saint Francis *et al.* which I quoted at the beginning of this essay; but it is the principle of life of his plays. We find it in its clearest presentation in the opposition between Father Keegan and Tom Broadbent in *John Bull's Other Island* and between Major Barbara and Undershaft—where the moral scales are pretty evenly weighted and where the actual predominance of the practical man, far from carrying ominous implications, produces a certain effect of reassurance: this was apparently the period—when Bernard Shaw had outgrown his early battles and struggles and before the war had come to disturb him—of his most comfortable and self-confident exercise of powers which had fully matured. But these opposites have also a tendency to dissociate themselves from one another and to feature themselves sometimes, not correlatively, but alternatively in successive plays. In *The Devil's Disciple* and *The Shewing-up of Blanco Posnet*, the heroes are dashing fellows who have melodramatic flashes of saintliness; their opponents are made comic or base. *Caesar and Cleopatra* is a play that glorifies the practical man; *Androcles and the*

Lion is a play that glorifies the saint. So is *Saint Joan*, with the difference that here the worldly antagonists of the saint are presented as intelligent and effective.

Certainly it is this theme of the saint and the world which has inspired those scenes of Shaw's plays which are most moving and most real on the stage—which are able to shock us for the moment, as even the "Life Force" passages hardly do, out of the amiable and objective attention which has been induced by the bright play of the intelligence. It is the moment when Major Barbara, brought at last to the realization of the power of the capitalist's money and of her own weakness when she hasn't it to back her, is left alone on the stage with the unregenerate bums whose souls she has been trying to save; the moment when Androcles is sent into the arena with the lion; the moment in the emptied courtroom when Joan has been taken out to be burned and the Bishop and the Earl of Warwick are trying each to pin the responsibility on the other. It is the scene in *Heartbreak House* between Captain Shotover and Hector, when they give voice to their common antagonism toward the forces that seem to have them at their mercy: "We must win powers of life and death over them . . . There is enmity between our seed and their seed. They know it and act on it, strangling our souls. They believe in themselves. When we believe in ourselves, we shall kill them . . . We kill the better half of ourselves every day to propitiate them." It is the scene in *Back to Methuselah* when the Elderly Gentleman declares to the Oracle: "They have gone back to lie about your answer [the political delegation with whom he has come]. I cannot go with them. I cannot live among people to whom nothing is real!"—and when she shows him her face and strikes him dead.

But now let us note—for the light they throw on Bernard Shaw in his various phases—the upshots of these several situations. In *Major Barbara*, the Christian saint, the man of learning, and the industrial superman form an alliance from which much is to be

hoped. In *Androcles and the Lion*, written in 1913, in
Shaw's amusing but least earnest middle period, just
before the war, Androcles and the lion form an alliance, too, of which something is also to be hoped,
but go out arm in arm after a harlequinade on the
level of a Christmas pantomime. In *Heartbreak
House*, which was begun in 1913 and not finished till
1916, the declaration of war by the unworldlings
takes place in the midst of confusion and does not
lead to any action on their part.

In *Back to Methuselah*, of the postwar period, the
Elderly Gentleman is blasted by the Oracle in a
strange scene the implications of which we must stop
to examine a moment. The fate of the Elderly Gentleman is evidently intended by Shaw to have some
sort of application to himself: though a member of a
backward community in which people have not yet
achieved the Methuselah-span of life, he differs from
his fellows at least in this: that he finds he cannot
bear any longer to live among people to whom
nothing is real. So the Oracle shrivels him up with
her glance.

But what is this supposed to mean? What *is* this
higher wisdom which the Elderly Gentleman cannot
contemplate and live? So far as the reader is concerned, the revelation of the Oracle is a blank. The
old system of Bernard Shaw, which was plausible
enough to pass before the war, has just taken a terrible
blow, and its grotesque and gruesome efforts to pull
itself together and function give the effect of an um-
brella, wrecked in a storm, which, when the owner
tries to open it up, shows several long ribs of steel
sticking out. The Life Force of the man and woman
in *Man and Superman* no longer leads either to human procreation or to social-revolutionary activity.
The Life Force has been finally detached from socialism altogether. In the *Intelligent Woman's Guide*,
Shaw will reject the Marxist dialectic as a false religion of social salvation; but the Life Force is also a
religious idea, which we have always supposed in the

past to be directed toward social betterment, and
now, in *Back to Methuselah*, we find that it has mis-
fired with socialism. Socialism has come and gone;
the planet has been laid waste by wars; the ordinary
people have all perished, and there is nobody left on
earth but a race of selected supermen. And now the
race of superior human beings, which was invoked in
Man and Superman as the prime indispensable condition for any kind of progress whatever but which
was regarded by Shaw at that time as producible
through eugenic breeding, has taken here a most
unearthly turn. It has always been through the superman idea that Shaw has found it possible to escape
from the implications of his socialism; and he now no
longer even imagines that the superior being can be
created by human idealism through human science.
The superior beings of *Back to Methuselah* are people who live forever; but they have achieved this superiority through an unconscious act of the will. When
they have achieved it, what the Life Force turns out
to have had in store for them is the mastery of ab-
struse branches of knowledge and the extra-uterine
development of embryos. Beyond this, there is still
to be attained the liberation of the spirit from the
flesh, existence as a "whirlpool in pure force." "And
for what may be beyond, the eyesight of Lilith is too
short. It is enough that there is a beyond."

Humanity, in *Back to Methuselah*, has dropped
out for the moment altogether. The long-livers of the
period of progress contemporary with the Elderly
Gentleman are not the more "complete" human beings, with lives richer and better rounded, which Marx
and Engels and Lenin imagined for the "classless society": they are Shavian super-prigs who say the cut-
ting and dampening things which the people have
always said in Shaw's plays but who have been ab-
stracted here from the well-observed social setting in
which Shaw has always hitherto presented them. And
the beings of the later epoch are young people playing in an Arcadia and ancients immersed in cogita-

tions, alike—both cogitations and Arcadia—of the bleakest and most desolating description. There is in *Back to Methuselah* nothing burning or touching, and there is nothing genuinely thrilling except the cry of the Elderly Gentleman; and that, for all the pretense of revelation, is answered by a simple extinction.

In the *Tragedy of an Elderly Gentleman*, the Elderly Gentleman is frightened, but his tragedy is not a real tragedy. *Saint Joan* (1924) is an even more frightened play, and, softened though it is by the historical perspective into which Shaw manages to throw it through his epilogue, it was the first genuine tragedy that Shaw had written. The horror of *Back to Methuselah* is a lunar horror; the horror of *Saint Joan* is human. The saint is suppressed by the practical man; and even when she comes back to earth, though all those who exploited or destroyed her are now obliged to acknowledge her holiness, none wants her to remain among them: each would do the same thing again. Only the soldier who had handed her the cross at the stake is willing to accept her now, but he is only a poor helpless clown condemned to the dungeon of the flesh.

v

Back to Methuselah is a flight into the future; *Saint Joan* is a flight into the past. But with *Heartbreak House* Bernard Shaw had already begun a series of plays in which he was to deal with the postwar world and his own relation to it in terms of contemporary England—a section of his work which, it seems to me, has had too little appreciation or comprehension.

Heartbreak House has the same sort of setting and more or less the same form as such Shavian conversations as *Getting Married* and *Misalliance*; but it is really something new for Shaw. There is no diagram of social relations, no tying-up of threads at the end. *Heartbreak House*, Shaw says in his preface, is "cultured leisured Europe before the War"; but the play, he told Archibald Henderson, "began with an atmosphere and does not contain a word that was foreseen before it was written," and it is the only one of his plays which he has persistently refused to explain. "How should I know?" he replied, when he was asked by his actors what it meant. "I am only the author." Heartbreak House, built like a ship, with its old drunken and half-crazy master, the retired adventurer Captain Shotover, is cultured and leisured England; but the characters are no longer pinned down and examined as social specimens: in an atmosphere heavily charged, through a progression of contacts and collisions, they give out thunder and lightning like storm-clouds. Brooding frustrations and disillusions, childlike hurts and furious resentments, which have dropped the old Shavian masks, rush suddenly into an utterance which for the moment has burst out of the old rationalistic wit. For once, where Bernard Shaw has so often reduced historical myths to the sharp focus of contemporary satire, he now raises contemporary figures to the heroic proportions of myth. —An air-raid brings down the final curtain: Heartbreak House has at last been split wide. The capitalist Mangan gets killed, and there is a suggestion that they may all be the better for it.

But in 1924 the Labour Party came to power, with Ramsay Macdonald as Prime Minister. Macdonald had been a member of the Executive Committee of the Fabian Society, and he brought with him two other Fabians, Sidney Webb and Sydney Olivier, who took the portfolios of Minister of Labour and Secretary of State for India. When Macdonald was reelected in 1929, he was accompanied by no less than twenty Fabians, of whom eight were cabinet members. The Fabians had now achieved the aim which was to have been the condition for the success of their ideas: they had "interpenetrated" the government. But in the meantime the competition of the British Empire with the German had culminated in a four years' war; and in England of after the war, with the top manhood of her society slaughtered and the lower classes laid off from their wartime jobs, and with English commercial domination further damaged by the United States, the influence of the Fabians could do little to bridge over the abyss which had been blasted between the extremes of the British class society. The best measures of the Labour Government were able to accomplish no more than just to keep the unemployed alive; and when the capitalists began to feel the pinch, they openly took over control. Ramsay Macdonald, in 1931, became Prime Minister in a Nationalist government and cleared his socialists out of office.

At the moment of the second accession of the Labour Party to power, Shaw had written *The Apple Cart*, in which Macdonald is caricatured as Proteus, the Prime Minister of a labor government. This government is represented as really controlled by Breakages, Limited, a great monopoly which opposes industrial progress for the reason that it has an interest in perpetuating the inferior and less durable machinery that requires more frequent repairs. But one finds in *The Apple Cart* no comment on the Fabianism, which, after all, has been partly responsible for Proteus: the blame is laid at the door, not of that socialism by interpenetration which has ended by itself being interpenetrated, but of something which Shaw calls "democracy"; and what is opposed to the corrupt socialism of Proteus is not socialism of a more thoroughgoing kind, but the super-constitutional-monarch, King Magnus. Again, Shaw has given the slip to his problems through recourse to the cult of the superior person.

Yet in 1931, after the final collapse of the Labour Government, Bernard Shaw visited Russia and, by applauding the Soviet system, incurred unpopularity in England for the first time since the war. In the same year, he wrote *Too True to Be Good*, a curious "political extravaganza," in which he turns back upon and criticizes his own career. Here the theme of the bourgeois radical of the eighties, disillusioned with himself under stress of the disasters of the twentieth century, is treated in the same vein, with the same kind of idealist poetry, now grown frankly elegiac and despairing, which Shaw had opened in *Heartbreak House* and which had made the real beauty of *The Apple Cart*.

A rich young English girl of the upper middle class is languishing with an imaginary illness in a gloomy Victorian chamber, fussed over by a Victorian mother. Into this sickroom erupt two rebels: a young preacher and a former chambermaid, who is an illegitimate child of the aristocracy. The chambermaid has been masquerading as the heiress's trained nurse, and she and the preacher have a plot to steal the heiress's pearl necklace. The girl comes to from her megrims and puts up an unexpected struggle. The preacher becomes interested in his victim and says that he has always wondered why she does not steal the necklace herself. Why doesn't she take it and go and do what she pleases, instead of staying home with her mother, moping and fancying herself sick? Why doesn't she let him and his accomplice sell the necklace for her, taking 25 per cent of the price apiece and giving her the other 50? The girl enthusiastically agrees, and while she is getting dressed to go with them, the preacher jumps up on the bed and delivers one of those live-your-own-life sermons with which Shaw, in the nineties, made his first success. Then he is off—in the excitement of his rhetoric, at first forgetting the necklace, which the heiress has to remind him they need.

All three sail away together to an imaginary Balkan country reminiscent of *Arms and the Man*, where they are able to do whatever they like but where their revolt turns out to lead to nothing and eventually to bore them to death. Shaw has evidently put into *Too True to Be Good* a sort of recapitulation of his earlier themes, the shams of bourgeois society: the capitalistic doctor of *The Doctor's Dilemma* is as much a fraud as ever; the pompous British military officer, though retaining an air of authority, has practically ceased even to pretend to be anything other than a fraud and is quite willing to leave the command to a private (drawn from Lawrence of Arabia), if he can only be left in peace with his water-colors; the old-fashioned materialist-atheist who is also the most rigorous of moralists, of the type of Roebuck Ramsden in *Man and Superman*, has lived through into a world where his morality has no power to prevent his son's turning thief, etc. Finally everyone except the preacher sets out for the "Union of Sensible Republics."

The preacher is left alone on the shore, abandoned between two worlds. He had come too late for the old and too early for the new. He had had the courage once to steal a necklace but he hadn't carried through his idea. He had given it back to the owner and they had made common cause together: the liberated bourgeoise girl had gotten 50 per cent of the price, the radicals only 25 apiece. In this last scene, the darkness comes, the clouds gather; the morale of the preacher breaks down. He can only go on explaining and exhorting, whether or not he has anything to say. A keen wind is blowing in, and it may be the breath of life, but it is too fierce for him to bear.

This, Shaw tells us, is a political fable; and now he is to return to politics proper. In *On the Rocks* (1933), he appears to drive himself into a corner as he has never before done and then comes out with a political position which still manages to be somewhat equivocal.

The first act shows a liberal Prime Minister, hard beset during a period of depression. Pall Mall and Trafalgar Square are full of excited crowds. The Prime Minister, on the verge of a breakdown, can think of nothing to do except to call out the police against them, but he is dissuaded by the Police Commissioner himself and finally induced to go away for a rest. He has just been visited by a labor delegation who have impressed him with the importance of Marxism, and he takes volumes of Marx and Lenin away with him.

When the curtain goes up on the second act, the Prime Minister has read Marx and Lenin; but the effect upon him is unexpected. He has gained an insight into economic motivation, an understanding of the technique of making use of it; but he has not been converted to socialism: he has worked out, on the contrary, an exceedingly clever scheme for preserving the capitalist state through a program, essentially fascist, of partial nationalization and taxation of unearned incomes. He will conciliate the various social groups which would normally be antagonistic by promising a concession to each. The plan seems bidding fair to succeed when it runs aground on Sir Dexter Rightside, the Liberal Prime Minister's Tory colleague in a coalition National Government. Sir Dexter represents the blind conservatism which sticks to the *status quo* through sheer obstinacy and inability to imagine anything else: he threatens to put colored shirts on "fifty thousand patriotic young Londoners" and to call them into the streets against the proposed program of the government. The Prime Minister has to give up his attempt, but he is now forced to face his situation: "Do you think I didn't know," he confesses to his wife, "in the days of my great speeches and my roaring popularity, that I was only whitewashing the slums? I couldn't help knowing as well as any of those damned Socialists that though the West End of London was chockful of money and nice people all calling one another by their Christian names, the lives of the millions of people whose labor was keeping the whole show going were not worth living; but I was able to put it out of my mind because I thought it couldn't be helped and I was doing the best that could be done. I know better now! I know that it can be helped, and how it can be helped. And rather than go back to the old white-washing job, I'd seize you tight around the waist and make a hole in the river with you . . . Why don't I lead the revolt against it all? Because I'm not the man for the job, darling . . . And I shall hate the man who will carry it through for his cruelty and the desolation he will bring on us and our like."

The shouting of the crowd and the crash of glass is suddenly heard outside. The people have broken into Downing Street. The police begin to club them and ride them down. The people sing, "England, arise!"

Sir Arthur Chavender's more or less liberal fascism has been defeated by the reactionary fascism of his Tory colleague in the National Government, with whom he is indissolubly united. (There is no question any longer of the superior man: King Magnus has disappeared from the scene.) There is a third point of view, opposed to both, but this, also, sounds rather fascist. Old Hipney, the disillusioned labor veteran, who speaks for the dissatisfied classes, seems to be looking for a Man on Horseback, too: "Adult suffrage: that was what was to save us all. My God! It delivered us into the hands of our spoilers and oppressors, bound hand and foot by our own folly and ignorance. It took the heart out of old Hipney; and now I'm for any Napoleon or Mussolini or Lenin or Chavender that has the stuff in him to take both the people and the spoilers and oppressors by the scruffs of their silly necks and just sling them into the way they should go with as many kicks as may be needful to make a thorough job of it." But Chavender declines the job; and the people begin throwing bricks.

The conclusion we are apparently to draw is that parliamentary fascism must fail; and that we may then get either a Lenin or a Mussolini. Is this also a final confession of the failure of Fabianism, which depended on parliament, too?

In any case, at the end of this play, we have come in a sense to the end of Shaw. With the eruption of the uprising, we should be plunged into a situation which could no longer be appropriately handled by the characteristic methods of his comedy. He is still splendid when he is showing the bewilderment of the liberal governing-class prime minister: it is surprising how he is still able to summon his old flickering and piercing wit, his old skill at juggling points of view, to illuminate a new social situation—how quick and skillful he is at describing a new social type: the communist viscount, with his brutal language, which shocks his proletarian allies. But with the shouts and the broken glass, we are made to take account of the fact that Shaw's comedy, for all its greater freedom in dealing with social conditions, is almost as much dependent on a cultivated and stable society as the comedy of Molière, who had his place in the royal dining-room and depended on Louis's favor for the permission to produce his plays. Shaw, as much as Molière, must speak the same language as his audience; he must observe the same conventions of manners. And further than *On the Rocks*—in depicting the realities of the present—we feel that he cannot go.

Then we realize that, after a detour of the better part of half a century, of almost the whole of his artistic career, Shaw has only returned to that Bloody Sunday of 1887 when the Socialists had headed a demonstration and been driven away by the police; and we remember, apropos of Molière, that the most celebrated of British dramatists for a long time found it impossible to get a theater in London for *On the Rocks*.

Shaw's most recent pieces are weaker. *The Simpleton of the Unexpected Isles* (1934) is the only play of the author's which has ever struck me as silly. In it, the Day of Judgment comes to the British Empire, and the privilege of surviving on earth is made to depend upon social utility. But, by setting up a purely theocratic tribunal, Shaw deprives this scene of social point: the principle of selection is so general that it might be applied by the fascists as readily as by the socialists, at the same time that the policy of wholesale extinction seems inspired by an admiration for the repressive tactics of both. The play ends with a salute to the unknown future, which, like the vision of infinity of *Back to Methuselah*, seems perfectly directionless. *The Millionairess* (1936) makes a farce out of the notion that a natural boss, deprived of adventitious authority, will inevitably gravitate again to a position where he can bully and control people, and sounds as if it had been suggested by the later phases of Stalin.

Here it cannot be denied that Bernard Shaw begins to show signs of old age. As the pace of his mind slackens and the texture of his work grows looser, the contradictory impulses and principles which have hitherto provided him with drama begin to show gaping rifts. In his *Preface on Bosses* to *The Millionairess*, he talks about "beginning a Reformation well to the left of Russia," but composes the panegyric on Mussolini, with the respectful compliments to Hitler, to which I have already referred.

Yet the openings—the prologue to *The Simpleton*, with its skit on the decay of the British Empire and the knockabout domestic agonies of the first act or two of *The Millionairess*—still explode their comic situations with something of the old energy and wit; and the one-acter, *The Six of Calais*, though it does not crackle quite with the old spark, is not so very far inferior to such an earlier trifle as *How He Lied to Her Husband*. It is interesting to note—what bears out the idea that Shaw is at his best as an artist—that the last thing he is to lose, apparently, is his gift for pure comic invention, which has survived, not much dimmed, though we may tire of it, since the days of *You Never Can Tell*.

And he has also maintained his integrity as a reporter of the processes at work in his time—in regard to which his point of view has never been doctrinaire but always based on observation and feeling. He has not acted a straight role as a socialist; a lot of his writing on public affairs has been nonsense. But his plays down to the very end have been a truthful and continually developing chronicle of a soul in relation to society. Professionally as well as physically—he has just turned eighty-one as I write—he is outliving all the rest of his generation.

Nor can it be said that the confusions of his politics have invalidated his social criticism. Of his educative and stimulative influence it is not necessary today to speak. The very methods we use to check him have partly been learned in his school.

1938

THE VOGUE OF
THE MARQUIS DE SADE

The interest in the Marquis de Sade has been steadily increasing in Europe ever since 1909, when Guillaume Apollinaire published a volume of selections from his work and thus brought him into general currency. Though his influence on the Romantic movement was considerable—Sainte-Beuve, writing in the forties, considered it equal to Byron's—it remained largely unacknowledged, as his books were not openly published and rather surreptitiously read. But the Dadaists, at the end of the First World War, delighted in him as a blaster of inhibitions, and broke down the inhibition against mentioning his name; and the Surrealists inherited him from them and have put him among their prophets. The late war, for reasons I shall discuss in a moment, has brought him again to the fore of the French literary consciousness, and so much has been recently written about him that the subject is in danger of becoming a bore, and he is sometimes, I understand, referred to as the Marquis de Fade. The most important authority on Sade is a writer named Maurice Heine, a former Communist of a very ancient vintage, since he was eliminated, in 1923, from the staff of the Communist *Humanité*, when he opposed the suppression of free discussion in the councils of the Party. Heine's interest in the queer Marquis was evidently partly inspired by this passionate libertarianism, for the Marquis, in his dubious way, was a fierce libertarian, too. Heine virtually devoted the rest of his life to running down and publishing Sade's work and vindicating his reputation. He is said to have reduced himself to penury buying up Sade's manuscripts. Heine did not, unfortunately, live to complete the biography he had undertaken, but some drafts for it and his scattered papers on the subject have been collected in a volume, under the title *Le Marquis de Sade*, by his friend M. Gilbert Lely, who is carrying on the torch and has himself published a volume of selections: *D. A. F. de Sade*. There have been two books on Sade in English, the more recent (1934)—*The Marquis de Sade: A Short Account of His Life and Work*—by that intrepid anthropologist Mr. Geoffrey Gorer, who has made a contribution to the subject by disengaging from Sade's partly pornographic novels his philosophical, religious, political and social ideas.

All three of these books are written with the bias of the Sade cult. The Marquis constitutes, unquestionably, one of the hardest cases to handle in the whole history of literature. He began writing novels to pass the time during his thirteen years of imprisonment in Vincennes and the Bastille, and they run to Richardsonian length. (His dates are 1740–1814.) They are unique and most uncomfortable productions, which alternate between descriptions of orgies on an impossible multiple scale, which may horrify the reader at first but which soon become routine and ridiculous, and vehement disquisitions, in the vein of the eighteenth-century *philosophe*, which are mostly intended to justify them. The Marquis has, thus, against him that he is often repulsive and often dull, and often both at once. He has usually hitherto been ignored by the French in their histories of their literature, and he is not even mentioned by Saintsbury in his work on the French novel.

But the Marquis does have his importance, and to

outlaw him thus is quite unjust—especially on the part of critics who devote considerable space to such a writer as Restif de la Bretonne, who, if somewhat less improper than Sade, has been also less influential. This unfairness is perceived by the champions of Sade, and they distort the picture the other way in their fanatical attempts to right it. The special difficulty that Sade presents to anyone who tries to arrive at a serious estimate of him is that he was neither quite mad nor quite sane. The perplexed head doctor of Charenton, the insane asylum in which the Marquis was confined during the last eleven years of his life, put the situation correctly when he explained, *"Cet homme n'est point aliéné. Son seul délire est celui du vice."* The Marquis was a man of strong intellect and a certain amount of literary ability, who in prison had had leisure for enormous reading but who was also what is called nowadays a compulsive neurotic of a violent and incurable kind. To the defense of his impulse to cruelty he brought an inflexible will and a contemptuous, obstinate pride that moved the Romantics to admiration and that still commands a certain respect. But this impulse was a lifelong obsession that gets in the way of his success as both a literary artist and a thinker. Signor Mario Praz, the author of *The Romantic Agony*, a study of the literary influence of Sade, has very firmly made this point and, as a result, has been treated rather sniffishly by both Heine and Mr. Gorer.

But both Heine and Mr. Gorer—as well as M. Lely —have been betrayed into howling absurdities by their eagerness to explain this obsession away. Their urbane attempts to gloss over the horrid chronicle of Sade's aberrations and the madly inappropriate interpretations that they sometimes try to put on his work have at moments reached the point of high comedy. M. Lely writes tender little poems to Sade and prints on the cover of his book the strange slogan *"Tout ce que signe Sade est amour."* Mr. Gorer tries to give the impression that the Marquis was a sober

and luminous thinker, with the good of humanity
at heart, in whose mouth butter wouldn't melt. You
would never find out from Mr. Gorer's book the real
tenor of his subject's life; you would hardly suspect
the main content of his work. "Although the sexual
element," says Mr. Gorer, "is present" in the early
versions of *Justine* (a triumph of understatement),
they cannot be "considered obscene"—a remark that
can be given meaning only if we assume that obscen-
ity must always for Mr. Gorer imply the use of the
French equivalent of four-letter words, which, it is
true, do not make their appearance till the rewritten
fourth edition. When he comes to explain away the
various exploits of Sade that made him an object of
concern to the police and nearly cost him his life,
Mr. Gorer becomes hilarious if one reads him after
examining the courtroom records and the memo-
randa of the Paris police, which Maurice Heine himself has published. Mr. Gorer represents Sade as a
courteous and considerate gentleman—one gets a distinct impression that he has been to an English public school—persecuted by vulgar harlots. Yet it is plain
from these documents and others that the Marquis
had for years done his best to enact the elaborate and
sinister debauches which he afterwards described in
his novels. In that great age of "libertinage," a good
deal must have been permitted to a noble with powerful connections like Sade; still, Sade was always getting into trouble in different places and with different people, and always for the same kind of offense.
The various frightened girls who ran to the police
about him, declaring that he had tried to poison them
or beaten them or tortured them or threatened to kill
them, the father who tried to shoot him, had not
picked up from his novels the bizarre and deleterious
ideas that they accused him of trying to carry out, for
these books had not been written yet; and, on the
other hand, the persistent recurrence in the fiction
he eventually produced of practices exactly similar to
those with which he had been charged would cer-

tainly show a strong predilection. It comes to seem, then, a masterpiece of euphemism when we find Mr. Gorer writing of the episode at Marseille, for which Sade was condemned to death, that the Marquis was "almost certainly exploring conscientiously and practically all possible extensions of sensual pleasure." (The use here of the great British phrase "almost certainly" is a truly wonderful touch.) Yet Mr. Gorer is only improving on a tenet of the Sadist faith established by Maurice Heine: that the allegedly poisoned bonbons offered on this occasion to some prostitutes, one of whom, the only one who ate them, was at once seized with agonizing cramps, were, in reality, nothing worse than aphrodisiacs. In the literature of the Sade cult, this case is always referred to as *"l'affaire des bonbons cantharidés."* But there is not a shred of evidence for assuming that they were not intended, if not to kill the girls, at least to have painful results, and the behavior of Sade himself, as reported by one of the girls, seems decidedly to show that they were. Why should a dose of cantharides produce convulsive cramps? We know that the heroes of Sade's novels want never to increase their partners' pleasure but always to make them unhappy, and that poisoning is one of their specialties.

No: one cannot blame Sade's family for locking him up. His wife had stood by him through years of this. He had at one time maintained in his Provence château a harem of both sexes, his reckless experiments with which became so alarming and troublesome that it was surely not unnatural for the Marquise's mother—not able to avail herself of the resources of modern psychiatry—to have him put away in Vincennes. The defenders of Sade have diverted attention from the propriety of this step by raising the issue of the quite different action of Napoleon, at a later date, in consigning the Marquis to an asylum. This latter was merely an incident of Napoleon's policy of censorship. The real objection to leaving him at large—though he was denounced as an enemy of morals—was that, just having published a scurrilous book about Josephine and Napoleon, he was regarded as a subversive force.

In the meantime, the Revolution had freed him from the Bastille. His wife would never see him again, but his sons seem to have done what they could for him. He found a mistress whom he appears to have been fond of and who was certainly loyal to him— he was evidently attractive to women—when he got into trouble again. He worked for the Revolution, and he actually served for a time as a judge on one of its tribunals, in which role—no doubt much to her astonishment—he got his mother-in-law and her family off when, in one of the queerest of confrontations, they happened to be brought before him. He exercised his influence so often in favor of sparing the accused that the bloodthirsty officials of the Terror began to suspect his revolutionary zeal and had him locked up again for the crime of "moderantism." His behavior had, however, been perfectly consistent. Having had his own head in jeopardy at the time of the Marseille affair, he had long opposed capital punishment on the ground that, since every crime was the result of a "natural" impulse, it was unjust to kill people for committing them. He was now confined in a prison where the guillotine was set up under the windows and where, he writes in a letter, "we buried eighteen hundred in thirty-five days, a third of them from our unfortunate house." His own turn eventually came, and he was saved from being beheaded only by the fall of Robespierre the night before his execution was scheduled. Did this frighten the Marquis or disgust him with blood? On the contrary, it probably afforded him a certain satisfaction in confirming his so often declared belief that the destructive lust of humanity represents our essential nature. He is funny in his saturnine way about the moral pretensions of the Revolution: "It is amusing that the Jacobins in the French Revolution should have wished to destroy the altars of a God who talked exactly their language, and even more extraordinary that those who detest and wish to destroy the Jacobins should do so in the name of a God who talks the same language as the Jacobins. If this is not the *ne plus ultra* of human absurdity, I should like to know what is." In a letter from the Bastille, after defending his materialistic philosophy, he ends with the following declaration: "Well, there's a letter that's calculated to prolong my captivity, isn't it? You can tell those prolongers from me that their prolongation is completely futile. They could leave me here ten years and they'd take me out no better, believe me, than I was when I went in. Either kill me or accept me as I am, for Devil take me if ever I change—I've told you that the beast's too old—there's no hope for him any more—the most decent and candid and delicate of men, the tenderest and most indulgent idolater of my children, for whose happiness I'd go through fire, scrupulous to the last degree about not wanting to corrupt their morals or mess up their minds or make them in any respect adopt my ideas, adoring my relatives (my own, I mean)—any friends I still have left, and above all my wife, whom I only want to see happy, and to whom I very much wish to make up for my many youthful indiscretions—because it's true that *one's own wife should not be exposed to that*—I felt this and told her so more than six months before I came here; she is my witness. Those are my virtues—as for my vices—unrestrainable rages—an extreme tendency in everything to lose control of myself, a disordered imagination in sexual matters such as has never been known in this world, an atheist to the point of fanaticism—in two words, there I am, and so once again kill me or take me like that, because I shall never change."

But nobody wants to take him. The conventional people won't touch him, and his defenders, as I say, will not face him. They like to repeat Apollinaire's statement that their hero was "the freest mind that ever existed," though he was certainly one of the most constrained. His peculiar tastes had instigated him to boldness in some directions, but he could never get away from his manias and had to make all his work and his thought eternally revolve around them. Even his pamphlet on the Revolution—anonymously reprinted, it is curious to note, at the time of the Revolution of 1848—turns out to be leading us up to the usual self-justification. One sometimes feels a certain disingenuousness in the attempts of these defenders to whitewash him. They seem to be excited by his atrocities at the same time that they are trying to tell us that Sade was the most charming man in the world and wouldn't have hurt a fly. M. Lely, for example, is himself rather sentimental in a vein that would have made Sade bellow. The Sadists have even looked up and reverently photographed—as if it were Buddha's Bo Tree—the sordid old iron staircase to the third floor of the house in Marseille where the attempt to poison the prostitutes took place. Among these enthusiasts a certain soft and sly tone prevails. It is characteristic of the cult of Sade that a friend of Heine, M. Georges Bataille, quoted by M. Lely, should refer to Heine as *"ce personnage séduisant,"* assuring us that he was "one of the gentlest and best bred men I have ever known," but remark a little further on that, one day at a political meeting, he "produced a revolver, fired at random and slightly wounded his wife in the arm."

So let us not try to disguise the congenital, the compulsive and inveterate sadism of the life and works of the Marquis de Sade. What, then, is he worth to the world? More than you might expect. His difficulties with his own aberrations made him interested in those of other people, and he brought to this whole so long outlawed subject a certain scientific point of view. He always likes to document himself, and he will tell you in a note that, fantastic though some hair-raising episode may sound, it is based on an actual case that recently came to light in a certain provincial city. He compiled—in *Les 120 Journées de Sodome*—the first systematic catalogue of sexual abnormalities, to the number of six hundred, for he discriminated many nuances; he anticipated Freud in perceiving that sexual constitution was determined at an early age and that a sexual element was present in all family relationships; and he had also the anthropological approach, for he was constantly invoking travel books to show that there is no sort of practice that is not somewhere the accepted thing. He was something of a scientist, something of a philosopher, something of a man of letters, and—if you can stand him at all—he is not without interest in any of these roles. He has even at moments some merit as a writer. Sade's cardinal defect as a novelist was his infantile inability to transpose his erotic fantasies into terms of the real world. The horrors that are perpetrated by his characters are made to take place in a kind of void: they rarely have any of the consequences that they would in actual life, and that they did, to his sorrow, for Sade himself. Yet it is true, as Heine suggests, that *Les 120 Journées de Sodome* had beaten all the Gothic novels hollow before most of them had been written; and it is true, as M. Lely claims, that some of its hideous characters —the financier, the bishop, the duke, and the judge, who represent the corruption of the old regime (Sade was a sharp observer of abnormal and vicious types) —show a power akin to Balzac's. But what is most striking about Sade is that, wordy and repetitious, implausible and disgusting though he tends to be, he gives expression to human malignance in a characteristically extreme and abstract eighteenth-century way that makes it forever impossible not to recognize the part it plays in all fields of human activity.

With the Surrealists and in some other quarters, the appeal of the horrific Marquis has been that of an upsetter of conventions and a purveyor of violent thrills. But there have been other reasons lately for the interest in Sade and for the curious forms it has

sometimes taken. In Europe, since the Second World
War, the professional intellectual has found himself
under a frightening pressure: he has had to try in
some way to accommodate—morally, intellectually—
in the world that has been conceived by the ordinary
educated man, the murderous devices for large-scale
murder, for suffocating, burning or blowing up one's
enemies, that the professedly Christian countries
have lately been going in for as heartily as the Odin-
worshipping Nazis, the Emperor-worshipping Japa-
nese, or the officially atheist Russians; and here is a
writer, the Marquis de Sade, of whom one knows
that he always insisted that such things were perfectly
normal and who tried to reason about them. The
atrocities he loves to describe do not today seem as
outrageous as they did before. Even writing in 1934,
Mr. Gorer was able to say that "the century and a half
which have passed since [the writing of *Justine* and
Juliette] have more than justified [Sade's] gloomiest
prognostications." M. Albert Camus, in a chapter on
Sade in his recent *L'Homme Révolté*, points out that
Sade's most sickening imaginations are now seen to
be well on the conservative side. And there is also the
disposition to find the Marquis himself not so bad as
he used to be thought. Certain writers have attempted to demonstrate that this man whose whole
work is a blasphemy was fundamentally or potentially
religious, arguing that the recognition of evil leads
the way to the love of God and that Sade's lifelong
quarrel with the Deity is a proof that he believed in
His existence. The result of consulting the work of a
professional diabolic to find some way of coming to
terms with the forces of destruction that threaten one
is, thus, to be moved to attempt to tailor for this
diabolic an aspect more acceptable and "human"—
that is to say, less psychopathic. The Marquis
accepted these forces; he had evolved a code of behavior, a proposed set of legislative reforms, a whole
system of philosophy based on them. May he not,
then, have made some sense? May he not have been

an excellent, if embittered, man, who desired to save his own soul, to procure the welfare of the human race?

Now, the Marquis did not make sense; he did not love the human race. But he does have his definite importance in the history of Western thought, and there is a gap if we leave him out. Signor Praz has filled up this gap in the domain of imaginative literature, and he has indicated the role that Sade plays in the politico-philosophical field. In this latter, the Marquis appears as the opposite pole to Rousseau, and if we do not allow him his place, the picture remains incomplete. To the rebellious but ingenuous mind of Rousseau, it came as a revelation that men were "naturally" good and that it was only institutions that had led them astray. To Sade, also nonconformist, also biassed by abnormality, it seemed obvious that crimes and perversions were prompted by tendencies that we had in common with all the rest of "Nature," and that the error of institutions was their effort to censor these tendencies. The logic of Sade, of course, reduces the argument from Nature to absurdity, but then so does the logic of Rousseau. We want to put to them both the same question: Are not our moral and legal codes also the products of natural instincts? But it was difficult still in that age to conceive of man as an animal with certain superior faculties, in the light of which he tries to discipline his so diverse natural instincts for purposes he strongly feels but is unable to formulate definitively (as they tried to do with everything in the eighteenth century) since he never can see to the end of them; and in the meantime the Rousseauist doctrine was in need of a correction, a contradiction, that it got with a vengeance in Sade. The utopians of the eighteenth century were eventually to have their complement in the cynical practicality of Napoleon; and in the interval the two conceptions had been hopelessly, disastrously, mingled in the sadistic idealists of the Terror. The Russian Marxists of our own century have arrived at an even more insidious confusion of the ideal of human improvement with a gospel of internecine strife; and the Marquis de Sade still stands as a reminder that the lust for cruelty, the appetite for destruction, are powerful motivations that must be recognized for what they are.

But, except for the Surrealist, the connoisseur of horrors, the relisher of sensations for their own sake, it is difficult to see how Sade can meet any other need. He tends only toward annihilation. Though he justifies himself by appealing to Nature, he also turns against Nature for having made him what he is: "Is it a being so contemptible, so odious as this that has given me life for no other purpose than to make me take pleasure in what injures my kind?" Nor does he shrink from destroying himself, for, like his characters, he is what is called today masochistic as well as what is called sadistic. He furiously announces again and again that he would like to wipe out the human race, to pulverize the universe: "It is she [Nature] that I desire to outrage. I should like to spoil her plans, to block her advance, to halt the course of the stars, to throw down the globes that float in space—to destroy everything that serves her, to protect everything that harms her, to cultivate everything that irritates her—in a word, to insult all her works." One of Sade's most extraordinary scenes is that in *La Nouvelle Justine* in which the misanthropic chemist encountered on Etna explains that he has mastered a method for producing artificial eruptions, and expresses a strong desire to devastate the whole of Sicily. He will be watching from a mountain, he says, and copulating with the goats. He will not even have to depend on another human being for the pleasure of indulging his lust. The last interest that ties him to others will have been repudiated. Now, grotesque though this scene may sound, it is quite close to recent states of mind. It is probable that the fascination at present exerted by Sade is due partly to the vertiginous excitement of a destructiveness that is ultimately self-destructive. One had the impression at moments during the bombings of the last war that people derived satisfaction from a reckless letting-go of power that might also annihilate the wielder of power. And Adolf Hitler, who presided over the holocaust, had something of Sade's insane chemist. He lived in such alienation from the ordinary natural instincts that he was probably not up to a goat, and he was thinking of himself, in any case, as a character in a Wagner opera; but he had certainly set off Etna when he burned himself up in the bunker. The mad exhilaration in power, the contempt for human life had been there, and he had led many others to share it—men who, unlike him, might equally well have been more or less amiably associating with their fellows instead of wiping out one another's cities.

To encourage this impulse is the ultimate blasphemy—far more terrible than the Voltairean jeering at theology or the Byronic defiance of law—and it is Sade's queer unique distinction to have declared it with the ultimate audacity.

In Sade's will, one of the most effective things he wrote, he invoked complete oblivion. After explaining that he wants to be buried in a particular copse on his country estate and that there is not to be "a ceremony of any sort," he lays down these specific directions: "As soon as the grave has been filled, the place is to be sown with acorns, in order that thereafter, the earth of the aforesaid grave being overgrown and the copse grown up as it was before, the traces of my tomb may disappear from the face of the earth, as I flatter myself that my memory will be erased from the mind of men, except for the few who have been kind enough to love me till my last moment and of whom I shall carry to the grave a very pleasant recollection." But we have not been able to forget him. We have never been able to shake him off, because we know that he is not entirely mad, not entirely out of touch with reality—that, nauseous and "hipped" though he is, he is harping on something

that is sometimes felt by other human beings who
seem to be sane. Let us hope that his moment is passing. That his prestige as a contemporary prophet of
human self-immolation to the forces that humanity
generates, as well as his use as a bogy to horrify the
bourgeoisie, may already now be declining is suggested by two excellent studies published since
1951—the chapter about him in Camus's new book,
referred to above, and the long paper by Mlle. Simone
de Beauvoir ("Faut-il Brûler Sade?") in the Decem-
ber, 1951, and January, 1952, numbers of Sartre's
magazine, *Les Temps Modernes* (this last perhaps
the very best thing that has yet been written on the
subject)—in which his ideas are coolly criticized and
the man himself brought into the clinic as a special
psychological case. They seem to make a new era in
the study of Sade.

                                                                1952

ABRAHAM LINCOLN: THE UNION AS RELIGIOUS MYSTICISM

The Collected Works of Abraham Lincoln, a project of the Abraham Lincoln Association, edited by Roy P. Basler, has just been published by the Rutgers University Press. This edition includes all the writings in the Nicolay and Hay *Works* as well as everything subsequently published, and it incorporates—its most important feature—all the hitherto unpublished material, released in 1947, of the Robert Todd Lincoln papers. The new *Works*, with this and other additions, contains almost twice as many items as all the previous editions combined, but this constitutes in actual quantity only a quarter as much material. The editing, in which Marion Dolores Pratt and Lloyd A. Dunlap have assisted Mr. Basler, is remarkably satisfactory, for it is scrupulous about dates and explains all possible references, supplying extracts from relevant documents such as letters and newspaper articles. The books themselves—nine volumes in all, of which the last, containing the index, is still to come—are well printed and easy to read. The format, in blue and gray, is the work of Mr. P. J. Conkwright, the designer of the Princeton Jefferson, and has a certain uniformity with this. Altogether, a distinguished job.

The great value of the new edition is, of course,

that it makes it possible to study Lincoln at first hand
—his ideas and his dealings with the world—in a more
consecutive fashion and on a much fuller scale than
before. In the period that is covered by the first three
volumes—that is, up to the time of the first inaugura-
tion—there is little of great interest that is new. For
the ordinary reader it would be enough, for the pre-
Presidential years, to acquaint himself with the material in Mr. Basler's admirable selection, *Abraham
Lincoln: His Speeches and Writings,* which provides
one of the most direct and most easily available ways
of making contact with Lincoln. But only a little more
than a quarter of this anthology, compiled before the
release of the new material, is devoted to the years
of the Presidency, which occupy five-eighths of the
Collected Works, and one can get the sense of these
years only by going through the day-by-day record revealed in the new edition. The pressure and suspense
of this period, the tenacity of Lincoln's purpose, his
control over his government in Washington and his
hold on his army in the field, his rigor with himself
and with others, which occasionally administers sharp
reprimands yet more often withholds impatient letters, a rigor that adopts as routine an insistence on
justice and mercy—all this makes these volumes ab-
sorbing. They bring us into touch with the powerful
force that, faced by disaffection in the North as well
as by the Southern rebellion, was able both to ener-
gize and to discipline the effort of the Union cause,
and that no one could successfully challenge till the
bullet of Booth cut its current.

To read Lincoln thus in bulk is to meet a being
very different from the Lincoln of humorous folklore
and sentimental legend. Except in the debates with
Douglas and some of his early productions, there is
little humor in these volumes, and only the gravest
sentiment. The dignity of the public utterances and
of the official correspondence of the Presidency is only
infrequently varied by some curtly sarcastic note to a
persistently complaining general or an importunate

office seeker. As for the style and the temper of intellect, with their tautness and their hard distinction, they could scarcely have differed more from those of his most popular biographer, the amorphous and coarse-meshed Sandburg, whose sprawling immense compendium eventually had Lincoln sprawling. There have probably been more bad romantic books—not, of course, to deny Sandburg his value—written about Abraham Lincoln than any other American figure, with the exception of Edgar Allan Poe. Let us try to get rid of the legend and approach him as if for the first time by going direct to his writings and to the memoirs of the people who knew him well.

One of the things that strike us most, when we do this, is that Lincoln was on much less familiar terms with certain of his popular eulogists than these like to be with him. The raw realities of his early years— the sordidness of his family life, the boorishness of his first beginnings—are uncompromisingly presented in the memoir of his law partner William Herndon, and the public has always found them repellent, but Herndon throws into relief Lincoln's genius and his will to succeed, as the more romantic writers do not. From those who knew Lincoln best, we learn that he was naturally considerate but essentially cold and aloof, not caring much, as Herndon tells us, about anyone but his wife and children. He seems always to have had the conviction of his own superiority. The legend of the log cabin, the illiterate father, the rail-splitting, the flatboat and all the rest has had the effect of vulgarizing Lincoln even in making him a backwoods saint. He seems to have believed that his mother was the illegitimate daughter of a Virginia planter, but, whatever his origins were or whatever he believed them to be, he knew that, by physical strength, by sound character, by brains, and by personal charm, he had been able, with no other advantages, to establish himself as a person of importance in pioneer Illinois, where most people started from scratch and you had to have real abilities in order to command respect.

Though Henry Adams makes a point of telling us that Lincoln struggled with his gloves at a White House reception, we never feel that he is seriously ill at ease or that he felt himself at a disadvantage. "With all his awkwardness of manner," wrote Don Piatt, a journalist who had seen a good deal of him, "and utter disregard of social conventionalities that seemed to invite familiarity, there was something about Abraham Lincoln that enforced respect. No man presumed on the apparent invitation to be other than respectful. I was told at Springfield that this accompanied him through life. Among his rough associates, when young, he was leader, looked up to and obeyed, because they felt of his muscle and its readiness in use. Among his associates at the bar it was attributed to his wit, which kept his duller associates at a distance. But the fact was that this power came from a sense of reserve force of intellectual ability that no one took account of save in its results." John Hay, who was Lincoln's secretary and saw him at close range all the time he was in the White House, insisted that it was "absurd to call him a modest man. No great man is ever modest. It was his intellectual arrogance and unconscious assumption of superiority that men like Chase and Sumner could never forgive." It was this, too, that made it possible for him to exercise an unfailing magnanimity almost incredible in a politician and that permitted him to keep Chase in his Cabinet when the latter was working against him and allowing Chase's followers to undermine him in leaflets that Lincoln declined to read. Herndon tells us that Lincoln was envious of Douglas, but this envy could not have lasted long, for, though he was beaten by Douglas in their contest for the Senate, the campaign so increased his own prestige that it made possible his candidacy for the Presidency. This is not the place to try to go deeply into the intricacies of Lincoln's psychology. I want to bring out the strength of his moral and intellectual qualities. But it ought to be said that Lincoln was a most peculiar case as a leader who came up from poverty. As is apparent from his relations with Douglas, who made certain attempts to high-hat him in the course of their travelling debates, he had little of the animus of the underprivileged. He started his political career with the party of the propertied interests, the Whigs, and though he sympathized profoundly with the slaves, he did not much resent their masters, always saying that if they of the North had found themselves in the same position, they would undoubtedly have behaved like the planters. His devotion to the United States was based on his firm conviction, derived from his own experience, that our system allowed a poor man to succeed, and he feared the Know-Nothing movement, which was working for discrimination against the recent German and Irish immigrants, just as he feared the extension of slavery, because it aimed to deprive other men of the chance to enjoy this advantage. Yet Lincoln had grown up in pain—I shall not attempt to discuss how his origins and character had brought this about—and he was more or less in pain all his life. There was a manic-depressive element—as appears from his own explanation of them—in the humorous stories and readings which his Cabinet sometimes found so incongruous. If his intellect was rigorous and his will tenacious, his emotional mood was despondent. He identified himself with suffering, not merely in the case of the Negroes but also with the suffering involved in the war, which, as President, he had to prolong.

Two descriptions of Lincoln by persons who knew him bring out his intellectual qualities. "Mr. Lincoln's perceptions," said Herndon, in a speech after Lincoln's death, "were slow, cold, clear, and exact. Everything came to him in its precise shape and color. To some men the world of matter and of man comes ornamented with beauty, life, and action, and hence more or less false and inexact. No lurking illusion or other error, false in itself, and clad for the moment in robes of splendor, ever passed undetected or unchallenged over the threshold of his mind—that point which divides vision from the realm and home of thought. Names to him were nothing, and titles naught—assumption always standing back abashed at his cold intellectual glare. Neither his perceptions nor intellectual visions were perverted, distorted, or diseased. He saw all things through a perfect, mental lens. There was no diffraction or refraction there. He was not impulsive, fanciful or imaginative, but cold, calm and precise." Add to this the following passages from the letters of the Marquis de Chambrun, only recently published in a volume of *Impressions of Lincoln and the Cival War.* "Mr. Lincoln," he says, "stopped to admire an exceptionally tall and beautiful tree growing by the roadside and applied himself to defining its particular beauties: powerful trunk, vigorous and harmoniously proportioned branches, which reminded him of the great oaks and beeches under whose shade his youth had been passed. Each different type he compared, in technical detail, to the one before us. His dissertation certainly showed no poetic desire to idealize nature; but if not that of an artist, it denoted extraordinary observation, mastery of descriptive language and absolute precision of mind. . . . No one who heard him express personal ideas, as though thinking aloud, upon some great topic or incidental question, could fail to admire his accuracy of judgment and rectitude of mind. I have heard him give opinions on statesmen and argue political problems with astounding precision. I have heard him describe a beautiful woman and discuss the particular aspects of her appearance, differentiating what is lovely from what might be open to criticism, with the sagacity of an artist. In discussing literature, his judgment showed a delicacy and sureness of taste which would do credit to a celebrated critic."

This brings us to Lincoln's style, which was highly developed in the literary sense and yet also instinctive and natural and inseparable from his personality in all of its manifestations. This style pervades his speeches, his messages to Congress, his correspondence with his generals in the field as well as with his friends and family, his interviews with visitors to the White House and his casual conversation. Mr. Basler, in a study of Lincoln's style, prefixed to his volume of selections, makes the important point that the literary education of Lincoln was a good deal more thorough than used to be thought. "A careful examination," he says, of the books on elocution and grammar "which Lincoln studied both in and out of school will not impress anyone with Lincoln's poverty of opportunity for the study of grammar and rhetoric. It is safe to say that few children today learn as much through twelve years of formal schooling in these two subjects as one finds in the several textbooks which Lincoln is supposed to have studied." For it is true that the schoolbooks of the early nineteenth century taught not only the mechanics of writing—that is, of grammar and syntax—but also the art of rhetoric—that is, of what used to be called "harmonious numbers" and of dramatic and oratorical effectiveness. Now, Lincoln's writing, though his spelling was weak, was usually correct and careful; he had evidently acquired at an early age a pretty highly accomplished technique with words. Here is a passage from a private letter dealing with personal matters, written by Lincoln in his thirty-third year: "The second [cause of his correspondent's melancholy] is, *the absence of all business and conversation of friends,* which might divert your mind, and give it occasional rest from that *intensity* of thought, which will sometimes wear the sweetest idea threadbare and turn it to the bitterness of death." Here, in the final phrases, the balance of vowels and consonants, the assonance and alliteration, the progression from the long "e"s of "sweetest idea," over which one would want to linger, to the short and closed vowels of "bitterness of death," which chill the lyrical rhythm and bite it off at the end—

all this shows a training of the literary ear that is
not often taught in modern schools. The satirical
"Letter from the Lost Townships," written in 1842,
which nearly cost Lincoln a duel, handles colloquial
language with a similar sense of style (it is a quite
successful experiment in the vein of frontier humor
that Mark Twain was to bring to perfection), and
the poems that Lincoln wrote three years later, when
he revisited his old home in Indiana, show even a
certain skill in a medium in which he was less at
home. He is describing a neighbor who had gone insane and whose daft doleful singing he now remembers:

> *I've heard it oft, as if I dreamed,*
> *Far-distant, sweet, and lone;*
> *The funeral dirge it ever seemed*
> *Of reason dead and gone.*
>
> *To drink its strains, I've stole away,*
> *All silently and still,*
> *Ere yet the rising god of day*
> *Had streaked the Eastern hill.*
>
> *Air held his breath; the trees all still*
> *Seemed sorr'wing angels round.*
> *Their swelling tears in dew-drops fell*
> *Upon the list'ning ground.*

The *Eulogy on Zachary Taylor*, delivered in
1850, has moments, when he is striving for eloquence,
of resorting to a kind of constricted blank verse. Yet
in prose, as in verse, he is working for the balance
of eighteenth-century rhythms, and he soon learns
how to disembarrass these of eighteenth-century
pomposity. He will discard the old-fashioned orna-
ments of forensic and congressional eloquence, but
he will always have at command the art of incanta-
tion with words, and will know how to practice it
magnificently—as in the farewell to Springfield, the
Gettysburg speech and the Second Inaugural Address

—when the occasion and his own emotion prompt it. Alone among American Presidents, it is possible to imagine Lincoln, grown up in a different milieu, becoming a distinguished writer. But actually the poetry of Lincoln has not all been put into his writings. It was acted out in his life. With nothing of the deliberate histrionics of the Roosevelts or of the evangelical mask of Wilson, he created himself as a poetic figure, and he thus imposed himself on the nation. For the molding of American opinion by Lincoln was a matter of style and imagination as well as of moral authority, of compelling argument and obstinate will. When we put ourselves back into the period, we realize that it was not at all inevitable to think of it as Lincoln thought, and we come to see that Lincoln's conception of the progress and meaning of the Civil War was indeed an interpretation that he partly took over from others but that he partly made others accept.

What *was* this interpretation? Like most of the important products of the American mind at that time, it grew out of the religious tradition of the New England theology of Puritanism. The struggle to abolish slavery, the war between North and South had come to present themselves in the light of a Christian crusade, of an apocalyptic battle between good and evil. Of this mental and moral atmosphere you will find a brilliant expression in the novels of Mrs. Stowe, and a strange and haunting description in Francis Grierson's *The Valley of Shadows*. You can see it in a minstrel song like *The Year of Jubilo* as well as in the "terrible swift sword" of God of *The Battle Hymn of the Republic*.

Let us, however, begin by examining Lincoln's view of the war as a crisis in American history and his conception of himself as an American leader. Both of these emerge very early. Lincoln felt himself close to the Revolution. He had been seventeen when Jefferson died; his great hero was Henry Clay, who, in putting through the Missouri Compromise of 1820, had averted a break with the slave interests. It was clear to Lincoln from his youth that the survival of the Union might still be threatened, and he already had dreams of defending it. In a speech on *The Perpetuation of Our Political Institutions*, made before the Young Men's Lyceum of Springfield in 1838, when Lincoln was twenty-nine, he mounts up to the following climax: At the time of the American Revolution, he says of its heroes and leaders, "all that sought celebrity and fame and distinction, expected to find them in the success of that experiment. . . . They succeeded. The experiment is successful, and thousands have won their deathless names in making it so. . . . This field of glory is harvested, and the crop is already appropriated. But new reapers will arise, and *they*, too, will seek a field. It is to deny, what the history of the world tells us is true, to suppose that men of ambition and talents will not continue to spring up amongst us. And when they do, they will as naturally seek the gratification of their ruling passion as others have so done before them." You may think that the young Lincoln is about to exhort his auditors to follow the example of their fathers, not to rest on the performance of the past but to go on to new labors of patriotism, but the speech takes an unexpected turn. "The question, then, is, can that gratification be found in supporting and maintaining an edifice that has been erected by others? Most certainly it cannot." He has been, it seems, preparing to deliver a warning: "Towering genius," he tells them, "disdains a beaten path. It seeks regions unexplored. . . . It *denies* that it is glory enough to serve under any chief. It scorns to tread in the footsteps of *any* predecessor, however illustrious. It thirsts and burns for distinction; and, if possible, it will have it, whether at the expense of emancipating slaves or enslaving freemen. Is it unreasonable then to expect that some man possessed of the loftiest genius, coupled with ambition sufficient to push it to its utmost stretch, will, at some time, spring up among us? And when such a one does, it will require the people to be united with each other, attached to the government and laws, and generally intelligent, to successfully frustrate his designs."

The effect of this is curiously ambiguous: it is evident that Lincoln has projected himself into the role against which he is warning them. And a little less than two years later we find one of his political speeches winding up with the following peroration: "The *probability* that we may fall in the struggle *ought not* to deter us from the support of a cause we believe to be just; it *shall not* deter me. If ever I feel the soul within me elevate and expand to those dimensions not wholly unworthy of its Almighty Architect, it is when I contemplate the cause of my country, deserted by all the world beside, and I standing up boldly and alone and hurling defiance at her victorious oppressors."

The Lincoln who went to Congress in 1847 had long ago discarded such eloquence, but the Lincoln who debated with Douglas in 1858 was already outranging his opponent by making slavery a moral issue; and when, in 1864, he was running for President the second time and his leadership seemed seriously threatened, he again made a strong impression by reasserting the absolute iniquity of slavery. There was nothing of demagoguery in this. This moral stand of Lincoln's against slavery was based, we cannot but feel, on a sharper and deeper judgment than Theodore Roosevelt's attack on the trusts or Woodrow Wilson's vague gospel of the New Freedom or Franklin Roosevelt's cavalier baiting of the economic royalists. Though an attentive and adroit politician, Lincoln carried, and carries, a moral conviction perhaps unique in American politics. He struck home to his public with this in his famous Cooper Institute speech of February 27, 1860. It begins with a historical analysis, carefully documented, of the status of slavery under the Constitution, proceeds to a firm formulation of the policy of the Republican Party—in which he has the task of dissociating himself from the insurrectionary methods of John Brown—and ends, not with a rhetorical flourish, but with the following now-famous passage: "If slavery is right, all words, acts, laws and constitutions against it are themselves wrong, and should be silenced, and swept away. If it is right, we cannot justly object to its nationality—its universality; if it is wrong, they cannot justly insist upon its extension—its enlargement. All they ask, we could readily grant, if we thought slavery right; all we ask, they could as readily grant, if they thought it wrong. Their thinking it right, and our thinking it wrong, is the precise fact upon which depends the whole controversy. Thinking it right, as they do, they are not to blame for desiring its full recognition, as being right; but, thinking it wrong, as we do, can we yield to them? Can we cast our votes with their view, and against our own? . . . Neither let us be slandered from our duty by false accusations against us, nor frightened from it by menaces of destruction to the Government nor of dungeons to ourselves. *Let us have faith that right makes might, and in that faith, let us, to the end, dare to do our duty as we understand it.*"

Along with this stiffening of moral conviction went a faith that became quite mystical. There is no question that Lincoln, in his earlier phase, had been what was then called a freethinker. Herndon tells us that the young Lincoln had been associated, during his years at New Salem, with persons who had been strongly influenced by the skepticism of the eighteenth century, and that he had read Voltaire, Volney and Tom Paine. Later, in Springfield, when Herndon had brought to the office the books of Darwin, Spencer and Feuerbach, Lincoln had dipped into these. "He soon grew into the belief," says Herndon, "of a universal law, evolution, and from this he has never deviated. . . . Mr. Lincoln believed in laws that imperiously ruled both matter and mind. With him there could be no miracles outside of law; he held that the universe was a grand mystery and a miracle.

. . . There were no accidents in his philosophy. Every event had its cause. The past to him was the cause of the present, and the present, including the past, will be the cause of the grand future, and all are one, links in the endless chain, stretching from the infinite to the finite. Everything to him was the result of the forces of Nature, playing on matter and mind from the beginning of time," which would continue to do so "to the end of it . . . giving the world other, further, and grander results." Herndon says that Lincoln did not believe "that the Bible was the special divine revelation of God, as the Christian world contends," and he goes on to tell us that in his middle twenties, before he had left New Salem, he even composed a long essay setting forth his views on religion, which he wanted to bring out as a pamphlet. But when he read it to the proprietor of the general store in which he was then working, his employer asked to look at it, then quickly thrust it into the stove. In 1842, when Lincoln delivers a remarkable address before the Springfield Washington Temperance Society, it is quite evident that his hopes for the world are still confined to a human utopianism that does not yet embody the will of God. "Of our political revolution of '76 we all are justly proud," he says. "It has given us a degree of political freedom far exceeding that of any other of the nations of the earth. In it the world has found a solution of that long mooted problem as to the capability of man to govern himself. In it was the germ which has vegetated, and still is to grow and expand into the universal liberty of mankind." The march of this cause of political freedom "cannot fail," he continues, "to be on and on, till every son of earth shall drink, in rich fruition, the sorrow-quenching draughts of perfect liberty. Happy day, when, all appetites controlled, all passions subdued, all matters subjected, *mind*, all-conquering *mind*, shall live and move, the monarch of the world. Glorious consummation! Hail fall of Fury! Reign of Reason, all hail!"

But when Lincoln was running for Congress in 1846, his Democratic opponent, a Methodist preacher, denounced him for infidelity. Lincoln then made a point of writing and publishing in a local paper a statement of his religious views, the only one he ever made, which seems to have satisfied his public. When we examine it closely, however, we see that this clarification is not really a confession of faith; it does not commit Lincoln to anything. He speaks of a Doctrine of Necessity in which he had once been "inclined to believe," but explains that he has ceased to discuss it, and ends by remarking that he would not care to support any man for office "whom I knew to be an open enemy of, and scoffer at, religion"—on the ground that no man "has the right to insult the feelings, and injure the morals, of the community in which he may live." Herndon had admitted that the Doctrine of Necessity had a conception of divinity behind it: "He firmly believed in an overruling Providence, Maker, God, and the great moral of Him written in the human soul. His—late in life—conventional use of the word God must not by any means be interpreted that he believed in a personal God. I know that it is said Mr. Lincoln changed his views. There is no evidence of this." This overruling Providence, this Deity, which we find, in proportion as Lincoln achieves political prominence, taking the place of such words as "reason" and "mind" in such an utterance as the Temperance Society speech, wears sometimes the more secular aspect of the creative or the fatal operation of "history."

The conception of history as a power that somehow takes possession of men and works out its intentions through them is most familiar today as one of the characteristic features of Marxism, in which it has become the object of a semireligious cult and has ended by supplying the basis for a fanaticism almost Mohammedan. But it was very widespread in the

nineteenth century, at a time when the scientific
study of the past had not yet disentangled itself from
the doctrine of a divine Providence. When we find
Lincoln speaking as follows, in 1858, in the course of
his debates with Douglas, we can feel this menace of
history as a superhuman force that vindicates and
overrides and makes of mankind its instruments:
"Accustomed to trample on the rights of others, you
have lost the genius of your own independence, and
become the fit subjects of the first cunning tyrant who
rises among you. And let me tell you that all these
things are prepared for you by the teachings of history, if the elections shall promise that the next Dred
Scott decision and all future decisions will be quietly
acquiesced in by the people."

But he needed something more in keeping with the
Scriptural religious conceptions of the majority of his
fellow-Americans. His Methodist competitor for Congress had come close to doing him damage, and he
must now have made a deliberate practice of stating
his faith in the Union and his conviction of his own
mission in terms that would not be repugnant to the
descendants of the New England Puritans and the
evangelism characteristic of his time. In this he went
much further than Herndon, with his basis in Darwin
and Spencer, was willing to recognize. We find Lincoln, in his First Inaugural, describing the situation
in the following terms: "If the Almighty Ruler of nations, with His eternal truth and justice, be on your
side of the North or on yours of the South, that truth
and that justice will surely prevail, by the judgment
of this great tribunal, the American people," and
"Intelligence, patriotism, Christianity, and a firm re-
liance on Him who has never yet forsaken this favored
land, are still competent to adjust, in the best way, all
our present difficulty." He is to revert several times in
the years that follow to the attitude of God toward the
war, and as the months of fighting drag on, he becomes less and less sure that the moral issue is per-

fectly clear, that the Almighty Ruler of nations is committed to the side of the North. "The will of God prevails," we find him writing in what was labelled by Nicolay and Hay a *Meditation on the Divine Will*, a note, found after his death, that dates from the autumn of '62, when he had been discouraged by McClellan's failures. "In great contests each party claims to act in accordance with the will of God. Both may be, and one must be, wrong. God cannot be for and against the same thing at the same time. In the present civil war it is quite possible that God's purpose is something different from the purpose of either party; and yet the human instrumentalities, working just as they do, are of the best adaptation to effect his purpose. I am almost ready to say that this is probably true; that God wills this contest, and wills that it shall not end yet. By his mere great power on the minds of the now contestants, he could have either saved or destroyed the Union without a human contest. Yet the contest began. And, having begun, he could give the final victory to either side any day. Yet the contest proceeds." Two years later, in a letter to a Quaker lady, "we hoped," he writes, "for a happy termination of this terrible war long before this; but God knows best, and has ruled otherwise. . . . Surely he intends some great good to follow this mighty convulsion, which no mortal could make, and no mortal could stay." This line of speculation culminates in the Second Inaugural Address. "Both," he writes there of the North and the South, "read the same Bible, and pray to the same God; and each invokes His aid against the other. It may seem strange that any men should dare to ask a just God's assistance in wringing their bread from the sweat of other men's faces; but let us judge not that we be not judged. The prayers of both could not be answered; that of neither has been answered fully. The Almighty has his own purposes," etc.

We are far here from Herndon's office, closer to Harriet Beecher Stowe. If the need to express himself in phrases congenial to his public may have had some part in inducing Lincoln to heighten and personify the formulas of his eighteenth-century deism, if it is true that as the war went on and gave rise to more and more disaffection, it became more and more to his interest to invoke the traditional Lord of Hosts, it is nevertheless quite clear that he himself came to see the conflict in a more and more religious light, in more and more Scriptural terms, under a more and more apocalyptic aspect.

All this is the vision of the Civil War, the interpretation of its meaning, that—influenced, of course, himself by the "climate of opinion" of the North— he fixed in the minds of the Union supporters. It was rightly said by Alexander H. Stephens, the Vice-President of the Confederacy, that "with Lincoln the Union rose to the sublimity of religious mysticism." Should we, too, have accepted this vision if we had been living in Lincoln's day? Can we be sure we should have voted for Lincoln, that we should even have wanted him as a candidate, in the election of '64? The war was then in its fourth year, and hundreds of thousands of men had been killed without, as it seemed to many, having brought a decision nearer. Lincoln had just called for a draft of half a million more, though the draft of the summer before had set off a series of riots in New York in which a thousand people had been killed or injured, Negroes had been shot and lynched, and Unionists' houses had been burned to the ground. The writ of habeas corpus had been suspended then, and one of Lincoln's bitterest critics, Vallandigham, had been sent to jail for the duration of the war for denouncing the administration (though his sentence was later commuted to banishment behind the Confederate lines). The President had vigorously defended, in a reply to Democratic criticism that shows his argumentative style at its most cogent, his suppression of civil liberties. Yet Lincoln was again elected, and we do not doubt now

that he was right, for what would it mean to say that
he was wrong? Under his leadership, the Union was
preserved, the Negroes were liberated, the Confederacy unconditionally surrendered. Lincoln's conduct
of the Civil War is generally now accepted as one of
the most conclusive and most creditable episodes of
our history. If the war left a lasting trauma, and re-
sulted in, not an apocalypse, but a period of materialistic progress, on the one hand, and disillusionment
for idealists, on the other, these are matters about
which we have rarely thought and even less often
spoken. We have, in general, accepted the epic that
Lincoln directed and lived and wrote. Since it was
brought to an end by his death the moment after the
war was won, we are able to dissociate him entirely
from the ignominies and errors of the Reconstruction
and to believe he would have handled its problems
better.

But let us see what Lincoln's epic leaves out. Of
the strategy of the economic interests at work in the
Civil War that has been analyzed by Charles A.
Beard in his admirable chapters on the war in *The
Rise of American Civilization*—which themselves
seemed so unconventional only twenty-five years ago
—you will get no inkling from Lincoln, because he
had none himself. During the years of the war, the
tariff, which benefited American manufacturers and
which the South, in its own interests, had been trying
to keep down, was raised higher than it had ever been
before; the government presented enormous grants to
the various railroad companies; and a threat of high
wages was met by the Immigration Act of '64, which
authorized importing labor under terms of contract
that are said by Beard to have resembled the earlier
indentured servitude. At the end of the Civil War, the
industrialists were firmly in the saddle, but of what
was implied for the future of the country by this
progress of industrialization Lincoln had had no idea.

He refers on several occasions to the relations of
capital and labor, and does not seem to be aware how

completely the Republican Party is already the champion of the former, for he always comes to the conclusion that capital overrates its importance, since labor can get along without capital, but that capital cannot get along without labor, and is, in fact, as he says, "the fruit of labor, and could never have existed if labor had not *first* existed." Though he examined the mechanical devices that were brought to him in the years of his Presidency and is said to have readily grasped them, he does not seem to have been much impressed by the development of machinery in America or even much interested in it. In a speech before the Wisconsin State Agricultural Society, in 1859, on the eve of his election to the Presidency, he takes rather a dubious view of the prospects of the steam plow, and a lecture delivered the same year on the subject of "Discoveries, Inventions, and Improvements" is a curious production for its period and was understandably not a success, since most of Lincoln's time was devoted to extolling the value to humanity of language and the art of writing, the only discovery, invention or improvement that appears to have excited his enthusiasm. This is quite characteristic of him, for he evidently felt that the use of the word was the only technique he needed; for him, it had been also a discovery and an improvement. Nor did he compensate for his indifference to industry by a sympathetic solicitude for agriculture. He does not seem to have looked back with pleasure on his boyhood labors on his father's farm, much publicized though these were, and when he writes to a friend who is working the land, it is usually in the vein of "I am so glad it is you not I who are trying to run that farm." Though he tells his Wisconsin audience that, since the farmers are the largest group, they are "most worthy of all to be cherished and cultivated," he hopes that he is not expected to flatter the farmers "as a class" or "to impart to you much specific information on agriculture," since, he says, "you have no reason to believe, and do not believe, that I possess it." Lincoln begins as a

provincial lawyer and soon becomes a politician of
more than provincial importance. His real vocation
was for what we call statesmanship, and, as a statesman, he was entirely absorbed by the problems created
by secession—though, under pressure of the necessity
of winning the war, he was forced to become something of a military strategist. From the moment that
his advent to the Presidency was greeted by the guns
of Fort Sumter, he had of course little opportunity
to occupy himself with anything else.

It is partly these limitations that give Lincoln's
career its unity, its consistency, its self-contained
character. He is not tempted to dissipate his energies;
he has no serious conflicts of interest. Everything
hangs together. He is conscious from the first of his
public role, not only in relation to the history of his
country but also in relation to the larger world, for
which all the old values will be modified, the social
relations altered, if it is possible to prove to it the
practicability of the principles of the Declaration of
Independence. With conviction and persistence he
performs this role, and he is always articulate in it.
Every word that he utters belongs to the part, but in
order to appreciate Lincoln's lines, you have to see
the whole drama. A foreigner who knew nothing of
our history might be able to hear the music of the
Second Inaugural and the Gettysburg Address yet at
the same time not fully grasp the reasons for the
powerful emotional effect that they have on Lincoln's
fellow-Americans; as for the letter to Mrs. Bixby, such
a visitor might be quite at a loss to account for the
elaborate trouble that has been taken to track Mrs.
Bixby down and to authenticate that the letter is
really by Lincoln. These things must be known in
their contexts, where they speak to us with all the
power of Lincoln's inspired conception of his role in
the Civil War.

The dreams and premonitions of Lincoln are also
a part of this vision, to which they contribute an
element of imagery and tragic foreshadowing that one

sometimes finds in the lives of the poets (Byron's last
exploit or Dante's visions) but that comes to seem almost incredible in the career of a political figure: Lincoln's recurrent dream of a ship on its steady way to
some dark and indefinite shore that seemed to mean
that the war would be going well, since it had always
been followed by a victory; his strange hallucination,
after the election of 1860, when, lying exhausted on
a sofa, he saw in a mirror on the wall a double reflection of his face, with one image paler than the
other, which Mary Lincoln had taken as a sign that
he would be elected to a second term but that he
would not live to complete it. He repeated this story
to John Hay and others the night of his second election, and a few days before his death he spoke of a
more recent dream, in which he had seen a crowd
hurrying to the East Room of the White House and,
when he followed them, found his own corpse laid
out and heard voices saying, "Lincoln is dead." In
Springfield, he used to predict to Herndon, "Billy, I
fear that I shall meet with some terrible end." But
although he had been shot at in '62 when he was
riding in the streets of Washington, he would not
have a bodyguard; he explained that he wanted the
people to know that "I come among them without
fear." He would take walks in the middle of the night
alone. It was only in November of '64 that four plain-
clothesmen were posted at the White House. On his
way back from Richmond after its surrender, he read
to his companions on the boat the scene from *Mac-
beth* that contains the lines:

> *Duncan is in his grave,*
> *After life's fitful fever he sleeps well.*
> *Treason has done his worst. Nor steel, nor poison,*
> *Malice domestic, foreign levy, nothing,*
> *Can touch him further.*

The night before he was murdered he dreamed
again of the ship approaching its dark destination. He
had foreseen and accepted his doom; he knew it was

part of the drama. He had in some sense imagined this drama himself—had even prefigured Booth and the aspect he would wear for Booth when the latter would leap down from the Presidential box crying, "*Sic semper tyrannis!*" Had he not once told Herndon that Brutus was created to murder Caesar and Caesar to be murdered by Brutus? In that startlingly prophetic speech of twenty-seven years before to the Young Men's Lyceum in Springfield, he had issued his ambiguous warning against the ambitious man, describing this figure with a fire that seemed to derive as much from admiration as from apprehension —that leader who would certainly arise among them and "seek the gratification of [his] ruling passion," that "towering genius" who would "burn for distinction, and, if possible . . . have it, whether at the expense of emancipating slaves or enslaving freemen." It was as if he had not only foreseen the drama but had even seen all around it, with a kind of poetic objectivity, aware of the various points of view that the world must take toward its protagonist. In the poem that Lincoln lived, Booth had been prepared for, too, and the tragic conclusion was necessary to justify all the rest. It was dramatically and morally inevitable that this prophet who had overruled opposition and sent thousands of men to their deaths should finally attest his good faith by laying down his own life with theirs.

1953

THE PRE-PRESIDENTIAL T. R.

The first instalment of *The Letters of Theodore Roosevelt*, published by the Harvard University Press, is an event of considerable interest, which may do something to restore the prestige of a somewhat staled reputation. The first two volumes of a series that is eventually to run to eight have as subtitle *The Years of Preparation* and cover the period from 1868, when Roosevelt was ten years old, through the Presidential campaign of 1900, when he was elected to the Vice-Presidency on the ticket with William McKinley. T. R. was a prodigious correspondent, and the letters in the whole series will represent a selection of "only about ten thousand" from an "estimated hundred thousand that are available." It has been complained by one reviewer that even this tithe is too many, but it is probably appropriate and inevitable that Roosevelt should be taken in a bulk that corresponds with his enormous energy and the crowding day-by-day business, both personal and official, that he so much enjoyed transacting. The result is, in any case, for one who looks back on the later Roosevelt of 1909–19—unwillingly retired from politics, dissatisfied, blaring and boring—to revive one's respect for the early T. R. and make one feel that,

in our recent perspective, he has been rather unfairly
eclipsed by Wilson and Franklin D.

Before going on to this subject, however, a word or
two ought to be said about the edition itself. It is one
of those modern jobs that are the products of collab-
oration. The title page announces that the letters have
been "selected and edited by Elting E. Morison,"
with John M. Blum as Associate Editor and John J.
Buckley as Copy Editor, but Mr. Morison's introduction makes it plain that a number of other persons
have also made contributions, and the impression is
that nobody has adequately coördinated or checked
on the work of the various editors. The touch of
misplaced coyness in Mr. Morison's introduction
suggests an uneasy awareness of this.

The worst feature, perhaps, is the index. Any incomplete index is a nuisance, and this is one of the
most incomplete that the reviewer has ever encountered. If you should look up Henry James in this list-
ing, you would not find any reference to a letter of
the early eighties in which Roosevelt mentions his
first meeting with him at the St. Botolph's Club in
Boston; and if you should look up Frank H. Cushing,
the anthropologist, a very important man in his field,
you would find no reference at all, though Roosevelt
twice mentions meeting him. The family of Eleanor
Roosevelt come off particularly badly both in the index and in a large chart that undertakes to show the
family relationships. There is no mention in either of
these of Mrs. Franklin D. Roosevelt's two brothers
(she appears in the chart as an only child), though
they are mentioned more than once in the text, and
the second reference to her in the index is listed by
the number of the letter in the series instead of, according to the system adopted, by the number of the
page on which it occurs. The circumstances as well
as the date of the death of Mrs. Roosevelt's father,
Theodore's brother Elliott, though there are several
letters about it, are left unexplained in the notes.

These notes are characterized, in general, by a

similar incompleteness, combined with an irritating garrulity. Mr. Morison disclaims any effort to elucidate such well-known names as Mark Twain or Grover Cleveland (though it might be a good idea to have the latter's terms of office indicated). He says that it is more to the point to throw light on such forgotten topics as Little Egypt and Cahenslyism, but, though he includes a brief mention of this latter subject in a note on Cardinal Gibbons, he does not tell us who Cahensly was or how the movement originated. The notes on literary subjects are full of irrelevant information and gratuitous criticism that is often rather badly expressed. We are told, for example, that Charles A. Dana was an editor of "perverse independence," that Agnes Repplier was "a familiar essayist of rare charm and insight," that John Fox, Jr., married Fritzi Scheff, that the novels of Marion Crawford were distinguished by "a high romance and a kind of baroque glitter," and that the literary activities of Arlo Bates were "all in the genteel and benign tradition." Along with these ineptitudes and this waste of space, one finds a neglect of allusions that really need to be explained. What, for example, is the article by Roosevelt mentioned on page 572? What is the article by Adams (and which Adams?) mentioned on 289? What is the poem of Kipling's on which Roosevelt comments on 909? Nobody's dates are listed, so it is never possible to tell how old anybody is. The chronology of the "principal events" in Roosevelt's life, which does not include his trips to Europe, his early schooling or the births of his children, is, up to his governorship, of an inadequacy that is hardly believable.

Theodore Roosevelt, as these letters show, was fortunate in his early surroundings and the situation to which he was born. The first sections of the correspondence take us into a well-to-do family of the New York of the seventies and eighties, where the adored mother and father and sisters and brother,

sheltered by the cozy shrubbery of a house at Sagamore Hill, embraced by its ample piazza, seem multi-
plied ad infinitum in the world beyond Oyster Bay by
innumerable cousins and uncles and aunts. The children are taken abroad, climb Vesuvius and
see Karnak in their teens, and at home they learn to
ride their ponies, collect ornithological specimens,
and celebrate the Fourth of July with much popping
of firecrackers. "I do not think there is a fellow in
College," Theodore writes to his father from Harvard
at the age of eighteen, "who has a family that love
him as much as you all do me, and I am *sure* that
there is no one who has a Father who is also his best
and most intimate friend, as you are mine." "It seems
perfectly wonderful," he writes at the same time to
his mother, "in looking back over my eighteen years
of existence, to see how I have literally never spent
an unhappy day, unless by my own fault!" And a year
and a half later, at the time of his father's death, he
addresses his sister Corinne: "My own, darling, sweet,
little treasure of a Pussie . . . I do hope you and
Muffie are enjoying yourselves. Dear little one, you
can hardly know what an inestimable blessing to a
fellow it is to have such a home as I have. Even now
that our dear father has been taken away, it is such
great and unmixed pleasure to look forward to a visit
home." To his mother: "I have just been looking over
a letter of my dear Father's in which he wrote me
'Take care of your morals first, your health next, and
finally your studies.' I do not think I ever *could* do
anything wrong while I have his letters." And this
early picture seems to merge into that of the son's
own household, still at Sagamore Hill, but populated
with six children instead of four, where he loves to
play bear with them when they are little and read
them *Hereward the Wake* when they are older, where
he takes them for sails on the Sound, encourages them
to camp out at night, and is delighted when they name
their pets after distinguished Roosevelt ancestors and
heroes of the Spanish-American War.

In this matrix, an ideal is conceived of the role of the United States in the world at the end of the nineteenth century and of the role of Theodore Roosevelt as a citizen of the United States. It is the definition of this ideal in relation to pressures and events that makes this first instalment of letters interesting. The slogans of the later Roosevelt—the big stick and the strenuous life, malefactors of great wealth, race suicide and all the rest of it—were to become such journalistic clichés, as the caricaturists' teeth and glasses were to make a cliché of T. R. himself, that it may come as a surprise to find that Roosevelt first met his age as a serious and thoughtful young man who formulated and was ready to fight for a personal philosophy of life. How this age presented itself to him, what he had to contend against, he has stated in his *Autobiography*: "In the reaction after the colossal struggle of the Civil War our strongest and most capable men had thrown their whole energy into business, into money-making, into the development, and above all the exploitation and exhaustion at the most rapid rate possible, of our natural resources—mines, forests, soil, and rivers. These men were not weak men, but they permitted themselves to grow shortsighted and selfish; and while many of them down at the bottom possessed the fundamental virtues, including the fighting virtues, others were purely of the glorified huckster or glorified pawnbroker type—which when developed to the exclusion of everything else makes about as poor a national type as the world has seen. This unadulterated huckster or pawnbroker type is rarely keenly sympathetic in matters of social and industrial justice, and is usually physically timid and likes to cover an unworthy fear of the most just war under high-sounding names."

The elder Theodore Roosevelt, whom the son so much admired, had himself been a business man, a banker and a glass importer, but, product of a Dutch burgher family long resident in New York, he had interested himself in civic causes and been among the founders of the Metropolitan Museum and the Natural History Museum. In the son, a high sense of noblesse oblige was obviously developed early. At Harvard, he shows a sharp class-consciousness that would hardly at the present time be stated in so bald a way: when writing to his sister that he ranks nineteenth in a class of two hundred and thirty, he says, "Only one gentleman stands ahead of me." He made a point of teaching Sunday school at college—which he found uncongenial work—and he was already studying natural history with something of scientific method. He corrected his physical frailty by resolutely, at the cost of some battering, taking lessons in boxing and wrestling. In a letter to E. S. Martin, the editor of *Life*, written in 1900, he was to explain, in connection with this training, that "In most countries the 'Bourgeoisie'—the moral, respectable, commercial, middle class—is looked upon with a certain contempt which is justified by their timidity and unwarlikeness. But the minute a middle class produces men like Hawkins and Frobisher on the seas, or men such as the average Union soldier in the civil war, it acquires the hearty respect of others, which it merits." In the meantime, he had written to his sister and her husband in 1889, at the time when he was Civil Service Commissioner: "I feel it incumbent on me to try to amount to something, either in politics or literature, because I have deliberately given up the hope of going into a money-making business."

He had further corrected the Manhattan burgher by a dose of the hard-living West. "You would be amused to see me," he writes Henry Cabot Lodge in the summer of 1884, when starting out for the Big Horn Mountains, "in my broad sombrero hat, fringed and beaded buckskin shirt, horse hide chaparajos or riding trousers, and cowhide boots, with braided bridle and silver spurs. I have always liked 'horse and rifle,' and being, like yourself, 'ein echter Amerikaner,' prefer that description of sport which needs a buckskin shirt to that whose votaries adopt the red coat. A buffalo is nobler game than an anise-seed bag, the Anglomaniacs to the contrary notwithstanding." He went to live, after his first wife's death, when he was still in his middle twenties, on a ranch he had bought in Dakota, and tried his nerve against cougars and grizzlies, grappled resolutely with roundups and forest fires, walked up squarely to the insults and ridicule of homicidal saloons and retaliated for the inroads of horse thieves. The opposite of a "gentleman" in New York or Boston was a "mucker" or a "mick." A cowpuncher was something quite different, a free man whom a gentleman Easterner could hardly even call an equal because one had to prove one's equality to *him*. This experience was extremely important to Roosevelt's whole career. It was one of the influences that went to determine his democratic conception of what it meant to be an American, and it enabled him to bring to the Presidency a firsthand sense of the West that no President before him had had.

Toward the new crop of millionaires that had come crowding in since the Civil War and the ostentatious spending they encouraged, the young Roosevelt was patronizing or contemptuous. "The Leiter wedding," he writes, "went off in fine style, and really in very good taste." The Roosevelts had "never liked" the Bradley Martins and declined an invitation to their pretentious ball of 1897. "We were immensely amused," he later notes when he and his wife meet the Martins somewhere, "by the intense seriousness with which they regard themselves and their ball." But he announces that, as Police Commissioner, he will "have to protect it by as many police as if it were a strike," and declares that the outcry against it has almost made him "retract" his refusal to go. "Do you see," he writes Lodge in 1887, "how the Newport cads have taken up the Duke of Marlborough?" Later, in 1895, when a marriage has been arranged between the Duke and Consuelo Vanderbilt, he exclaims to the same correspondent that "The exhibition of snobbery in regard to the Duke of Marlborough this fall has been loathsome." (None of the names in the above quotations is to be found in the defective index, and a footnote explains erroneously, in connection with the first Marlborough reference in a letter of 1887, that the Duke was then "about to marry Consuelo Vanderbilt"—at a time when she was ten years old!) On Americans such as Henry James and William Waldorf Astor, who went to live permanently in England, he imposed a kind of excommunication, denouncing the novels of the former and declining to meet the latter on the occasion of his return to the States. "I hope you will be presented at court," he writes to his sister Anna. "In your position you ought to be"; but adds immediately, "What snobs the Hays are! They have no business to bring out their daughter abroad. If you see Gussie Jay give him a hint that if he educates his children abroad he will lose all chance of being returned to our diplomatic service, and ought to lose it." On the subject of a correspondent to the London *Times,* he expresses himself with something like fury: "He is more British than the British. He is the kind of man who makes me a ferocious jingo." In the next letter—to Henry Cabot Lodge, on March 13, 1896—the word "Americanism" first occurs.

What did Roosevelt mean by this term? By the end of the First World War, it had become a mere cant word of politicans brandished vaguely to create the impression that one's opponent was an undesirable foreigner or corrupted by foreign ideas. But Roosevelt had given it a meaning; it was a concept he had had to invent as an antidote to those tendencies in the national life that he found himself sworn to resist.

Americanism implied an ideal of disinterested public service for the benefit of the American community, and an approach to this community that differed from the "alien"-baiting tactics of the later exploiters of the term in insisting on a complete impartiality, a rigorous abstention from prejudice, in dealing with race, color, nationality, religion or social status. These letters are full of expressions that complement the passages quoted above. "There is really a touch of comedy," he writes to Carl Schurz in 1895, when he is Police Commissioner of New York, "about attacking me as an 'illiberal,' 'nativist' and 'know nothing;' I have not got a drop of that kind of blood in me; it is alien to my whole nature. I do not care a rap. Taking the matter of promotions and reductions inside this force, the two last reductions I made were of native Americans who were Republicans, as the local politicians took care to inform me; and to fill their places, and to fill three other vacancies, I promoted five men, all of them, I believe, born in this country, but four of them of Irish and one of German parentage. The four Irish I believe were Catholics. My own only two personal appointments, my secretary and messenger, are both Catholics of Irish parentage." "As you know," he wrote Maria Longworth Storer, "I always treat Catholics and Protestants exactly alike, as I do Jew or Gentile, as I do the man of native American, German, Irish or any other kind of parentage. Any discrimination for or against a man because of his creed or nativity strikes me as infamy." It is impossible to go through this correspondence of Roosevelt's early official life without becoming convinced that he pretty consistently lived up to this principle —though one notes that, in 1899, when Carl Schurz happens to differ from him politically, he refers to him invidiously as "that prattling foreigner."

We see him, also, as Civil Service Commissioner and as Police Commissioner of New York, doing his best, at the cost of much obstinate resistance to private pressure and public abuse, to remove public service from politics. His conception of himself was that of a benevolent dispenser of justice who rewarded merit and punished wrongdoing. His insistence on human worth and his method of dealing man to man were quite natural to him and not a pose, because handling people of different kinds—whipping them in a fight, making them like him, making them do what he wanted—was a sport that he enjoyed like big-game hunting. The record of his adventures in the state legislature—getting the hang of the Irish politicians, honest and dishonest; acquiring as his closest ally a storekeeper from an Adirondacks crossroads; and in one case defending a bill against "one or two members of the committee who were pretty rough characters" by flourishing the leg of a broken chair—makes quite exhilarating reading.

The vicissitudes of Roosevelt's relations with Tom Platt, the Republican boss of New York, come out in these letters in a striking way. "Platt's influence is simply poisonous," he writes in September, 1895, at the time he is Police Commissioner. "I cannot go in with him; no honest man of sincerity can." The next March he has been obliged, in order to attain a certain objective, "to go in with the Platt men. . . . It was of course the only thing to do; but it was very disagreeable having to do it." Yet, in the days of his governorship, he did his best to get along with Platt and to minimize the shock of those policies of which he knew Platt would disapprove by regularly writing or seeing him—he even comes to close his letters with "warm regards to Mrs. Platt." But this formally friendly tone blows up in 1900 with a memorable declaration of independence: "You say that we must nominate some Republican who 'will carry out the wishes of the organization,' and add that 'I have not yet made up my mind who that man is.' Of one thing I am certain: that, to have it publicly known that the candidate, whoever he may be, 'will carry out the wishes of the organization' would insure his defeat. . . . It is not the business of a governor to 'carry out the wishes of the organization' unless these wishes coincide with the good of the party and of the state."

Roosevelt's breakfasts with Platt, which took place quite openly at the latter's hotel and got to be a kind of institution, were reprobated by those whom Roosevelt, writing in his *Autobiography*, characterized as "solemn reformers of the tom-fool variety." One finds in these letters, also, a whole series of retaliatory blasts against editors like Godkin and Villard, who were intransigent in their war against bossism, and Republicans like Carl Schurz and John Jay Chapman, who, disgusted with Republican corruption, ran an independent Good Government ticket. These attacks are all too often devoid alike of taste and of justice, yet it is impossible, reading these letters, not to sympathize to some extent with Roosevelt in his doctrine of "practical politics," his insistence that the uncompromising kind of reformer, who refuses to yield anything to expediency, can never put through his reforms; that politics is a matter of adapting oneself to all sorts of people and situations, a game in which one may score but only by accepting the rules and recognizing one's opponents, rather than a moral crusade in which one's own stainless standard must mow the enemy down. Roosevelt's attitude here was akin to his attitude toward expatriates: it was priggish and craven, he thought, to deplore conditions in the United States yet at the same time to raise one's eyebrows at anybody who rumpled his waistcoat by plunging into the plebeian melee. In the United States of that era, one sees, among the noble spirits, so many embittered critics, so many neurotic cranks, that it is cheerful to look on at the spectacle of a well-educated and public-spirited man, not merely attempting to formulate an ideal of Americanism that will discredit the pawnbroker and the huckster but punching it out on their own ground with the sordid political boss, the arrogant millionaire, the bought senator, the exploiter of tenements, the Spanish War profiteer—all those types from whom so many of his stratum shrank, with whom they refused to contend.

Americanism in foreign affairs had also its definite meaning. The expressions of bellicosity in these letters may antagonize, but they will not surprise anybody who remembers T. R.'s fulminations against the peace policy of Woodrow Wilson. "Frankly," he writes in 1889 to Cecil Spring Rice, "I don't know that I should be sorry to see a bit of a spar with Germany; the burning of New York and a few other seacoast cities would be a good object lesson on the need of an adequate system of coast defences," and, in 1895, to Henry Cabot Lodge, at the time of our dispute with England over the boundary of Venezuela, "Let the fight come if it must; I don't care whether our seacoast cities are bombarded or not; we would take Canada." His interpretation of the Monroe Doctrine was carried to extreme lengths: "I believe," he writes in 1893, "in ultimately driving every European power off of this continent." But what is unfamiliar and more impressive is the first Roosevelt's grasp of world affairs and the scope of his historical imagination, especially as shown in the series of letters to Cecil Spring Rice. I doubt whether either Woodrow Wilson, for whom the history of Europe seems to have figured, like the chronicles of the Bible, as a remote source of moral instances, or Franklin D. Roosevelt, whose comprehensive knowledge of land and sea seems to have been mainly cartographical, would have been capable of such a survey of Europe, America and Russia, past and present and future, as Theodore sends Spring Rice on August 13, 1897. The unexpected feature of these letters is the absence of jingo rant and the freedom from cocksureness of the long-range views.

There is a similar curious contrast between the extreme manifestations of Roosevelt's egoism and his moderate estimate of himself in his soberer moments of self-appraisal. Of his governorship, one finds him boasting to Cecil Spring Rice, "My own business goes on fairly. At any rate, for this year I have had an absolutely honest administration from top to bottom in this State, and an absolutely efficient one, too." And his confidence in his abilities, his exultant satisfaction in his own achievements, completely takes the bit in its teeth at the time of his letters from the Spanish War, in which he really does make it appear that his storming of San Juan Hill (or what he believed to have been San Juan Hill) was virtually the whole of the Cuban campaign. The relentlessly prolonged correspondence with Henry Cabot Lodge and other allies in Washington in his subsequent (unsuccessful) attempt to obtain the Medal of Honor are embarrassing and exasperating. Yet he writes to Andrew D. White, "Do you know, I have come to the conclusion that I have mighty little originality of my own. What I do is to try to get ideas from men whom I regard as experts along certain lines, and then to try to work out those ideas." Just as in his *Autobiography* one of the most impressive passages is that in which he explains that the "successes" he has "won" are not of the kind due to genius but the products of "hard labor and the exercise of my best judgment and careful planning and working long in advance," and in which he goes on to tell how, in spite of a natural timidity, he had trained himself, by discipline and practice, to face his first self-imposed dangers of bad horses, Western gunmen and large ferocious animals.

Of the demagogue of the later years, the rabid and self-righteous Roosevelt, who diverted attention from his questionable acts by brutal denunciations; of the red-faced and beefy ex-President whom one saw during the First World War pounding his left palm with his right fist and bombarding his hearers with dogmatic opinions, delivered in a high-pitched voice, that no question or objection could touch; of the self-produced mask of the public man, excreted in public debate to protect and fortify himself, to frighten and reassure others—of this crude ventriloquial oracle, there are already some signs in these letters. He early gave in to the habit of accusing his opponents and critics of "dishonesty" and "deliberate falsehoods." He must often, from the start of his career, have had to deal with outrageous examples of both, but it was one of his less amiable traits (somewhat redeemed by the fact that he seems to have been, though a truculent, a not really ill-natured man) that he never gave his critics the benefit of assuming good faith on their part, of admitting that they might be mistaken. "I therefore denounce its statements," he writes in 1891 of an article in the Delphi *Journal* (the editors of the correspondence do not tell us where Delphi was) that may well have deserved his indignation, "as mere wanton and malicious falsehoods, which its editor knew to be wanton and malicious falsehoods at the time they were written." But we find him a year later declaring that an article in the *Nation* is "so foolish, so malignant, so deliberately mendacious and so exultant that it fairly made me writhe to think of the incalculable harm to decency that scoundrelly paper, edited by its scoundrelly chief, Godkin, has done." By 1899, Republicans like Senator Hoar, who happened to differ from Roosevelt on the subject of annexing the Philippines, were "little better than traitors." And treason is now added to his stock accusations. By 1900 we find him writing, apropos of the election of that year, in which McKinley ran against Bryan, "I cannot express the anger and contemptuous indignation with which I regard the cultivated men from Schurz and Godkin down to the smaller vermin like Jack Chapman and Erving Winslow who at this great crisis show themselves traitors to their country." But these aspects of Roosevelt's character may be left for consideration till the later instalments of the letters appear. In the meantime, the general impression of the pre-1900 Roosevelt is attractive and even inspiring.

1951

THE HOLMES-LASKI
CORRESPONDENCE

The correspondence between Justice Holmes and
Harold J. Laski extended over nearly nineteen years—
1916–35. It has been published almost *in toto* in two
volumes, comprising sixteen hundred and fifty pages,
by the Harvard University Press: *Holmes-Laski Letters*, under the editorship of Holmes's literary execu-
tor, Mr. Mark DeWolfe Howe, with a foreword by
Mr. Justice Frankfurter. Mr. Howe has supplied careful notes that identify, wherever possible, the innumerable authors and books discussed by the two
correspondents, and has added a biographical appen-
dix that gives somewhat fuller accounts of the more
important persons mentioned. There is a complete,
an ideal index, that runs to a hundred and twenty-
three pages.

This reviewer has read the whole correspondence
with never flagging fascination and has found it the
perfect resource for railroad trips and bedtime entertainment, but everyone may not feel the same interest in the earlier phases of the "liberal" movement—
about which, during the years when Laski was teaching at Harvard and associated with the *New Republic*,
before he returned to England in June, 1920, we get
a good deal of inside information—nor will everyone,
perhaps, care to follow the whole of the detailed rec-

ord of Laski's inveterate book-hunting, about which
he sends Holmes a bulletin in practically every letter.
Yet the letters make such easy reading, they are so full
of gossip and wit and alert comment on current happenings, and the correspondents are both so extraordinary, that the book may be recommended to anyone
with a taste for the informalities of intellectual and
political history.

Before going on to discuss the personalities of the
two celebrities and their curious relationship, one
ought to call attention to one element of unusual interest. Though the exchange between Holmes and
Laski deals mainly with law and politics, it is full of
incidental observations on all sorts of philosophical
and literary subjects. You have Holmes's rediscovery
of Melville in 1921—he thought that *The Scarlet Letter* seemed thin beside *Moby Dick*—with his expression of regret that he had not, as a small boy in
Stockbridge, "tried to get hold of the (if my memory
is right) rather gruff taciturn man that I saw in my
father's study." You have his many interesting references to Henry James: "I think," he writes in a letter
of 1925, "there was something big in H. James, but I
think that with all his preoccupation he wanted something of the gentleman and that it tells in his choice of
subjects and sometimes in his writing. This is a thing
that I wouldn't say except in confidence and I will
not develop it." You have his candid and critical
opinions of the Adamses, Charles Eliot Norton and
James Russell Lowell. There is a brilliant remark
about Santayana in a letter of 1924: "In a general
way his thinking more than that of other philosophers
coincides with mine. But he has a patronizing tone
—as of one who saw through himself but didn't expect others to." This Laski can hardly rival when he
writes in his next letter: "For ability to dwell on the
heights, to move with sure foot amid great conceptions, I think George Eliot is unsurpassed. Meredith
had her quality; but when he tried to express it he was
like a man trying to speak with a fishbone deliberately

stuck in his throat." In his literary judgments, Laski is less penetrating and more conventional, for, in general, he accepted the English canon. Holmes accepted nothing that he had not examined and approved: "I can't see," he writes when he is ninety, "why they seem to take the author of *Walden* (I forget the name) so seriously." One of the most amusing features of the interchange is the efforts of both these connoisseurs of literature to understand what it is that the French admire in Racine. Holmes is still worrying about this at the age of eighty-six, and Laski is only beginning to get a little light on the subject when, in a letter written four years later, he tells Holmes of hearing a Frenchman recite the poet's verses.

These letters, however, are a good deal more than an entertaining commentary on books and events. They throw into relief, I believe, certain aspects of Holmes and Laski in a way that nothing else has yet done, and they stimulate long-range reflections on the characters and careers of the two men.

In Harold Laski's case, this revelation brings out some disquieting problems, which both Mr. Howe in his preface and Mr. Justice Frankfurter in his foreword have had to handle with tact. These problems are treated with candor in Kingsley Martin's *Biographical Memoir* of Laski, and I propose to make use of this excellent book in this as well as in other connections. The great scandal about Harold Laski, regretted by all his friends and sometimes used against him by his enemies, was his habit of unscrupulous romancing. He would freely invent stories that had often no basis whatever in fact about people he did not know but whom he claimed to have met and talked with, exploits that he had not performed, scenes that had never occurred and books that he had never read. It is obvious that these falsehoods of Laski's represented a genuine aberration, because they were entirely gratuitous. Laski *was* on confidential terms with distinguished and famous people; he *did* have a phenomenal memory, and he *was* immensely learned; he *did* have an uncanny knack of picking up unsuspected treasures from the shelves of secondhand-book dealers. From what motive, then, could he have allowed himself to bewilder and trouble his friends, to leave traps for his biographers and editors, and to make himself ridiculous in retrospect by providing in his personal letters so much evidence against himself?

More and more, as we read his correspondence with Holmes, it becomes a distracting preoccupation to try to guess which of his stories are false and to check up on his conflicting statements. I would wager, for example, that the following is purely a pat invention: "The outstanding thing was a talk at Shaw's between him and Barrie about the art of the theater; each quite right, and each shouting the other down with grim energy. Shaw insisted that Barrie fled from ideas as though to possess them would defile his virginity; Barrie said that Shaw always shouts sermons at the top of his voice and that if one of his characters seeks to come to life he promptly murders it. Pinero, who was there, amused me greatly; for him the whole art of plays was how you got the actor on and off the stage —and the notion of a function in drama beyond interesting or pleasing situations clearly puzzled him. Half the time he listened as a noble of Louis XIV might have overheard a conversation of two Jacobins." Did Shaw and Pinero and Barrie really consort together? Do celebrities perform in private ever quite so consistently in character? And yet we cannot be sure, and we presently begin to feel that we cannot be sure of anything.

Even Holmes, who was so loyal to Laski, occasionally pounces on him. When he reads about an interview in the course of which his friend, now returned to England, has said that he found Woodrow Wilson "easy to work with," Holmes demands to know "where and what" this was, and Laski is prompt to reply that the interviewer has misreported him. Yet the old

man has swallowed without comment a good many
other dubious statements—perhaps because the incon-
sistencies, in the early correspondence, at any rate,
are usually introduced rather far apart. At one point,
Laski tells the Justice that he has just read the complete works of Thomas Hardy, but then, in
subsequent letters, he will mention from time to time
that he has been reading some novel of Hardy's that
he had not known before. He claims in three different
years—1926, 1928 and 1929—to have just been completely baffled by Agatha Christie's detective story
The Murder of Roger Ackroyd. Yet the discrepancies
sometimes come closer together. In a letter of January 9, 1926, he announces that he has purchased in
Amsterdam an engraving of Voltaire by Moreau le
Jeune, and in a letter of February 13th that he has
bought the same picture "last week" in England. It
was certainly careless of Laski, on the occasion of a
visit to the Continent, to report a long conversation
with Georg von Below, a German historian, whom he
describes as a "delightful old man," when von Below,
as the editor tells us, had at that time been dead three
years. And, in spite of his many reports of conversations with Arnold Bennett, the index to Bennett's
diary does not show a single reference to Laski.*

In these letters one gets the impression that Laski
became more reckless under pressure of his busier life
and in proportion as Holmes, who was ninety in
1931, grew mentally dimmer and less attentive. One

*In a review of the Holmes-Laski correspondence by
Mr. Kingsley Martin that has appeared, since this was
written, in the *New Statesman and Nation* (August 8,
1953), he tells us that, "Most of the anecdotes [Laski]
relates were of real events but his own achievements were
far more remarkable than those which he related with
pride in his letters to America. It was as if he were afraid
to be thought boastful if he told the truth, whereas it
was only fun if he transformed it into an improbable
yarn. I always knew that Harold was really a friend of
Franklin Roosevelt because he did not boast of being
one."

of Laski's last efforts to amuse the old man is an incredible succession of witty remarks—one of which, only two letters before, he has attributed to someone else—supposed to have been fired off by "a young don" at "the high table of Christ Church." "And all this in one evening," adds Laski, with one of his circumstantial touches, "from a lad whose specialty is vector analysis." We finally come to feel that these letters were composed for a character in a novel, that they are more or less plausibly concocted for a brilliant young professor of politics with the run of the London intellectual world, who is supposed to be writing to a friend in America.

Yet Laski was a real person and a person of some importance. Though his boasting suggests megalomania and his habit of romancing frivolity, he was actually not only a well-equipped scholar and an able political thinker but a fighter for unpopular ideals whose career as a whole is an example of singularly disinterested devotion. About the things that were essential to his subject, he did not mislead his students, and he did not, so far as I know, allow any improvisations to get into the text of his books. He was trying to expound what he thought was the truth, and he was willing to go to bat for it. From the moment one recognized this and learned to discount what was specious, one found, in one's personal relations with Laski, that he inspired respect and affection—which, in Holmes's case, he knew how to return with modesty as well as warmth. Mr. Martin has shown him at his best as a teacher who labored over as well as inspired his pupils and even sometimes helped them out with money; as an adroit and judicial arbitrator who served for twenty-four years on the British Industrial Court that decided disputes between the Treasury and Civil Service employees; and as a political adviser to Labour who was able to play in England a role for which, it would seem, no one else was precisely fitted.

I shall return to this role in a moment, but I want

first to advance a theory, also suggested by Kingsley Martin's memoir, that would partly account for Laski's queer incongruities. I had not had any idea, before reading Mr. Martin, of the self-confined character of the Jewish world in which Laski had grown up in Manchester or the struggle he had had to break out of it. His parents had come from Poland, and his father, a successful businessman, was the recognized leader of the Jewish community. The Laskis were rigorously orthodox, and they practiced all the Mosaic regulations about eating and drinking and washing, wearing phylacteries and keeping the Sabbath. Harold was sent to a Gentile school, but this English education ran parallel with his Jewish training without ever being allowed to impinge on it. This must have created a split in his mind, for it eventually gave rise to rebellion. The time came, says Mr. Martin, when Harold said to his father, "I am English, not Polish; an agnostic, not a Jew. I cannot reconcile Maimonides with Mill, nor *Ann Veronica* with the Mosaic Law." He was allowed to go to Oxford, but before he went he had managed, at eighteen, to marry, without telling his parents, a young non-Jewish girl, a lecturer on eugenics and a champion of woman suffrage, who was also at odds with her family. This precipitated a terrible crisis. The two young people were separated. Harold's allowance was stopped till the term began at Oxford, and he was told by the elder Laski that unless he renounced his marriage or persuaded his wife to become a Jew, he would not be given a penny from the moment he graduated. Harold flouted this ultimatum, and when he later emerged from Oxford in 1914, he set out to make a living for himself and his wife, and, physically unfit to serve in the war, he accepted a history lectureship at McGill University in Montreal. Two years later he went to teach at Harvard, where he remained till 1920. While in America, he studied the United States, made lasting American friends, and acquired an American accent. He was undoubtedly one of the foreigners who knew most about this country and understood it most sympathetically, and when he finally returned to England to function for the rest of his life as a professor at the London School of Economics, he never ceased to make the effort to interpret the two countries to one another. Later on, he lectured in Russia and attempted, in a lesser way, the same kind of two-way interpretation between the West and the Soviet Union.

Harold Laski was thus incessantly and in every situation practicing what Stephen Potter calls "clubmanship"—a branch of "oneupmanship" that involves playing one milieu off against another. In Laski's case, he had in his repertoire the English, the Jewish, the American and the Soviet Russian worlds. He was always the informed outsider, full of insight, anxious to be helpful, but not unwilling to score and capable of deadpan mischief. It was also true, I suppose, that he felt he had to out-Oxford Oxford by an exhibition of easy accomplishment. To have known Harold Laski and watched him in action is to find oneself now equipped to appreciate the tone of his letters in a way that would hardly be possible for a reader who had never seen him. He was almost elfishly small and looked frail, rather frailer than he really was. With his spectacles and his round black eyes, which defied such a description as "beady" by force of the high-powered intelligence brought out by the owlish lenses, and which were usually more lively than the rest of his face, his appearance was perennially youthful, as of a schoolboy who was stumping his elders or innocently waiting for someone to pick up one of those buzzing matchboxes that give the effect of an electric shock. I was told years ago by a friend who had crossed on a boat with Laski of his method of dealing with a man who was boring the other passengers by his pompousness and self-importance. Laski sat down and wrote this man a note that purported to come from the captain, apologizing for not having realized before that there was so distinguished a person aboard and for not having done him the honors of the captain's table, and inviting him to dine with him that evening tête-à-tête in his cabin. And in Laski's correspondence with Holmes, he occasionally lets his friend see him in the act of pulling somebody else's leg. "Another," he writes of a man whom he had met at a dinner of judges in London, "was, I gather, a great swell in commercial cases; but he seemed most interested in incomes at the Bar, wherefore I led him up the garden gracefully. He said that J. Simon was making sixty thousand a year, so I invented a quite imaginary Bonville-Smith (don't you think Bonville a neat touch?) who now makes £100,000 and never appears in Court. The others nodded solemnly, and the poor judge was quite persuaded by the third glass of port that he knew of him vaguely, but had no idea he did so well."

It is amusing for the present writer to read Harold Laski's comment on a dinner that was given for him by the *New Republic* on one of his visits to the States: "I dined too with the *New Republic* and felt they were as solemn as a gathering of Baptists met to do justice to the Scarlet Woman of Washington." I was present at this dinner, and can testify that the attitude toward Laski was certainly solemn. The old *New Republic* group had found out about Laski's fictions just before he went back to England in 1920—when someone had happened to see Colonel House and learn from him that he did not know Laski, just after the latter had impressed his friends by reporting a long conversation with Woodrow Wilson's advisor—and the dreadful thing had been passed along, like the secret of the Glamis Horror, to their successors of the later group. We were constantly suspicious of him, yet we always gave him a dinner when he returned to America, and he had for us a real prestige. It was not the Scarlet Woman of Washington that made the *New Republic* solemn but the splendor and the scandal of Harold Laski. The tiny guest of honor, gleaming through his round glasses, with something of the schoolmaster's manner that overlay the im-

pulses of the schoolboy, would sit plying us affably
with questions and evincing a courteous interest, help-
ing us out with the precise figures on some such matter
as an ancient plebiscite in some faraway country,
which nobody could contradict. When he had
claimed, on one of these occasions, to have been told
something or other in confidence by a certain Soviet
official and was reminded by somebody present that
this man had not at that time been a commissar, he
ignored the interpolation and passed easily on to
something else, with an authority one could not
challenge.

Paradoxically—incredibly, as it seemed to some—
this authority was not a fraud. From what was it derived? First of all, from Laski's undoubted compe-
tence as an international critic with a grounding of
all-around reading and authentic information. The
small boy at a disadvantage, who, puny of physique,
had pitted his will against the steam-rollering vested
interests of orthodox Judaism, one-hundred-per-cent
Americanism and the formidable class structure of the
British Empire had made of his intellect an instrument that could analyze and estimate these great
social entities as few members of them could do for
themselves. He had performed for the liberal press of
both England and the United States the service of
acting between them as a kind of liaison man, and
Mr. Martin makes one feel that for England he
performed a unique service in keeping English students of politics in touch with the rest of the world.
(I cannot do justice to Laski's books, since I have
never done more than look into them.) But the power
that Laski exerted had, beyond this, another, an ultimate source—a vision (in the Jewish sense, prophetic) both of the larger forces that were working in
the social world and of what he desired that world to
become. He not only watched politics intently, he bet
on and worked for those movements and groups that
he thought would help to realize his vision. He succeeded in maintaining this long-range vision through

all the years of the second war as few figures in politics could, and not only brought constant pressure to prevent the abuse of civil rights and to curb the excesses of the censorship but consistently urged that Labour should not be diverted by the national crisis from insisting on social reforms.

Yet in Laski's imagination—for all his considerable shrewdness—lay his weakness as well as his strength. There was always something perhaps not quite sound in his relation to practical realities. His conversational and epistolary inventions were the least important part of this, but they indicated a discrepancy more serious. In some sense, Laski lived in a dream—a dream full of actual data, with its foundations in a real grasp of history, and made vivid with first-hand impressions of a variety of modern societies, but a dream that did not, nevertheless, quite make the right contact with life. One comes to the conclusion, in following Laski through Kingsley Martin's biography, that his steady and considered refusal, up to his later years, to follow the advice of such friends as the Webbs, who wanted him to stand for Parliament or otherwise take a more active part in politics, was prompted by a warning instinct that such a role would impose conditions with which he was unfitted to cope. In his rallying to Soviet Russia at the time when the Stalinist Terror had made the regime least defensible, his capacity for fantasy became quite alarming; and he certainly sometimes behaved in a very unrealistic way when he was Chairman of the Labour Party, after it came to power in 1945. He had by that time become a world figure for the Socialists of Western Europe—an intellectual, a "theoretician," whom the Leftists of the Continent could understand —and he went around abroad making speeches in which he promised a number of things that he and other Leftists wanted but that neither Bevin nor Attlee had any intention of granting, till the latter had to cut him short and rebuke him for his "irresponsible statements."

Mr. Martin takes account of one aspect of this curious performance of Laski's—he was here playing truant to his Party—when he writes in this connection that "no man, however disinterested or clever, can accomplish by letter, conversation and private memorandum the feat of changing the policy of a great party, since that is based not on the wishes or opinions of individuals, but on the interests of classes and groups." It had been unrealistic already, in the heat of the 1945 election, for Laski to sue the *Daily Express* for its story that he had advocated, at a public meeting, "revolution by violence." A denial would have been enough, but Laski insisted on fighting and evidently could not conceive that the verdict might go against him in the event that a jury should fail to grasp the difference between advocating violent revolution and advocating peaceful revolution in order to avert violence. Having always had the freedom of the classroom and of the Left intellectual world, he does not seem to have been aware of how much less secure his position was in relation to the general public, and his losing his case was a terrible shock, for it upset his fantasy about his life. It is probably significant that he specially complains of his feeling that he has been "called a liar." His death less than four years later—when he was still only fifty-six—was probably due partly to this rebuff. But he was sensitive to the force of the shock because, nervously and physically, he had worn himself out in the effort to save the cause of Labour, with which he had associated his vision. He had stoutly stood up to the ordeals of the war, and he now threw away his last strength travelling about and speaking at innumerable working-class meetings. He had always been a dedicated man. He had always given the world all he had, to the verge of exhaustion; one finds in Holmes's letters a constant solicitude lest the younger man shall burn himself out. Laski's love of human beings was real, and he was exceptional in class-conscious England by reason of his complete lack of snobbery—for he lived in an unfashionable section of London and he gave to his hundreds of visitors of all statuses, nations and races the same ready attention and patient consideration. He was admirable with his working-class audience. Though he could not help coming to them a little in the role of the fancy Oxford don, he talked to them without constraint, and he knew how to talk to their children. Harold Laski was genuinely kind; one never for a moment had the feeling, as happens with professional politicians, that his electioneering affability was a mask for some hardness or meanness. As for his fantasies, they were no more reprehensible than the commoner kinds of vice that we easily forgive in gifted men and that often do more harm than Laski's, since it was Laski himself who most suffered from his failure in realism. If he had been a poet, like Shelley, instead of a political thinker, his delusions and the croppers they cost him would have been sanctified along with his highest work. Mr. Martin has done well to minimize them and to emphasize that Laski's career was brilliant, courageous and useful, and had behind it a backbone of hard work that contradicted his apparent facility.

But what value and what fascination did this visionary elusive creature possess for old Justice Holmes, who disagreed with most of Laski's premises and thought most of his ideals nonsense, who was scrupulous about every word he wrote, and who did not, till he was over ninety, allow himself the self-indulgence of dropping a book he had once begun? The easy and obvious answer is probably to some extent true: Holmes had no children and needed a son, and certainly Harold Laski, who continued to the end of his life to find it a considerable strain to revisit his Manchester family, was badly in need of a father. He even needed a Jewish father, and I believe that Holmes filled this role. But in order to understand how it came about we must go back to Holmes's own beginnings.

The key to a good deal in Holmes is to be found in his experience of the Civil War. How taxing and searching this experience was may be seen from his war letters and diaries, which have been published by Mr. Howe under the title *Touched with Fire*. Holmes went through some of the worst of the fighting; he was wounded three times and constantly expected to be killed; he saw his regiment all but wiped out. In dating his subsequent letters, even in writing to persons whom he did not know well, he seems rarely to have failed to note the anniversaries of the battles of Ball's Bluff and Antietam, at both of which he had been wounded. He had been swept into the struggle on the tide of the New England abolition movement, but his ardor cooled off in the course of the war, and he always remained distrustful of exalted states of mind connected with moral crusades. He mentions this again and again in the course of his correspondence with Laski. At one time when he was thought to be dying, as the result of his wound at Ball's Bluff, he had resisted as unworthy an impulse to pray to that traditional God in whose existence, when sound and sane, he had decided he did not believe, and he came out of the Civil War with some very grim and skeptical views, which supplied him with the permanent basis of his social and legal philosophy. He had seen a great political structure disrupted by a social issue and readjusting itself to the needs of war; he had seen the North and the South battering one another down into poverty, scorched earth and chaos; and this revelation of human institutions as provisory and precarious affairs, this spectacle of human nature reduced to its lowest terms in the simple battle for survival, must have had great importance in determining the then unconventional point of view from which he attacked the law—regarding it not merely as a sacred code, which had simply to be read correctly, but as a complex accretion of rules accumulated through more than a thousand years and representing the needs and demands of definite groups of people existing in particular places at particular periods of history. And the methods by which the states had had to settle their quarrel had seriously shaken his faith in the doctrine of human rights and the ideals of democratic government. He had come to believe that the only real rights were those that compelled themselves to be recognized, and he was always insisting that the right to kill, to enforce authority by violent means—even, in time of war, to suppress, as Lincoln had done, subversive or obstructive speech—is of the essence of any sovereign power, and that the function of the law is to put into effect the policies of this power. "The sacredness of human life," he writes Laski on October 26, 1919, "is a formula that is good only inside a system of law." "I repeat my old aphorism," he says on January 14, 1920, "that everything is founded on the death of men—society, which only changes the modes of killing—romance, to which centuries, that is generations, of dead, on the memorial tablets of a great war are necessary." Nor had the war made him more democratic; he was far from having been so favorably impressed by any of the common men with whom he had been thrown in the Army as Tolstoy's Pierre, in *War and Peace*, was by the peasant Karataev. "It's odd," he had written his parents, "how indifferent one gets to the sight of death—perhaps, because one gets aristocratic and don't value much a common life. Then they are apt to be so dirty it seems natural—'Dust to Dust'—I would do anything [for them] that lay in my power but it doesn't much affect my feelings."

It was the paradox of Holmes's career, which lent piquancy to his personality and made him a dramatic figure, that, holding these unpopular opinions, to which he gave frequent expression, he should have devoted himself to the service of the democratic government for which he had fought, attempting to interpret the will of the people in measures which he often disapproved—he speaks somewhere of telling some lady how much, as a private citizen, he detested a good many of the principles which, as a judge, he was bound to uphold—defending the liberties at which he scoffed and finally, being childless, bequeathing his money to the United States. Of the talented "intellectuals" who had taken part in the war and who had then had to function in a climate that did not encourage their highest aims, it was Holmes, perhaps, who succeeded in carrying through most consistently the serious role he had chosen and who came closest to doing his abilities justice. He had at first been afraid that the law might not turn out sufficiently rewarding in a spiritual and intellectual way. "There were," he told a college audience in 1897, "few of the charts and lights for which one longed when I began. One found oneself plunged in a thick fog of details—in a black and frozen night, in which were no flowers, no spring, no easy joys. Voices of authority warned that in the crush of that ice any craft might sink. One heard Burke saying that law sharpens the mind by narrowing it. One heard in Thackeray of a lawyer bending all the powers of a great mind to a mean profession. One saw that artists and poets shrank from it as from an alien world. One doubted oneself how it could be worthy of the interest of an intelligent mind. And yet one said to oneself, law is human—it is a part of man, and of one world with all the rest."

But working hard and working uphill were natural, perhaps necessary, for Holmes—the result of his Puritan heritage as well as of the discipline of his Army years. He had brought out of the war a character austere and not a little hard, a personality a little bleak, which his humor and his personal charm, his air of being a man of the world, could never completely embellish. This helped him to survive the Big Money era, whose temptations meant nothing whatever to him and whose demagogueries did not move him. But he suffered from its cultural sterility, and he complains of intellectual solitude. "I must vent a line of unreasoning—rage I was going to say—dissatisfaction is nearer," he writes in 1902 to Sir Frederick Pollock, in connection with the editorials about him at the time when he had just been appointed to the United States Supreme Court. "They are so favorable that they made my nomination a popular success but they have the flabbiness of American ignorance. I had to get appreciation for my book in England before they dared to say anything here except in one or two quarters. . . . It makes one sick when he has broken his heart in trying to make every word living and real to see a lot of duffers, generally I think not even lawyers, talking with the sanctity of print in a way that at once discloses to the knowing eye that literally they don't know anything about it. . . . I hope some one of the [legal periodicals] may have an intelligent word, but you can understand how at a moment of ostensible triumph I have been for the most part in a desert. . . . If I haven't done my share in the way of putting in new and remodeling old thought for the last twenty years, then I delude myself. Occasionally someone has a glimpse—but in the main damn the lot of them." And he writes Laski in 1925, from the country during a summer vacation, "You have a great advantage in England that you are all so near together that you can find intellectual companionship on every side. Whereas here it is nearly solitude outside my wife. However, one gets a spark here and there. I am afraid that letters giving one a puff, a natural incident of old age, hardly take the place of talk with people who keep you up to the mark. Brandeis is a great comfort in the winter, but he is not here."

"One gets a spark here and there." For Holmes—though he was then seventy-three—the prospect had brightened a little when the *New Republic* was founded in 1914 and the liberals began to take him up. He speaks of this in a letter to Pollock of February, 1917, in which he also introduces Laski: "We had here over Sunday a youth whom I wonder if you remember: Harold Laski, an unbelieving Jew with a *spécialité* for church history. He was distinguished at Oxford, I believe, then lectured at McGill and now does at Harvard. Beat the American champion at tennis [this, it seems, was another of his romances], is one of the very most learned men I ever saw of any age, is in his twenties and an extraordinarily agreeable chap. He goes with some of the younger men like Frankfurter and the *New Republic* lot, who make much of your venerable uncle and not only so, but by bringing an atmosphere of intellectual freedom in which one can breathe, make life to him a good deal more pleasant." This late recognition pleased Holmes. His prestige at the Harvard Law School seems steadily to have increased with the years, and he had begun to be accepted by the public, who knew little about his ideas, as a national sage and hero. But there was something else, I think, involved in his *rapprochement* with the "liberal" movement. The tradition of New England idealism, which Holmes had been forced to renounce when he came to discount the abolitionists and to realize the cost of the Civil War, still exerted on him a certain pull and made him feel a certain sympathy with the men of the later era who were working for what they called "social justice." He still hated what Mencken called "the uplift" and what Holmes called "the upward and onward." He shies away when he detects any symptoms that remind him of the fanaticisms of wartime. "He [Bertrand Russell] seems to me," he writes to Laski in September, 1918, "in the emotional state not unlike that of the abolitionists in former days, which then I shared and now much dislike—as it catches postulates like the influenza." Later—October 30, 1930—he writes, of Maurice Hindus's *Humanity Uprooted*, "His account of the Communists shows in the most extreme form what I came to loathe in the abolitionists—the conviction that anyone who did not agree with them was a knave or a fool. You see the same in some Catholics and some of the 'Drys' apropos of the 18th amendment. I detest a man who knows that he knows."

He had already been complaining by the end of the twenties that the *New Republic* was becoming "partisan," and he was later to complain more strongly of its further shift toward the Left. He grumbles and growls to Laski when the latter sends him books by himself or others that put challengingly the case for Socialism—for Holmes's economic views were a combination of Malthusianism with a doctrine of non-interference with what he called "the stream of products." Yet his colleague Louis Brandeis had prevailed on him at least to do a certain amount of reading on the condition of industrial communities, a subject, it seems, he had completely ignored, and one cannot read his correspondence with Laski without feeling that he was not wholly uninfluenced by his contact with Laski and the liberals. "All my life," he writes Laski on September 15, 1916, "I have sneered at the natural rights of man, and at times I have thought that the bills of rights in Constitutions were overworked—but these chaps [Faguet and Hazlitt, whom he had just been reading] remind me, if I needed it . . . that they embody principles that men have died for, and that it is well not to forget in our haste to secure our notion of general welfare." It is perilous—especially for someone who does not know the law—to explain the motivations of judicial decisions, but one gets, for example, a distinct impression that, between the decisions of Holmes in the Schenck and Debs cases, in which he upheld convictions under the wartime Espionage Act, and his dissent in the somewhat similar Abrams case, his new friends had been working on his conscience. In connection with Debs, he had written to Laski on March 16, 1919, in a vein that is almost apologetic: "The federal judges seem to me (again between ourselves) to have got hysterical about the war. I should think the President when he gets through with his present amusements might do some pardoning." It is clear that the liberals have not been happy about the Debs and Schenck decisions, and Laski greets the Abrams opinion with a veritable paean of joy.

There would be a long chapter to write, for which this is not the place, about the close self-identification with the Jews of the Old Testament of the Puritans escaping from England to what they called the Promised Land, and the profoundly Hebraic elements that persisted in the New England theology and the New England discipline of life. Though this theology had been seriously undermined by the middle of the nineteenth century through the rationalizing of Unitarianism, which had softened the creed of the elder Holmes, the apocalyptic vision of a better world—of America as the country of which Harriet Beecher Stowe says that she used to feel as a girl, after reading Cotton Mather's *Magnalia*, that "the very ground I trod on" was "consecrated by some special dealing of God's providence"—had been revived with ardor on the eve of the Civil War, and it had gone to the head of the youthful Holmes. Its ebb had left him high and dry—high in his moral ideals, dry in the thirst of the spirit. But a reaction against the materialism of the era of unscrupulous millionaires was to bring in time another revival of the traditional American idealism, which expressed itself in the several varieties of the struggle for a secular "better world," in which the American people were to be rescued—as they had once been from slavery—from poverty and exploitation, from the corruption of machine politics and the debasement of cultural standards, from domestic panics and foreign wars. For Holmes, the expectations of this movement rested on delusions and fallacies, yet he was certainly interested in it and even, one feels, rather stimulated by it. He acquainted himself with its literature (he had already twice read *Das Kapital*). And he came to admit that the tides of society might be setting in that direction, and

that if people should want such nonsense as Socialism, they would of course command the means to try
it. In July, 1926, he writes to Laski, apropos of a book
by R. H. Tawney, *Religion and the Rise of Capitalism*, "I wrote to him this morning and said, as bound,
after an appreciative word, that I was an old skeptic
and thought capitalism better than anything likely to
replace it but that I got more intellectual companionship from you young prophets than from the older
orthodox sages." These young prophets included, as
is always the case with movements for social betterment, a good many intellectual Jews, and with these
it is clear from his friendships—Brandeis and Morris
Cohen, Felix Frankfurter and Harold Laski—that
Holmes felt a special affinity. They had behind them
the same Biblical culture, and they shared—however
secular their faith, however practical their professional
activity—the conviction that what we do in this world
must have the sanction of non-worldly values and be
acted in the sight of eternity.

Thus Brandeis and Holmes, though they appeared
to differ on fundamental matters, were evidently
closer to one another than either was to any other of
his colleagues, and Holmes's affection for and interest
in Laski seem to have been a good deal more lively
than for any of his secretaries. Though Holmes, like
his younger admirers, had dispensed with the ancient
Jehovah, these latter must have felt that he figured
in his field as something of a priest and prophet as
well as a man of learning; as, at any rate, a lawgiver
and moralist who held himself quite superior to
worldly considerations. In Laski's case—in spite of
divergences of opinion that became more and more
pronounced—we feel that his attitude toward Holmes
is quite that of the loyal disciple of one of the great
modern Jewish thinkers or leaders whose position has
something of the rabbinical—Marx or Trotsky
or Freud, Arnold Schoenberg or Alfred Stieglitz.
What dignifies his whole correspondence with
Holmes—and not least when, by dint of whatever in-

ventions, he is still trying to amuse the old man, now
at ninety too feeble to answer—is its genuine emotion of piety. In this sense, he found in Holmes a
father. And on Holmes's side, the veteran of the Civil
War, who had continued to serve all his life an ideal
that he sometimes questioned, must instinctively
have felt at home with the minds of such men as
Laski, whose moral inspiration stemmed from the
same remote but still operant source as that mori-
bund New England tradition which, by the era of
Calvin Coolidge, could no longer nourish one much.
It may be that even Laski's extravagances, the excitement of a dream that could not become real, were
needed to quicken the interest of the stoical old sol-
dier-judge, to reawaken a flush of that fervor for the
destiny of human society which had been blighted on
the battlefields of the Civil War.

                                                      1953

ANCHOR BOOKS